AF821770

STUDIES IN HISTORY, ECONOMICS AND PUBLIC LAW

Edited by the
FACULTY OF POLITICAL SCIENCE
OF COLUMBIA UNIVERSITY

NUMBER 425

BRITISH METHODS OF INDUSTRIAL PEACE

A STUDY OF DEMOCRACY IN RELATION TO LABOR DISPUTES

BY
DUCKSOO CHANG

BRITISH METHODS OF INDUSTRIAL PEACE

A STUDY OF DEMOCRACY IN RELATION TO LABOR DISPUTES

BY

DUCKSOO CHANG, PH.D.

NEW YORK
COLUMBIA UNIVERSITY PRESS
LONDON: P. S. KING & SON, LTD.
1936

Copyright, 1936
by
Columbia University Press

PRINTED IN THE UNITED STATES OF AMERICA

. . . I am a Jew! Hath not a Jew eyes? Hath not a Jew hands, organs, dimensions, senses, affections, passions, fed with the same food, hurt with the same weapons, subject to the same diseases, healed by the same means, warmed and cooled by the same winter and summer as a Christian is? If you prick us, do we not bleed, if you tickle us, do we not laugh, if you poison us, do we not die? And if you wrong us, shall we not revenge? If we are like you in the rest, we will resemble you in that.

William Shakespeare: The Merchant of Venice, Act 3, Scene 1.

. . . For ye, brethren, were called for freedom; only use not your freedom for an occasion to the flesh, but through love be servants one to another. For the whole law is fulfilled in one word, even in this: Thou shalt love thy neighbor as thyself. But if ye bite and devour one another, take heed that ye be not consumed one of another.

St. Paul: The Epistle to the Galatians, 5: 13-15.

ACKNOWLEDGMENTS

THE following work is based upon materials collected principally in England in 1929-1932 largely through personal interviews and correspondence with officials of Government Departments, employers' associations, trade unions, and other institutions, such as the Industrial Court and the Joint Industrial Councils, as well as from various Government reports, documents, and trade journals. The author wishes to express his great indebtedness to the gentlemen who kindly supplied him with important information and advice. A special acknowledgment of appreciation is due to the British Museum Reading Room Staff whose excellent service and unfailing courtesy are a pleasant and happy memory.

Invaluable help has been received from Dr. Eveline M. Burns of Columbia University who carefully read the manuscript. Her detailed criticism and suggestions made necessary additional study and a great deal of revision. Professor Leo Wolman also kindly read the manuscript and offered comments of great value. Professor Lindsay Rogers, under whose guidance the study was begun, has generously given of his time to the supervision of its progress. Thanks are due to the late Professor Henry R. Seager who kindly went over the outline and made many valuable suggestions. Thanks are also due to Professor Arthur Macmahon for his kindness in reading proof and to Mrs. C. P. Killien for her criticism in points of diction. The author has no word adequately to express his appreciation of the continuous support, both moral and financial, of Mr. Sung-

Soo Kim, one of the founders and a former President of Bosung College, Seoul, Korea. Without his aid the author's long stay abroad would have been impossible.

In acknowledgment the author can only say that he is bound in great obligation and sincere gratitude to these teachers and friends for their inspiration, aid, and encouragement.

The following work is an attempt to present the British methods of industrial peace as a whole, to describe the actual modes of operation of the various peace agencies, to determine the relative importance of each, and to indicate the possibilities of further progress toward increased efficiency and better and more democratic industrial relations admittedly among the urgent needs of to-day.

DUCKSOO CHANG

OCTOBER 11, 1936.

CONTENTS

PAGE

CHAPTER IV

The Government Agencies for Industrial Peace, with Special Reference to the Industrial Courts Act, 1919

CHAPTER V

The Joint Industrial Councils System

CHAPTER VI

The Negotiation Machinery in the Five Major Industries

CHAPTER VII

Past Experiences and Future Prospects

CHAPTER I

Introduction: the Basic Questions of Industrial Peace

1. DEMOCRACY AND INDUSTRIAL PEACE

Modern industrial disputes in the various countries of the world differ in the circumstances under which they occur, vary in nature and in magnitude and are growing ever more complex. Differences naturally arise between capital and labor, not only over questions in regard to the division of industrial proceeds and the regulation of working conditions, but also increasingly over moot questions of industrial reorganization. No one superior mind can order a perfect peace, or devise a complete peace machinery, any more than the farmer can order a regular course for changeable weather or the tailor cut a uniform to fit all sizes of people.

A survey of the British methods of securing industrial peace reveals that their chief characteristics, which are many-sided and flexible, are a direct result of the British practical, voluntary and democratic approach to the complicated problem of industrial disputes. The full significance of the British experiment is still hidden in the deep vistas of the future. A careful study of the actual operation, results and possibilities of the system as a whole may teach us, however, the practical lessons of democracy in the solution of modern industrial ills inasmuch as the system has been developed by a nation that is not only one of the most highly industrialized and admittedly well governed democracies in the world, but also a pioneer in the field of modern industrialism and representative government. Certainly it will reveal the basic requirements of peace in the modern industrial community, on the one hand, and of their fulfillment in democratic ways, on the other.

Peace in the profound sense of the term is not a mere negative concept of the avoidance of strife, but a positive idea of the fruitful co-operation of all for the fullest possible development of each. If an avoidance of conflict is the maximum requirement of peace this demand may be fully met by a police State whose armed forces are strong enough to keep law and order. Such peace, or rather tranquility, does not suffice of course to fulfill the conditions under which a full life and profound satisfaction can be obtained by every individual in complete harmony with millions of other lives. Such harmony is the basic requirement of peace in the true sense. Questions as to what the conditions are, how to establish and maintain them, through what institutions, and a discovery of the actual forces operating against or for such institutions are involved in the broad quest after a rightful order of society, which is indeed the central theme of political science and the greatest concern of modern democracy.

For democracy is not a mere majority rule for the achievement of whatever end the majority may set up. Its true aim is to make certain " that no member of the community shall be denied the opportunity to live a full and free life." [1] The basic assumption of the principle is that each individual has an equal claim to be his best self, for he is an ethical end in himself. Life's opportunities are not, however, equal under the actual conditions of society, and history proves that every inequality in social position, wealth, power, and knowledge may be made an occasion for oppression and exploitation. Modern democracy requires therefore that each man's position and his inherent rights shall be guaran-

[1] The Liberal Inquiry, *Britain's Industrial Future*, p. xvii.

teed through his participation in the Government, through representation and free criticism, so that his opportunity to live a good and civilized life may be realized to the fullest extent in harmony with the equal claims of his fellow men.

Democratic governments are being strained on all sides by the increasingly disturbing elements of social unrest and industrial dispute, while their authority is being challenged by opposing principles of Government. It is a debatable question whether democracy differs greatly from its principal alternatives, Communism, on the one hand, and Fascism, on the other, in so far as the abstract ideal is concerned; there are certainly great differences between them, however, in the measures advocated for the realization of ideal social conditions. It is not within the scope of this monograph to discuss in detail the merits and demerits of different political theories, but it is pertinent to note the marked distinctions between the fundamental conceptions of life underlying the respective philosophies. Dictatorship, whether of the Italian or the Russian brand, means order and unity imposed from above and enforced by Government authorities for the supposed good of the common people incapable of governing themselves. The basic principle of democracy as practised in Great Britain is tolerance, the attainment of unity and order being sought, not through the omnipotent power of the State, which cuts the cloth of social life into uniforms, but by the free expression of the inmost spiritual and social nature of the average British citizen through various social institutions in many and diverse forms.[2]

Diversity and flexibility are two marked characteristics of freedom responsive to the deeper unity and order of a moving equilibrium of social justice. These characteristics of

[2] *Cf.* John Milton, *Areopagitica*; R. H. Tawney, Radical Social Reconstruction in Chapter V, *Labor and Capital after the War*, edited by S. J. Chapman.

democracy are conspicuous in the British scheme of industrial peace. In the first place they determine the immediate methods to be applied in the settlement of disputes, and secondly they supply the spirit by which the existing industrial order itself moves slowly but irresistibly toward a broader basis of industrial democracy, with increasing responsibility of the Government for industrial peace and social security. Neither the technique nor the spirit, therefore, may fully be understood without a clear conception of British democracy at large. It is after all the general attitude and temper of the British people as applied in the particular field of industrial relations that gives a distinct color to their methods of industrial peace.

2. TRADE UNIONISM AND INDUSTRIAL DEMOCRACY

The Industrial Revolution, which set the world in a new direction of civilization, presented features without parallel in the long history of the British nation. It had been planned by nobody. Nor was it possible for the narrow range of human intelligence to anticipate its future course and provide for all possible social evils that might arise out of it. The only practical way open to the nation in facing the grave social and political dangers resulting from the great industrial disturbances caused by the Revolution was by piecemeal legislation as each occasion arose and particular cases proved their merits. Out of the long process of such gradual remedies during the last century and a half there have appeared two principal institutions which we may call the two ends of the British framework of industrial peace, namely, the system of social security and the complete recognition of trade unionism. They are the chief elements in the British position which make it possible for the various agencies charged with the immediate task of adjusting industrial disputes to work smoothly and effectively.

It is not necessary to go into the long process of the growth of British trade unionism in detail. But the salient points must be mentioned, since the entire effectiveness of the British system of conciliation and arbitration depends on the power of organization of employers and workmen.

In the old days industry was regarded as a duty to the State, and naturally labor was strictly regulated in respect both of wages and freedom of movement. This was an inevitable result of the then widely held social theory that the acts of individuals should be governed, not by "private interests", but by "social needs" of the community as a whole, the representative authority of which was the Government of the day.[3] As the nation grew up, with a wider market and diversified industrial processes, this narrow policy of regulation from the small center of the governing classes became untenable. A reaction set in under the doctrine of laissez-faire, with Adam Smith as its principal theoretical champion. Every man was now regarded as being free to rise to the top; but the actual facts of the Industrial Revolution brought the factory and mining workers into practical slavery. Their only chance to get a square deal from their employers lay in their number and in concerted action, but this was against public policy as expressed in the law. For the prohibition of combination among workers, which had been incidental to the general policy of regulation of trade and industry by the State since the days of Edward III, was now made an explicit general law under the Combination Law of 1800.

As the thunder of the French Revolution rolled away and the political atmosphere cleared up, this general policy was gradually modified until it was completely reversed by the Trade Disputes Act of 1906. The first step in this direc-

[3] See Sir James F. Stephen, *A History of the Criminal Law of England*, vol. iii, ch. 30.

tion was taken in 1825 when Peel's Act was passed, granting the right of combination among the workers for the purpose of regulating their own wages and hours of labor.[4] A second step was taken in 1859 when the Molestation of Workmen Act was passed, legalizing picketing. By 1871 the Liberal Government of Mr. Gladstone had come to the conclusion that industrial disputes could be settled in an amicable fashion only by making the laws "neutral, just, and equal" as between employers and workmen and by leading them to compose their differences among themselves by reason and understanding rather than by the force of law. This changed attitude of the Government was due partly to the strong growth of trade unionism in spite of the law and partly to the wide spread of the system of voluntary conciliation and arbitration which had been introduced by Messrs. Mundella, Kettle, and David Dale in the hosiery, building, and iron trades.[5] The Trade Union Act of 1871 legalized the trade unions in their civil capacity by granting complete protection for their funds. Four years later Disraeli's Government passed the Conspiracy and Protection of Property Act, which further legalized trade-union actions taken in connection with a trade dispute, unless such an act, if committed by a single person, should be indictable as a crime. Direct punishment for a simple breach of contract of service was also done away with under the Employers and Workmen Act, 1875.

Thirty years later Mr. Campbell-Bannerman, another Liberal Prime Minister, recognized the beneficent nature of trade unions, and pleaded for their complete immunity from

[4] Robert M. Rayner, *The Story of Trade Unionism, from the Combination Acts to the General Strike*, pp. 6-21.

[5] Parl. Deb. (3rd Ser.), (204), 257, 2032; (205) 638, 808, 1173, 1381, 1911; (206), 778; Feb. 14, 1871, per Mr. Bruce, then Home Secretary.

any civil liability that might arise out of a trade dispute.[6] In response to his recommendation there was passed the Trade Disputes Act, 1906, which prohibits the court of law from entertaining any action against a trade union, its members or officials, in respect of any tortious act alleged to have been committed on its behalf.[7]

The Trade Union Act, 1913, further authorized trade unions to establish a political fund by a majority vote of their members for the purpose of carrying on political activities on behalf of the working class.[8]

The trade unions of England have thus at last been recognized by law as an established institution of the country. They are free to own property and to further both industrial and political contests. They may enroll hundreds of thousands of workers in membership and collect a great sum of money in fees. They may enter into binding and detailed industrial agreements with organized employers which, though beyond the recognition of the law,[9] are nevertheless effective means for securing a self-imposed common rule in

[6] As for the Taff Vale case which eventually caused the passage of the Trade Disputes Act 1906, see The Law Reports, K. B., 1901, vol. i, pp. 170-7; L. R. A. C., 1901, pp. 426-445; see also Report of the Royal Commission on Trade Disputes and Trade Combinations, 1906.

[7] Parl. Deb. (4th Ser.), (154), 1295, March 28, 1906, per Sir John Walton, then Attorney General; (155), 21, March 30, 1906, per Sir Campbell-Bannerman, 51; (162), 120, 1607; (163), 1349, 1452; (164), 145, 856.

[8] See Amalgamated Society of Railway Servants *v.* Osborn (1910), A. C., 87, p. 94; C. A. (1909), 1 ch. 163; Parl. Deb., Commons (5th Ser.), (38), 593; (41), 2975. This right of the trade unions to establish a political fund by a majority vote of their members has been restricted under the Trade Disputes and Trade Unions Act of 1927, which establishes what is called the principle of "contracting in" by individual members to make contributions to the fund.

[9] Industrial agreements made by a majority of those engaged in the weaving section of the cotton trade may be made legally binding on the section as a whole by Order of the Minister of Labor under the Cotton Manufacturing Industry (temporary provisions) Act of 1934.

the government of industry. All this is subject, however, to a controlling central principle of British trade unionism, the principle of free association, the cardinal faith of British democracy. Under this principle no one is obliged to join a trade union or to contribute to its fund against his will. In trade disputes both employers and workers are free to declare a lockout or strike as they may think fit, and it is a crime by direct violence or intimidation, to coerce anybody to work or to abstain from work. The industrial disputants may freely approach the Government with a view to securing intervention in their behalf, but under the Trade Disputes and Trade Unions Act of 1927 it is unlawful for them to coerce the Government by means of a lockout or strike or to cause great inconvenience to the community by " wilfull breach " of a contract of service with the local or any other public authorities. In case of emergency the Government is empowered, under the Emergency Powers Act of 1920, to take all measures necessary for securing the essentials of life to the community, without imposing, however, any form of compulsory military service, industrial conscription, or prohibiting any genuine industrial strike or lockout.

These safeguards of personal freedom, on the one hand, and of communal interests, on the other, are the two broad limits within which organized employers and workmen may lawfully pursue whatever objects they choose in their collective capacity. This policy of wide public recognition of the corporate actions of employers and workmen, with a strict prohibition of violence and intimidation, has produced significant results. These results are noticeable in the steadily growing importance of British trade unionism as an operative force in furthering the democratic control of industry [10] through such civilizing influences as organization, self-discipline, and education among the workers.

[10] *Cf.* Milne-Bailey, W., *Trade Unions and the State*, pp. 371-380.

3. SOCIAL SECURITY AND PEACE REQUIREMENTS

Combination alone is not enough to secure a real growth of the law-abiding spirit, sense of fair play, good will, and comradeship, conditions that are marked among British workers and are, after all, the surest bond of social co-operation. It is the basic principle of modern democracy that such a spirit cannot be produced at the point of the bayonet or by an order from the State. Coercion may secure outward conformity, but often through the sacrifice of the development of personality, the basic core of social cohesion and of social institutions. For human personality can not be shaped with the knife. It can grow only through the extension of personal experience governed by the conception of right. When a man controls himself by his own sense of right or wrong he exerts his will and reason, and thereby develops his personality. Coercion renders such an exercise of his spiritual powers impossible or unnecessary, to the great pauperization of his moral nature. Self-determination is as essential to moral responsibility and personal growth as it is to a democratic Government. In other words, personality must develop through the spiritual growth of each individual, not by coercion, but by wide and deep appreciation of the true meaning of the good and civilized life.[11]

Spiritual growth, however, is dependent upon favorable conditions in society just as the gloss of the violet appears only in the spring soil. The poor may be blessed, but obviously hunger is not conducive to the development of personal integrity, nor do long hours of labor, unhealthy working conditions, squalid dwellings, oppressive industrial management lead to the fuller knowledge and understanding of life. It is to eliminate, as far as humanly possible, such

[11] *Studies in Religious Education*, edited by Philip H. Lotz and L. W. Crawford, ch. 19, pp. 434-449; *cf.* also L. T. Hobhouse, *The Elements of Social Justice*, *passim.*

evil conditions and to replace them with such as are conducive to the growth of spiritual power that social institutions are created and maintained. For this purpose modern democracy requires the State to create and maintain a certain system of rights providing a decent standard of living for all its people. This is the positive side of the principle of liberty, liberty in the sense that a man feels free when his fundamental needs are satisfied and harmonized in a well ordered personality. In the same way a society is free when its members are satisfied in their basic requirements for existence and are associated in free co-operation, not only in the State, but in the daily exercise of industry, art, science, and religion.[12] It is, however, obviously beyond the power of the State to make of every citizen a scientist of Dr. Einstein's standing or a businessman of Mr. Ford's calibre. At best it can secure only a certain minimum standard of social security so that no man shall fall below the line of a decent living. This is the way along which British democracy has been travelling toward "the growth of an improved commonwealth" of free people.[13]

The British system of social security may be studied under three headings: the factory and mines legislation, minimum wage legislation, and social insurance against major contingencies of modern industrial life.

The principle of factory legislation had been firmly established by the first year of the Reformed Parliament. Its central idea as fully developed in the course of the century was to secure a national humane order in the factories so that no wage earner should be allowed to descend to conditions injurious to social health under undue economic stress. Broadly speaking, this idea was due to no particular person or class, though certain individual names, belonging to the

[12] G. von Schulze-Gaevernitz, *Social Peace*, pp. xix-xx.

[13] Parl. Deb., Lords (31), 5, July 29, 1918, per Lord Haldane.

well-to-do class, such as Owen, Peel, Hobhouse, Sadler, Fielden, and Lord Shaftesbury, appear most prominently in the legislative records.[14] It was due rather to the English people themselves, whose public opinion, facing an emergency created by the Industrial Revolution, set itself to the task of compelling the mill owners to behave as good citizens, obliged to recognize the rights of the men and women they employed. This was possible because, while the industrial crisis was new, the English were a people with a history from which they could draw inspiration and learn methods to meet the difficult situation. One of their old institutions was the Poor Law. It was as an extension of this system that the first Factory Act applying to the parish apprentices employed in the cotton and woollen mills was passed in 1802. Education had also kept alive among the governing class the humanism of the Classics,[15] while Christianity, another great steadying force of the past, was represented in such leaders as Wilberforce and Shaftesbury, whose noble and passionate work for humanity is still a source of inspiration in the British legislative records. Furthermore the British intellectuals of the 19th century were not uninfluenced by

[14] It is interesting to note that "class struggle to the finish" in the Marxian sense has been largely unknown in modern British political history. The cause of the oppressed factory children was taken up by Tories and Whigs, as well as by the workers themselves. Progressive national co-operation has also secured political reforms, trade unions legislation, public education, and social security measures. In going through the British Parliamentary records one is struck by the recurring and persistent note of the British sense of fair play and practical idealism, in which, perhaps, lies the secret of the British national cohesion and the ability of "muddling through" in dire times.

[15] *The Debate on a Motion of the Abolition of the Slave Trade in the House of Commons, April 18-19, 1791*, published in London, 1791, pp. 1-42, per Mr. Wilberforce; per Mr. Pitt, pp. 94-103; per Mr. Fox, p. 104; *The Debate on the Motion for the Abolition of the Slave Trade in the House of Commons, April 2, 1792*, published in London, 1792, pp. 1-63, 138-168, 106-126, per Messrs. Wilberforce, Pitt and Fox.

contemporary European thought in which humanitarian liberal views of life played such a prominent part.

It was almost inevitable under such circumstances that legislative interference on behalf of the unfortunate factory workers should come sooner or later. Lord John Manners was prophetic, indeed, when, in the course of debate on a factory legislation Bill, he said:

> As long as women had eyes to weep and the souls to pray, as long as men had hearts to feel, voices to utter, and hands to raise, so long this struggle (for factory legislation) would be continued; so long the ill gained victories (of the opposition) be fruitless.[16]

Freedom did not mean the unrestricted power of the rich to destroy the poor in the course of trade. Liberty in the widest and positive sense of the term meant only the liberation of each man's life in the form of fulfilment and self-realization through regulated social co-operation. Such was the underlying principle of the factory legislation, which has grown up from its small beginning with the parish apprentices in the cotton mills until it now covers the entire field of the manufacturing and mining industries. Naturally children and youth became the first object of remedial legislation, and women the next. A minimum degree of decency was secured first in the hours of labor, sanitation, safety, health, and, after a long struggle, in wages and education.

Children today are protected by the Maternity and Child Welfare Act of 1918 as well as by the Education Acts both in pre-school and school years. Entering upon industrial life the workers come under the protection of the Mines and Factory Acts with regard to their working conditions and of the Employers' Liability Act and Workmen's Com-

[16] Parl. Deb. (3rd Ser.), (89), 1106-7; Feb. 10, 1847.

pensation Acts in connection with industrial accidents and diseases, while in certain unorganized trades they are entitled to minimum wage rates which are legally enforceable under the Trade Boards Acts.

Finally the various contingencies that are inherent in modern industrial life came under the notice of the State and have been provided against by a more or less complete system of social insurance. Premature death, ill health, and unemployment are provided for by means of the Health and Unemployment Insurance Acts, under which the premium is shared by the State, the workman, and the employer. Upon reaching the age of 70, or 65 in certain cases, the poor and worn-out workers become entitled to a pension from the State. The actual amount of money accruing to the individual workman under these arrangements is not much,[17] but it does

[17] The maximum weekly pension rate under the Old Age Pensions Acts, 1908-1924, is 10s. for those aged poor whose yearly income does not exceed £26, 5s.; a widow's pension of 10s. per week, with additional 5s. for the eldest and 3s. for each other child under 14, is payable under the Widows', Orphans', and Old Age Contributory Pensions Acts, 1925-1931, which provide also an orphan's pension at the rate of 7s. 6d. per week. A full sickness benefit, under the National Health Insurance Acts, 1911-1932, is payable to an incapacitated workman at the rate of 15s. per week for men, 12s. for unmarried women and widows, and 10s. for married women, for a period of 26 weeks, after which a disablement benefit is payable at the rate of 9s. per week for men and 7s. 6d. for women. The unemployment benefit rates as operative in 1934 were:

	Men	Women
Adults	17s. Od.	15s. Od.
Young persons 18-21	14s. Od.	12s. Od.
Juveniles 17-18	9s. Od.	7s. Od.
Dependent's benefit	9s. for an adult and 2s. for each child	

The weekly Trade Board minimum time rates for lowest grade of experienced workers, as operative in December, 1930, ranged from 40s. od. in the Retail Bespoke Tailoring in Scotland to 61s. 6d. in the Tobacco Trade, for males, and from 22s. in the Aerated Water in Scotland to 41s. in the Brush and Broom, for females, while the weekly minimum wage

at least show the way in which democracy tries to help secure to every member of the community a minimum order of humane existence, if not " a full and free life " in its entirety.

4. THE GENERAL OUTLINE OF THE BRITISH SCHEME OF INDUSTRIAL PEACE

The economic security provided by social legislation and the status of labor assured by strong trade unionism are the chief pillars of the British system of industrial peace. The former provides an atmosphere of good will by securing a minimum of decent living to every member of the community, while the latter supplies the power of self-government to the employers and workmen. In this broad perspective let us proceed to examine the methods of adjusting industrial disputes, the main characteristics of which we have already described. The general plan consists, practically speaking, almost entirely of conciliation and arbitration, which are many in form according to the varying circumstances of different industries, but are essentially all of the same voluntary character.

Conciliation in the ordinary sense of the term as used in industrial negotiation is nothing but the coming together of the parties concerned with a view to arriving at an amicable settlement of their disputes, although the term is often used

fixed by the Wages Committee for ordinary adult agricultural workers ranged form 30s. to 34s. in September, 1934. A comparison has been made as between the unemployment benefits for a family of five, the Rowntree Poverty Line, the Human Needs Standard, and wages of unskilled workers operative in December, 1930, as follows:

Benefits	Poverty Line Standard	Human Needs Standard	Wages of Unskilled Labor
£. S. D.	£. S. D.	£. S. D.	£. S. D.
1. 12. 0.	1. 19. 8.	2. 16. 10.	2. 12. 5.

H. F. Hohman, *British Social Insurance and Minimum Wage*, pp. 262, 402-3; see the annual Reports of the Ministries of Health and of Labor.

where the method would be more properly described as mediation. Mediation is the exercise of good offices by a third party in order to avert an impending rupture between the disputants, or, if the rupture has already taken place, to bring them together as soon as possible without himself acting as an arbitrator. He may, however, sometimes make and even publish recommendations as to the best course to be followed, thereby facilitating what may be called arbitration by public opinion. Arbitration is the settlement by an impartial outside agency of an issue on which the parties have failed to agree. It may in character be compulsory, voluntary, or a combination of both. Thus, for instance, both the reference of an issue to arbitration and the observance of the findings may be made a matter of compulsion, or be left entirely to the agreement of the parties. The reference may be made compulsory, but not the observance of the findings, or the converse may be the case.

In the British system we find, on the one hand, the various voluntary agencies of conciliation, that have been developed in different industries in the varying course of history, and, on the other, the Industrial Court, which was established under the Industrial Courts Act, 1919, as a permanent court of voluntary arbitration. In between, stands the Ministry of Labor which occupies a definite position in relation to industrial disputes and is armed with certain statutory powers. So far as the settlement of industrial disputes is concerned its main function is mediation. The keynote of the entire system is the principle of voluntary agreement, which has a long history behind it and many great avenues of development in the future.

In the following two chapters a brief survey of the historical background of conciliation and arbitration will be made in order to provide a clear view of the rich soil of experience, out of which the existing system has grown up with native vitality. In the three subsequent chapters we propose to examine the actual operation, results, adequacy, and relative position of the Governmental and non-governmental agencies.

Broadly speaking, the Government policy on industrial disputes is, so far as possible, to remain in the background, allowing the employers and workers to settle their differences among themselves. In grave cases, however, the Government has power not only to make impartial inquiries and inform those directly involved as well as the public at large of the true facts at issue, but also to make recommendations as to the best course to be followed. In all cases Government service in conciliation and arbitration is available on a purely voluntary basis, the chief agency being the Ministry of Labor with its conciliation officers, on the one hand, and the Industrial Court, on the other. Conciliation is more of a preventive measure and precedes arbitration, which is often arranged by the conciliation officers after the parties have failed to come to an agreement on the issue. The Industrial Court was established with high hopes, but the narrow basis of its constitution and its limited power have been responsible for its failure as the chief co-ordinating authority of wage movement in the country as a whole. In a more limited field it is a rational, expedient, and inexpensive means of arbitration. The Civil Service, certain industries governed by Acts of Parliament, and other trade groups have regular recourse to it for settlement of their disputes.

The prime importance of the British system of industrial peace consists in the negotiation machinery of the various industries themselves. It is of two kinds; one simply for conciliation, the other the Whitley Scheme. The conciliation machinery in the major industries selected for the present study reveals several distinct features which deserve a careful study. In the first place it is not imposed by an outside authority, but has grown up more or less spontaneously, relying for its effectiveness on strong organizations of both the employers and the workmen. Secondly, in nearly all cases it is national in scope, if not in the actual determination of wage rates, at least in the review of trade disputes. It is in this respect that the different industries exhibit their greatest resourcefulness by presenting a rich variety of methods appropriate to their own individual cirsumstances. Thirdly, the various conciliation organizations do not meet regularly for discussion of the broader interests of the industries as a whole; they are concerned mainly with the settlement of wage questions and other conditions of employment. In other words, stress is laid on the divisional, rather than on the cooperative side of the industry. It was to meet this shortcoming of the ordinary type of negotiation machinery that the Whitley Councils were established in a number of industries, but for one reason or another the possibilities of the new scheme have not been fully developed.

The broad lessons of this study are summarized in the concluding chapter. There is no panacea, no final solution of the industrial differences that arise from the very nature of modern industrial organization. The practical mind of the British people has, however, worked out a system or systems which are manysided and are flexible enough to meet the difficulties arising under widely different circumstances. These systems nevertheless show an irresistible movement toward a broader basis of industrial democracy.

CHAPTER II

The Historical Background of Conciliation and Arbitration

I. THE EARLY EXPERIMENTS IN COMPULSORY ARBITRATION

A. The Cotton Arbitration Acts, 1800-1813

A brief survey of the historical background of British industrial conciliation and arbitration may serve us well as it reveals the rich soil of experience out of which the existing voluntary system has grown up with native vitality in close connection with the growth of trade unionism. The principle of voluntary conciliation and arbitration was first recognized officially in the Conciliation Act of 1896, which was passed after a long series of experiments in compulsory arbitration had been made and failed. The first experiment was tried in the cotton trade under the 1800 Cotton Arbitration Act, covering all cases of disputes between employers and workmen. When arbitration was made a general law by the Arbitration Act of 1824 the scope of this method of settlement was limited to the interpretation of existing contracts only. Two more general laws were passed subsequently in the form of the Councils of Conciliation Act, 1867, and the Arbitration (Masters and Workmen) Act, 1872, which were, however, stillborn and inoperative.

By the last part of the 18th century the old method of wage-assessment by the justices of the peace in session [1]

[1] The Statute of Apprentices of 1562 (5 Elizabeth c. 4) repealed all existing labor laws and resorted to a new method of wage regulation which had tentatively been tried in 1389 and 1427. It did not prescribe, as previously had been done, the actual wage rates for various classes of workers on a national scale, but delegated the power to the local justices

had become only a memory, except that prescribed by the Spitalfields Weavers Act, 1773,[2] which continued in force until 1824. Toward the end of 1795 a movement was started by Mr. Samuel Whitebread for minimum wage legislation on the lines of the Statute of Apprentices of 1562 with a view to alleviating the hardships caused by war and bad harvests. The Bill was defeated by the opposition of Mr. Pitt, who had become a devout follower of Adam Smith in the belief that "trade, industry, and barter would always find their own level, and only be impeded by regulations which violated their natural operation and deranged their proper effect. . . . If the price of labor could be made to find its own level, it would be much more desirable than to assess it by any arbitrary Statute, which, in the execution, was liable to abuse, on the one hand, and inefficiency, on the other."[3] Wages in the cotton industry were thus left entirely to the economic pull and push between employers and workers, and disputes arose over repeated reductions which between 1792 and 1800 brought the wage level, in certain cases, from 24s. down to 9s. a week. Furthermore cotton manufacture was then partly domestic and partly factory, frequent disputes arising over such technical matters as spoiled materials, bad workmanship, and the violation of agreed prices. It was in such circumstances that the Cotton Arbitration Act, 1800 (40 Geo. 3, c. 90) was passed in re-

of the peace requiring them to determine district rates at their general sessions at Easter, taking into consideration "the plenty and scarcity of the time and other circumstances," and to make a special and diligent enquiry twice a year into the good execution of the rates so determined.

[2] The Act (13 Geo. 3, c. 68) authorized the local authorities of the London districts to determine wage rates and other disputes arising between the master and journeymen silk weavers in the districts.

[3] Sir F. M. Eden, *The State of the Poor Laws*, 1797, vol. iii, Appendix 2, pp. 308-12; *cf. Select Committee Report on Petitions, Cotton Manufacture*, 1809 (111) 3, p. 331.

sponse to petitions presented by both journeymen and master cotton weavers in Lancashire and adjoining counties.

In their petition the operatives complained that their wages had been greatly reduced while the cost of living had been progressively rising. Their "oppression" had been effected by a powerful combination of the master weavers, a combination that was so much in "secrecy, wealth, and power" that it was entirely beyond the power of the poor petitioners to check. They prayed therefore that "a more speedy and summary mode" than that provided for under existing laws might be established for the general regulation of the cotton trade and for the establishment of wages therein. The master cotton weavers also prayed for the same relief. The petitions were referred to a special committee, which reported that in many cases the master weavers, on various pretenses, such as war, bad market, spoiled materials, and bad workmanship, were paying lower wages than they had agreed to and that extensive wage reductions had been effected. In the case of bad faith, the Committee said, the aggrieved workers could go to the magistrates for a remedy, but this they could not do on account of the expense involved or would not do for fear of losing their jobs. Even if they did, the justices were not generally well acquainted with the technical points at issue. In such circumstances a Mr. James Holcroft, secretary to the Association of Weavers at Bolton, suggested to the Committee that arbitration might answer the question. "Each party", he said, "would be at liberty to choose an arbitrator, a man who understands the nature of manufacture, and, according to the nature of the clause, to compel the other to justice," at a cost within the reach of the operatives. This suggestion was adopted in the Cotton Arbitration Act of 1800.[4]

[4] *Journal Commons* (55), pp. 261-2, 485-94, 679, 784; March 5, May 8, June 20, July 28, 1800.

The Act applied to England only, but covered all cases of disputes arising between employers and workmen engaged in the cotton trade, including wage disputes over both future and existing rates. Each party to a dispute was free to demand arbitration and to appoint an arbitrator. The arbitrators so appointed were authorized to summon and examine witnesses and to decide the case finally. Should they fail within three days to agree upon an award, they were required to refer the case for final settlement to one of the justices of the peace of the locality. Any party refusing either to submit to arbitration or to observe the findings was to be liable either to the payment of ten pounds in damages or three months' imprisonment.

The Act of 1800 was in successful operation in 1803, when a Select Committee, appointed by the House of Commons to consider petitions presented by cotton weavers, took evidence on its actual operation. Within less than three years more than 1,500 cases on such mixed subjects as wage contracts, bad materials, implements, workmanship, and the setting up of new patterns had been dealt with under the law. Out of a total of 100 cases handled by a Mr. Richard Needham, 50 or 60 were settled by the arbitrator, about 30 by the parties themselves, and 5 by the magistrates, about two-thirds of the awards being in favor of the operatives. It was thus proved that this method of settling disputes was cheap and speedy,[5] but it should be borne in mind that the disputes so settled were, in a majority of the cases, of relatively small importance and arose out of existing contracts rather than over the more vital questions of future wages. It is true that under the law individual workers were granted the right to demand arbitration in case they could not come

[5] The arbitrators accepted generally 2s. as a fair recompense, while the general expense in the ordinary court of law would have amounted to about 7s. The time taken up in the process of arbitration under the law was usually an hour, but sometimes two or more days.

to terms with their employers as to future rates of wages, but the law was not clear on what might be called collective arbitration between employers and workmen en masse. Certainly it was illegal for the workers to combine for the purpose of such collective action, and without the backing of such collective action the poor workers were practically in no position to enforce their right to arbitration against any determined hostile employers. This position was clearly shown in the years 1808-1811, when the cotton operatives in Manchester, Paisley, and other places turned, not to arbitration, but to minimum wage legislation and the old Act of 5 Elizabeth for a relief of their acute distress as a result of the repeated reductions in wages and the extravagant rise in the cost of living.[6]

There were certain other defects in the Cotton Arbitration Act of 1800. Firstly, arbitrators appointed by interested parties could not be expected to be unbiased and unprejudiced; secondly, there was no power to compel the arbitrators to proceed with their case; thirdly, in the course of time there appeared a number of professional arbitrators who stirred up unnecessary strife in order to fish in the troubled waters. Some of these defects were remedied in the Arbitration Act of 1804 (44 Geo. 3, c. 87), which authorized a justice of the peace to determine the dispute, if the parties so desired, or, at the request of either party, to nominate a number of referees, from among whom each party

[6] The cotton operatives' petitions presented to the House of Commons praying for minimum wage legislation were referred to a Committee presided over by Mr. Thomas Standley. This Committee professed an unbounded faith in the doctrine of laissez-faire. The cotton operatives then turned their attention to the old Elizabethan Act and started a movement for its application which resulted only in the repeal of the Act on April 15, 1813 (53 Geo. 3, c. 40) just in time to take away the powers of the justices of the peace to act at their Easter Sessions. *Report on Petitions (Cotton Manufacture)*, 1809 (111) 3, p. 331; 1810-11 (232) II, pp. 389-90; *Journal Commons* (68), pp. 172, 185, 229, 299, 308, 318, 335, 337.

should choose an arbitrator. The arbitrators so chosen were then required to meet within two days and determine the case finally and, failing agreement, to bring it immediately before the justice of the peace for a final settlement.

In view of the apparently successful operation of the Cotton Arbitration Act the Scottish cotton weavers presented a petition to the House of Commons in 1803, praying for its extension to Scotland with the necessary modifications. The request was granted in an Act passed on August 11, 1803 (43 Geo. 3, c. 151). This Act anticipated the amendments of the following year, but applied only to those disputes that might arise over "the price or prices to be paid for work done or in the process of being done." Ten years later this Scottish Act was extended to Ireland, (53 Geo. 3, c. 75) also in response to a popular demand of the Irish cotton weavers.[7]

This experiment of compulsory arbitration in the cotton trade is interesting for a number of reasons. Firstly, the old practice of direct regulation of wages by State authorities was formally and finally done away with; secondly the actual task of the adjustment of industrial disputes was primarily entrusted to those who were well acquainted with the trade in question rather than to the local authorities whose public office required quite a different set of qualifications; thirdly, the trade was still unorganized, leaving the individual workers to the mercy of their employers; and fourthly, the compulsory nature of the experiment still showed a remnant of the old spirit of the Elizabethan time when industry was regarded more as a public concern than as a strictly private affair. The new wine was poured into the old bottles. This will become clearer as we proceed further.

[7] *Journal Commons* (58), pp. 152, 216, 278, 422-3, Feb. 11, Mar. 1, 22, May 8, 1803; (59), pp. 187-8, Mar. 28, 1804; (68), p. 362, Mar. 30, 1813; *Minutes of Evidence before the Committee on Cotton Arbitration Act*, 1800, 1802-3 (114) 8, pp. 33-4; *Report of Committee on Cotton Manufacture*, 1803-4 (41) 4, p. 211.

B. The Arbitration Act, 1824

We have seen in the preceding chapter that the prohibition of combination among workers was made a general policy under the Combination Law of 1800. It was in the same Act that compulsory arbitration was prescribed for the settlement of industrial disputes generally. Apparently it was thought fair that, if the workers were to be deprived of their only means of self-help by the prohibition of combination,[8] they should in return have some protection from the law. Arbitration appeared best to serve this good purpose. Accordingly provisions on the lines of the Cotton Arbitration Bill, then under consideration by Parliament, were inserted in the Combination Bill. When the Bill came up for a third reading, however, Sir John Freeman, then Attorney General, objected to the arbitration clauses on the ground that the object of the measure "was to settle and appoint wages and not such differences as may arise on the contract itself." Mr. Pitt himself intervened, and the amendments later accepted changed the whole significance of the arbitration proposals, for the Combination Law, as finally passed, prescribed compulsory arbitration for the settlement of such minor cases as might arise over the interpretation of existing contracts, excluding the more important determination of future wage rates from its scope.[9]

Twenty-four years later the Combination Laws came under review by the Hume Committee which, in the course of its inquiry, found that the practice of industrial arbitration had been attended with good results and recommended that the various existing arbitration laws should be codified with necessary amendments. This recommendation was

[8] *Journal Commons* (61), p. 554, July 17, 1806; Appendix No. 99, p. 903.

[9] *Journal Commons* (55), pp. 707, 716-7, 730, 744, 772, 776; June 27, 30, July 4, 8, 1800; *Bills Public*, 1800, vol. 30, pp. 959, 961.

adopted in the 1824 Arbitration Act,[10] which applied the principle of compulsory arbitration to the settlement of all disputes arising between employers and workmen engaged in any trade, except disputes concerning future wage rates. The arbitration procedure itself did not differ much from that provided in the Cotton Arbitration Act, 1800, as amended in 1804, except for an important proviso to the effect that, should the parties to a trade dispute agree to refer their case to arbitration outside the law, such agreement might be taken as valid as though under the Act itself. The proviso proved subsequently a fertile soil for arbitration experiments.

The 1824 Arbitration Act was amended as to details once in 1837 (7 Will. 4 and 1 Vict., c. 67) and twice in 1845 (8 & 9 Vict., c. 77, 128).[11] The amendment of 1837 was favored by operative silk weavers in the Spitalfields, indicating that the Act of 1824 was still in operation in the trade. When the Act was amended in 1845, however, there were revealed not only the fundamental defect of the arbitration system as a means of protection for labor in lieu of trade combinations, but also certain new trends of thought in the industrial field. In a petition presented to the House of Lords, in May, 1845, the journeymen silk weavers in Chesh-

[10] The Act (5 Geo. 4, c. 96) was prepared by Joseph Hume, Sturgess Bourne and Peter Moor, who also framed the Combination Act, 1824. *Journal Commons* (79), pp. 29, 395-6, 408, 433, 443, 466, 476, 518, 521.

[11] By the amendment of 1837 the time limit within which a complaint could be lodged was extended from six to fourteen days and the jurisdiction of the justices of the peace was transferred from the locality where both parties resided to that of the party complained against. The amendments made in 1845 were concerned mainly with the furnishing of particulars in the hosiery and silk trades, making it compulsory to issue the particulars which were to be produced as evidence in case of trade disputes arising in the industries. *Journal Commons* (92), p. 606, July 7, 1837; *Journal Lords* (77), p. 249; *Journal Commons* (100), p. 464, May 19, 1845.

ire and other places complained that they could not seek redress of oppression by their masters in the Arbitration Act of 1824 because of a well founded dread of losing their employment. They, therefore, prayed their Lordships to establish local boards of trade, to be composed of masters and workmen in an equal number, with power "to regulate the proportionate number of apprentices, decide upon any abatement required by insufficient work, correct any inequality of price for the same work, and generally to superintend the operations of the trade."

A similar plea was presented to the Muggeridge Commission on the hosiery trade in 1845 by a Mr. William Felkin, who stated that the Arbitration Act of 1824 had not the confidence of the working class or of the employers. He was in favor of the establishment of a Council of Prud'hommes which, in his view, would operate to heal differences as they arose and to prevent abuses by combining the experiences of masters and men, whose ultimate interests were identical after all.[12] This idea of local trade boards was taken up, as we shall see presently, in the Councils of Conciliation Act, 1867. It was a direct reflection of the changing public attitude toward labor, and a herald of the great movement for collective bargaining, which in 1867 won its first official recognition by the Trade Union Commission, and has finally resulted in the establishment of the Joint Industrial Councils to be discussed in a later chapter.

There is some evidence that the Arbitration Act of 1824 was still occasionally invoked in the Spitalfields silk area in London in the years 1855-56, when a Select Committee was appointed by the House of Commons, with Mr. W. A. Mackinnon as chairman, to inquire into the expediency of establishing equitable tribunals for the amicable settlement of dif-

[12] William Felkin, *An Account of the Machine-Wrought Hosiery Trade*, 1845, London, p. 33; Lord Amulree, *Industrial Arbitration*, p. 55.

ferences between masters and operatives. Throughout the country as a whole, however, the Act had been "nearly inoperative", the Committee reported, hardly anybody, whether master or workman, resorting to it. The principal causes of this gross failure were believed to be that (1) the arbitration procedure under the law had too much the appearance of a criminal proceeding; (2) the magistrates were allied too closely with the manufacturing interests; (3) there was a reluctance to refer cases to the decision of an unknown set of arbitrators, that is to say there was no standing panel of expert arbitrators whose intimate knowledge of trade and impartial treatment of disputes could command the full confidence of the parties.[18]

The principal cause was, however, to be found in the change of the social and economic condition of the country at large. When the Cotton Arbitration Act was passed in 1800, the cotton trade was still partly domestic and partly factory. The trade was largely unorganized, and frequent disputes arose between individual employers and workmen over minor technical details. By the middle of the century, however, the factory system had reached an advanced stage both in its manufacturing process and in State regulation of working conditions. The workers were being organized and most work was done under the immediate supervision of the foreman in the factories. The occasions for minor disputes were greatly reduced under the changed circumstances. When they did arise they could be dealt with effectively by representatives of organized employers and workmen without any outside aid. The serious disputes came more and more to be concerned with such large questions as

[18] *Report of the Select Committee on Master and Operatives (Equitable Councils of Conciliation)*, 1856 (343) 13, p. 3; *Minutes of Evidence before the Committee*, pp. 156, 192, 197-8, per Mr. Hammil, a police magistrate for Worship Street, London.

future rates of wages and hours of labor, which were outside the scope of the Arbitration Act. On these matters the representatives of organized employers and workmen came together to confer directly as a result of the repeal of the Combination Laws, which had "crippled the energies of the capitalists and fettered the action of the workmen." [14] In other words, trade unionism had at last come to stay and began to break a new path in British industrial relationships, the end of which we have not yet reached.

C. *The Councils of Conciliation Act, 1867, and the Arbitration (Masters and Workmen) Act, 1872*

We have already seen that the Combination Act of 1825 was the first step in the recognition of labor's right to combine. It was indeed only a first step, for, while the workers might combine for their own immediate protection, it was still unlawful for them to combine on behalf of their fellow workers, or to strike on any question other than wages and hours of labor, such, for instance, as the introduction of piecework or machinery or the employment of apprentices or non-unionists, all of which it was then thought to be exclusively within the privilege of the management to decide. Picketing was also almost impossible under the wide interpretation given by the law courts to the intimidation clause of the 1825 Act. As late as 1853, Lord Palmerston himself stated in Parliament that the "mere presence of the picket might become an effective intimidation" to those workers who wished to continue work in order to support their families.[15]

No law can prevail, however, against the natural tendency of men to combine when their interests coalesce. Trade

[14] *The Report of the Select Committee on Masters and Operatives*, 1860 (307) 22, p. 443; Appendix No. 3, p. 104; see also Memorandum by Thomas Winters included in the same Report.

[15] Parl. Deb. (3rd Ser.), (125), 647; April 5, 1853.

unions grew up in spite of the law, and many bitter and disastrous strikes were fought, the most notable examples being the engineering and the cotton strikes in 1852 and 1853 respectively. It was under such circumstances that the House of Commons appointed the Mackinnon Committee in 1856, which, after an exhaustive examination of the subject matter, recommended the establishment of local courts of conciliation and arbitration to be elected by trade members with power to decide all questions except future rates of wages. This recommendation was criticised as a proposal for the creation of "a multitude of small Parliaments," but after prolonged discussion and many inquiries by Parliamentary Committees, it was finally adopted in the Councils of Conciliation Act, 1867 (30 & 31 Vict., c. 105), popularly known as Lord St. Leonard's Act.[16] Under the law the Home Secretary was authorized, upon a joint petition by masters and workmen engaged in any trade or trades within a locality, to license the formation of a Council of Conciliation, consisting of an equal number of members elected each year by qualified members of the trade concerned and presided over by an impartial chairman with a casting vote. All questions, except future rates of wages, were in the first instance to be referred to a standing Committee of Conciliation, and, upon failure of the Committee to agree, to the whole Council whose decision was final and enforceable under the Arbitration Act of 1824.

This elaborate machinery provided in the Act of 1867 anticipated a great deal of the later development of the tripartite system of arbitration court adopted under the Conciliation Act, 1896, which we shall presently discuss, but its very elaborateness rendered the machinery inoperative. In the first place such machinery required for its effective operation some administrative means, such as a central Gov-

[16] *Journal Commons* (111), pp. 58, 74, Feb. 19, 28, 1856.

ernment Department or its equivalent in the trade union officials, whose duty it was to see that the machinery worked, but there was no such administrative organ at the time. Secondly, the scheme was based, not upon the recognition of trade unionism as such, but upon the group spirit in the trade concerned, which, in fact, did not exist to any great extent. Thirdly, the elaborate machinery was perhaps inevitable in view of the compulsory nature of the scheme, which was really an antithesis of the growing spirit of voluntary conciliation and arbitration in the actual industrial fields. In the fourth place the elaborate scheme could not do anything about the future rates of wages which vitally affected the daily lives of the individual workmen. It was really a big hammer to crack a small nut, and nobody bothered much about it.[17]

The last attempt to prescribe compulsory arbitration for industrial disputes was made in the Arbitration (Masters and Workmen) Act, 1872 (35 & 36 Vict., c. 46), popularly known as Mr. Mundella's Act. By this time an important change had taken place in the public attitude toward trade unionism. In 1867 a Royal Commission was appointed to inquire into the activities of trade unions and their effects upon industry and industrial relations. The Commission went into various phases of trade union activities and was deeply impressed by the growing practices of voluntary conciliation and arbitration between organized employers and workmen, notably in the hosiery trade at Nottingham and the building trade in the Midlands. In the opinion of the Commission trade disputes were bound to arise on the difficult question of wages, whether trade unions continued to grow or not. The strike was a very rude method, to be avoided as far as possible. Compulsory arbitration was out of the question, because there was "no principle on which

[17] *Cf.* George Howell, *The Conflict of Capital and Labor*, p. 451.

the arbitrator may proceed," and because it was practically impossible "to bind so fluctuating a body as the workmen to any decision of a permanent character." The best hope for the peaceful settlement of industrial disputes lay in the steady growth of voluntary trade boards for conciliation and arbitration. Such trade boards would consist of an equal number of representative employers and workmen engaged in particular trades and would settle disputes arising in the trades concerned. They required no complicated machinery, no novel division of profits, no new method of business, no Act of Parliament. All that was needed was simply for certain representative employers and workmen to meet at regularly stated times and discuss around a table their common trade interests. Under such a system, the Report said, "there is not then that jealousy and distrust on the part of either employers or workmen which there would be if it were supposed that they were committing themselves beforehand to have important questions definitely settled by a board of arbitration in whose decisions they might not always feel confidence." [18]

The Minority Report, signed by Lord Lichfield, Thomas Hughes, and Frederick Harrison, struck the same note with more emphasis on arbitration and working rules, stating that there was a uniform approval "of a system of working rules agreed to between employers and employed, and still further of the existence of some recognized board of arbitration to give these rules consistency and to interpret their effect." These codes of rules and the boards of arbitration were in their nature spontaneous and could receive no direct aid from any legislative source. It was pointed out, however, that the existence of some associations or trade unions was essential to the formation of such codes of rules and boards

[18] *The 11th Report of the Royal Commission on Trade Unions*, 1869 (4123), p. 235; xxvii-xxviii.

of arbitration. Whatever measures tended to give "a permanent, legal and public character to unionism," the Report went on, would tend "to improve the existing unions and to fit them to co-operate in sound mutual agreement with employers." With this broad purpose in view the three members of the Royal Commission recommended that full legal recognition should be given to "all trade societies not tainted by any criminal character," and that increasing facilities should be given in all cases "where a code of rules exists under mutual agreement for the enforcement of the agreement against either party who has bona fide accepted it." [19]

The Minority Report was given effect in the Trade Union Act of 1871 with regard to trade union recognition, and in the Arbitration Act of 1872 [20] with regard to facilities for the enforcement of industrial agreements voluntarily entered into between employers and workmen. Under the Act the employer was authorized, on the occasion of the hiring of a workman, to deliver to him a printed copy of an agreement, which would become binding under the old Arbitration Act of 1824 unless rejected by the man within a certain specified period of time. This agreement might contain working rules, covering wage rates, hours of labor, or any other conditions of employment, and might designate a board of arbitration to give interpretation to the agreement.

The Act of 1872 was a twin brother of Lord St. Leonard's Act of 1867, though there were some notable differences between them. The 1867 Act provided more for the present, ruling future rates of wages out of its scope, while the 1872 Act made provisions more for the future since under the law the question of future wages could be arranged by

[19] *The 11th Report of the Royal Commission on Trade Unions*, pp. xxxi, xlix.

[20] The Bill was introduced on April 18, 1872, by Messrs. Mundella, Thomas Hughes and others.

agreement to be settled by arbitration. The Act of 1867 was primarily intended to encourage conciliation by local boards of trade, while the Act of 1872 was designed to facilitate arbitration by an impartial outside agency through written agreements. Both Acts concurred, however, in their presupposition that employers and workmen should come together voluntarily for the discussion of their common interests. In fact the Act of 1872 added nothing new to the growing actual practices of collective bargaining between employers and workmen, except the provisions made for the legal enforcement of industrial agreements. It came to naught in practical results as Mr. Mundella himself admitted in 1887.[21]

2. THE CONCILIATION ACT, 1896

A. Its Provisions

By 1891 when another royal commission on labor was appointed the voluntary boards of conciliation and arbitration had grown greatly both in number and influence. It will be recalled that when the Trade Union Commission of 1867 was appointed the voluntary boards were confined to the type of trade boards which were organized strictly on trade lines. By 1891 there had appeared a new type, the so called General or District Conciliation Boards, which were usually brought into being by co-operation between local Chambers of Commerce and Trade Councils for the purpose of settling any trade disputes arising in the locality. The number of the voluntary boards of the two types had reached 92 by 1894, and had settled 1,146 cases in the same single year, while the existing Acts of compulsory arbitration had seldom been put into operation, very few people even know-

[21] J. A. Mundella, *Industrial Association, in the Reign of Queen Victoria*, edited by Thomas H. Ward, vol. ii, p. 79; L. W. Hatch, *Government Industrial Arbitration*, pp. 395-97.

ing of their existence. It was generally recognized that the best guarantee for the enforcement of conciliation agreements and arbitration awards could be found only in the growth of effective trade unionism.

The Royal Commission on Labor of 1891 reported that in the well organized trades there was "every prospect of fewer outbreaks of industrial conflicts between employers and employed, due to the growing practice of consultations upon equal terms of representatives of either party in conference or standing joint committees, in spite of occasional serious disturbances." [22] The trade customs growing out of such mutual conference between organized employers and workmen were so strong that, even without assistance from the law, they could afford "an almost certain and practically sufficient guarantee for the carrying out of industrial agreements and awards."

Many witnesses examined by the Royal Commission had still faith in the efficacy of compulsory regulation of industrial relations, such as compulsory arbitration, legal prohibition of strikes and lock-outs, voluntary boards of conciliation and arbitration vested with legal powers, and the incorporation of the employers' and workmen's associations with powers to enter into legally binding collective agreements.[23] The Royal Commission rejected these proposals either as impracticable or undesirable, and recommended certain measures of a purely voluntary nature,[24] which were adopted in the Conciliation Act of 1896. The Conciliation Bill itself, as originally drafted, had proposed to invest the court of arbitration with certain legal powers, but Mr. Mundella, the father of the British conciliation boards, objected to "any-

[22] *The 5th and Final Report of the Royal Commission on Labor*, 1894 (C. 7421), p. 53.

[23] *Ibid.*, pp. 54-58.

[24] *Ibid.*, pp. 98-101.

thing like a court" in connection with industrial arbitration. The clause was omitted in Committee, and another clause was adopted declaring that the Arbitration Act of 1889 should not be applied to any settlement of an industrial dispute under the Conciliation Act.[25]

The Conciliation Act, 1896 (59 & 60 Vict., c. 30), definitely buried the past and ushered in the full forces of the new age. It repealed the three existing compulsory arbitration Acts of 1824, 1867, and 1872, and took a positive step toward helping and encouraging the growth of voluntary boards of conciliation and arbitration by the simple means of registration with the Board of Trade; such registration carried no special power or privilege with it. Provision was made also for informal consultation with those immediately concerned on the advisability of establishing trade or district boards of conciliation and arbitration (clauses 1 and 4). The Act charged the Central Government with the duty, or privilege, of intervention in trade disputes, and provided, for the purpose, a wide and very flexible method in order to meet every set of circumstances. The Board of Trade was authorized (1) to inquire into the causes and circumstances of any existing or impending trade dispute, (2) to take steps expedient for the purpose of enabling the parties to meet under an impartial chairmanship to be mutually agreed upon or to be appointed by the Board of Trade, (3) to appoint a conciliator or board of conciliation on the application of either party, or (4) to appoint an arbitrator upon the application of both parties to the dispute, (clause 2). In brief

[25] *Bills Public*, 1893-4 (4), p. 35; —1894 (2), pp. 651-55; —1895 (1), p. 459; —1896 (1), pp. 163, 399, 407; Parl. Deb. (4th Ser.), (37), 644, 660, 791; (42), 419, 423, 427; (43), 1427; Feb. 19, 20, June 30, Aug. 4, 1896, per Messrs. Ritchie, Bryce, Mundella, and Lord Dudley. The Arbitration Act of 1889 is concerned with business matters and grants the court of arbitration certain legal powers in regard to procedure and findings.

the Act provided the means of public inquiry, conciliation, and arbitration upon a purely voluntary basis, as each particular case might require.

B. Its Actual Operation

1. The Registration Clause

It is important to note how the registration clause has assisted the growth of the voluntary boards of conciliation and arbitration that provided the foundation upon which the British system of industrial peace has been erected. Technically speaking the clause failed of its purpose as the majority of the conciliation boards did not take advantage of it.[26] At the end of 1919 there were altogether 479 conciliation boards and joint committees, but only 13 of them had registered with the Board of Trade.[27] In a broader sense, however, the clause served a good purpose by facilitating the typical British method of doing things quietly and informally. It created an official link between the Government and the voluntary agencies for industrial peace. Immediately after the passage of the Conciliation Act in 1896, the Commercial, Labor, and Statistical Department in the Board of Trade, to which the administration of the Act was entrusted,[28] issued a circular to the various boards of con-

[26] Lord Amulree, *Industrial Arbitration*, p. 108.

[27] *Report on Conciliation and Arbitration by the Ministry of Labor*, 1921 (221), p. 12.

[28] The Labor Department originated in the Bureau of Labor Statistics, which was created in 1886 by Mr. Mundella, then President of the Board of Trade, for the purpose of collecting and publishing labor statistics so that labor disputes might be settled peaceably by arbitration or otherwise on the basis of reliable facts. In 1893 the Bureau was reorganized into a separate Labor Department consisting of a Commissioner for Labor, a chief Labor Correspondent, and a number of local correspondents. The main work of the new Department was, in addition to the collection of labor statistics, to conduct special inquiries into matters of various industrial interests and publish the *Labor Gazette*, a monthly magazine

ciliation and arbitration, calling their attention to the registration clause and stating that their registration would be of good service, not only in avoiding the overlapping of work between the Department and the voluntary boards, but also in keeping the public informed on the progress of conciliation and arbitration as a means of peaceful settlement of industrial disputes. Acting upon the advice contained in this circular the voluntary boards, both registered and unregistered, kept in close touch with the Board of Trade in their settlement of disputes and supplied it with detailed accounts of their proceedings, while the Board of Trade gave them every possible assistance in the form of necessary information, appointment of required arbitrators, and the promotion of their good cause generally.

That this close and informal co-operation between the Board of Trade and the voluntary agencies had been attended with good results was clearly shown in 1919 when the Industrial Courts Bill proposed to repeal the Conciliation Act of 1896. Mr. J. Jones, speaking on behalf of the Labor Party, stated that nearly every trade throughout the country had a

which is still being published by the Ministry of Labor. Government intervention in trade disputes was not thus orginally included among the activities of the Labor Department, but the course of events soon forced it to take administrative action, without Parliamentary authorization, in labor disputes, notably in the great coal strike in 1893 and the boot and shoe trade dispute in 1895. This position was regularized by the passage of the Conciliation Act, 1896. Under the new Act Government intervention grew steadily until in 1911 the work was separated from other functions of the Labor Department and placed under the sole charge of a new Chief Industrial Commissioner, the Labor Department itself becoming an entirely separate Department responsible for the administration of the Trade Boards Act, the Labor Exchanges Act, and the National Insurance (Pt. II) Act, 1911, in addition to its original work of gathering labor statistics. See Appendix to the Fourth Report of the Royal Commission on Civil Service, Minutes of Evidence, Q. 32-697, March 14, 1913, per Mr. G. S. Barnes, then Comptroller General of the Labor Department.

voluntary arrangement under the Conciliation Act of 1896. Any attempt to interfere with the arrangements under the Act would make considerable trouble and prevent the successful operation of the new measures proposed in the Bill. Mr. Arthur Henderson believed that, "in spite of failure to register," the Conciliation Act had acted as a stimulus to the setting up of conciliation boards. Another member observed that the Act of 1896 was an inducement to the establishment by employers and workmen of conciliation boards, which the Bill did not provide for. Sir Robert Horne in charge of the Bill was impressed and, admitting the value of the word conciliation, allowed the 1896 Conciliation Act to remain on the Statute Book "as a lamp" of hope to which, in case of trouble, people might turn their eyes.[29]

The consultation clause of the Conciliation Act has also furnished legal ground for the conciliation officers of the Board of Trade, in the settlement of disputes, "to suggest and establish means by agreement for the prevention of future strikes and better relations, more sympathy, between employer and employed, in spite of the hot enmity in which they might have been engaged."[30] This policy was responsible for the creation of the railway conciliation boards in 1907 and the conciliation board for the tramways department of the London County Council in 1909.

Under these circumstances the voluntary conciliation and arbitration boards increased both in number and in influence from year to year, as is shown opposite:[31]

[29] Parl. Deb. Commons (5th Ser.) (121), 441-444, Nov. 12, 1919.

[30] Lord Askwith, *Industrial Problems and Disputes*, p. 129.

[31] Compiled from the Board of Trade Reports on Strikes and Lock-Outs. The Board of Trade published detailed reports on the rules and organization of the voluntary boards in 1907 and 1910. See also the annual Reports of the Proceedings under the Conciliation Act, 1896.

Year	Trade Boards	District and General Boards	Total
1894	72	20	92
1895	72	21	93
1896	83	22	105
1909	260	17	277
1910	265	17	282
1911	277	16	293
1912	282	15	297
1913	310	15	325
1918	—	—	410
1919	—	—	479

It will be noticed in the table that, while the Trade Boards increased from 83 in 1896 to 310 in 1913, the District and General Boards decreased from 22 to 15. It may safely be inferred that as the Government's responsibility for trade disputes increased the influence of the General Boards receded. In other words the basis of organization for industrial peace was shifted from local to trade lines, with trade unionism as the main operative force. Another interesting feature was the increasing number of voluntary boards,[32] which made provision for the appointment of a conciliator or arbitrator by the Board of Trade in the case of a deadlock. This provision indirectly gave the public an opportunity to have a voice in the settlement of trade disputes. The practice has been more or less fully recognized in most of the negotiation machinery now existing in the well organized industries, notably in coal mining, railways, iron and steel, and in the cotton trades.

[32] The number of Boards with such a provision grew:

1897	2	1909	87
1901	35	1911	97
1903	41	1913	121
1905	48		
1907	60	1918	194

2. Government Intervention in Trade Disputes

For direct Government intervention in trade disputes a general plan of procedure was soon worked out as the Conciliation Act became widely known and increasingly used. Before the outbreak of the Great War the plan was a progress from the appointment of single conciliators and arbitrators to the establishment of ad-hoc courts of arbitration on a tripartite basis representing employers, workers, and the public, and from the system of ad-hoc courts of arbitration to the creation of a standing Industrial Council representing the industries of the country as a whole.

Under the actual operation of the Conciliation Act it was established within a year that "the presence of an impartial person able to mediate, to prevent the effect of personal asperities, to make suggestions, and to facilitate concessions," was a great benefit to both parties to a trade dispute,[33] and, accordingly, the Act became popular as the years wore on. The total number of applications for Government intervention made in the year, from July, 1896, to June, 1897, was only 31, but the number increased in 1910, 1911, 1912 and 1913 to 59, 68, 65, and 78 respectively. Out of a total of 610 applications made in the years 1896-1913, 417 (nearly 70 per cent) were joint applications, Government action without application from either party being taken only in 86 cases.[34] This growing public confidence was secured in the first few years by a group of men, whose service the Government was fortunate enough to obtain, either as single arbitrators or as conciliators. For instance, in a little over

[33] *The 1st Report of the Proceedings under the Conciliation Act*, 1896, p. v; *cf.* Lord Askwith, *Industrial Problems and Disputes*, p. 79.

[34] See the *Annual Reports of the Proceedings under the Conciliation Act*, 1896.

four years, from 1896 to 1901, Mr. G. R. Askwith,[35] (now Lord Askwith), was appointed an arbitrator 6 times and a conciliator, 4; Mr. Hudson, arbitrator 11 times; Sir William Markby, arbitrator 6 times and conciliator 3; Mr. Thomas Bell arbitrator 4 times. This repeated appointment of the same arbitrators or conciliators in case after case naturally developed in them an expert knowledge and skill in dealing with industrial disputes and gained them the confidence of the parties concerned.

In the course of time, however, it was found that the system of single arbitrators had certain drawbacks. The arbitrator had in many cases to rely for his decision solely upon the arguments and statements put forth by the parties, whose industrial position, it was alleged, he did not fully understand. To meet this difficulty a new system of arbitration court on a tripartite basis of representation was established in 1908. Three standing panels of arbitrators, called the chairmen's, the employers' and the workmen's panels, were formed by the Board of Trade after consultation with various leading trade organizations, from which the Board of Trade would appoint the actual members of an arbitration court as occasion might require.[36] The new scheme, really a reversion to the old system of arbitration provided in the 1867 Act, had the advantage of enabling the impartial chairman to secure the assistance of those who had intimate knowledge of the industrial and psychological background

[35] Mr. Askwith was subsequently appointed the Chief Industrial Commissioner and the Chairman of the Committee on Production. He did more than anybody else in the propagation of the cause of conciliation and arbitration in the British industrial fields. A pen sketch of him and his method of conciliation by Mr. Ben Tillett may be found in Lord Askwith, *Industrial Problems and Disputes*, p. 232; see also *ibid.*, pp. 78-83.

[36] *The 7th Report of the Proceedings under the Conciliation Act, 1896*, p. 135.

of the issue and were therefore able correctly to assess the arguments of the parties.

This system of ad-hoc courts of arbitration was, again, found defective in the fact that the arbitrators were ordinarily engaged in other vocations and only occasionally were called upon to act, without having any knowledge of what other arbitrators were doing, or any enduring principle to which decisions in any particular case should be related as closely as possible in view of the interdependence of modern industries. The Conciliation Act itself had given no indication of the principles to be pursued by the arbitrators nor any co-ordinating system of their activities. Another difficulty was the delay that was inevitable in the appointment of a court from a list of busy men occupied with other affairs, while speed at the psychological moment was essential to any settlement of industrial disputes.

With a view to overcoming these difficulties a standing Industrial Council was created in 1911, consisting of thirteen representatives each from organized employers and workers, with Sir George Askwith, appointed to the new office of Chief Industrial Commissioner, as chairman. The Council, which was to meet regularly in quarterly conferences each year, had a two-fold function to discharge. As a Parliament of industries, representing the industries of the country as a whole, the Government might refer to it cases for its considered opinion on specific matters; as a tribunal for the settlement of industrial disputes the parties concerned might, by agreement, refer to it their disputes either for an impartial ascertainment of the facts only or for specific recommendations as to the best course to be followed. Mr. Sydney Buxton, who was then President of the Board of Trade and responsible for the creation of the Council, stated that considerable progress had recently been made toward what he called " federated effort—combinations of trade-unions, on the one hand, and of federations of employers' associations, on the other, and that, from the point of view of trade disputes, trade and industry are far more interdependent than they used to be. While, therefore, a few years ago the creation of a National Conciliation Council, representing all the great industries, might have been thought to be premature, its existence is really now essential so that these matters can be considered as a whole." Such a national Council, he believed, would bring to bear on industrial disputes "a great range of advice, a great weight and a greater likelihood, therefore, of useful and acceptable action, especially before, rather than after, stoppage of work." Such a body would also enable the parties to appeal to it for a settlement of their disputes "without loss of dignity." [87]

It is a well established fact that modern industrial disputes are interlocked, that a great number of different industries are involved. For their well balanced adjustment it is essential, therefore, to have a broad representative authority such as that of the Industrial Council of 1911. This Council, however, did not do much work nor did it exist for long. It was established in a time of great industrial stress during the serious strikes of railwaymen, seamen, and dockers in 1911, without, apparently, much forethought on the part of the Government as to the future course of the Council or the difficulties with which it would be confronted. It was a rather hurried response to the popular clamor that something be done about industrial disputes, which were causing serious industrial disturbances. Many leading trade-unions and employers' organizations were consulted, but they were not represented on the Council in their collective capacities, their leading members being appointed only as individuals. The members of the Council were

[87] *The 9th Report of the Proceedings under the Conciliation Act, 1896*, pp. 2, 117-9.

appointed originally for one year and reappointed in 1912. Thereafter no renewal of appointment was made, and the Council was allowed to drop out of existence quietly. No published reason has been given for this, but it is quite probable that the experiment was discarded because it had failed either as a Parliament of industries or as a tribunal for the settlement of industrial disputes.

As an Industrial Parliament the Council could not claim power and authority based upon a thorough representation of the organized industries of the country as a whole. The difficulty of finding such a basis is immense. The 1891 Royal Commission on Labor had also considered the advisability of establishing such a "Higher Council of Labor," and reported that "regard being had to the number, magnitude, and complexity of industries in this country . . . it would be difficult by any system of nomination or election to compose a body of employers, workmen, and others, which would give general satisfaction as a central council thoroughly representative of all the interests concerned."[38] Lacking such authority, it was only natural that, when the Council presented an elaborate report in 1913 after much hard work, the Government did not take it "as the last word and as the best recommendation" that the most important leaders of capital and labor had ever jointly produced,[39] but tried to get the opinion of another body, namely, the Trades Union Congress which, without much discussion, brushed it aside as undesirable. In other words, the Industrial Council was not an Industrial Parliament.

As a tribunal for the settlement of industrial disputes, the Industrial Council was too large in its membership; moreover the personnel was chosen, not for their qualifications as members of a judicial court, but for the precise reasons

[38] *The Final Report*, pt. i, p. 103.

[39] Lord Askwith, *Industrial Problems and Disputes*, p. 181.

that Mr. Clynes rejected as undesirable in the course of a debate on the Industrial Courts Bill of 1919. He stated that the members of the proposed court should not be nominated or appointed by trade organizations, but should be persons "of experience, of known impartiality; judicially-minded and capable of estimating evidence and reaching a reasonable decision according to the revealed facts of the case."[40] The members of the Industrial Council were all busily and actively engaged in industrial warfare and were for this reason chosen as leaders of their organizations. If the Council was not fit to act as a judicial court, it was still more unfit to act, through committees, in the interest of conciliation which required speed at the right psychological moment with the right person on the spot. For these and other reasons the Council did not succeed with strike settlement. The first strike referred to it, the dock strike at Newport, Mon., in 1911, the Council failed to settle through a committee, and out of several meetings held in connection with the great coal-mining stoppage in 1912, nothing developed.

The general results of Government intervention in trade disputes in the years 1896-1913 may be briefly summarized as follows.[41] The total number of trade disputes dealt with under the Act was 696, of which about 65 per cent took place in the last six years of this seventeen-year period because of increasing unrest in the transport, engineering, and building trades. The number of disputes involving a stoppage of work was about equal to that of cases that did not lead to a cessation of work, namely, 345 and 351 respectively. Out of the total number of 696 cases dealt with, 538 cases were settled by conciliation and arbitration, conciliation

[40] Parl. Deb. Commons (5th Ser.) (120), 1724, Nov. 6, 1919.

[41] Compiled from the Annual Reports of The Board of Trade on the Proceedings under the Conciliation Act, 1896, and on strikes and lock-outs.

settling 98 cases which involved a stoppage of work and 74 cases that did not lead to a cessation of work, making a total of 172; while arbitration settled 112 cases of stoppage of work and 254 cases of non-stoppage of work, making a total of 366. The total number of workers involved in the actual stoppages of work was about 780,000, of whom about 696,000 were connected with cases settled by conciliation and 84,000 with cases settled by arbitration.

As for the relative positions of the various peace agencies in the settlement of actual stoppages of work the Conciliation Act played a leading part in so far as the number of workers affected was concerned, if not in the number of cases settled. The total number of stoppages of work settled by the various agencies in the period under discussion was 949, of which 210, a little over 22 per cent, were settled under the Conciliation Act, while the voluntary trade boards, general boards, and single arbitrators and conciliators settled 205, 59, and 475 cases, respectively, making a total of 739 which affected less than 500,000 workers as against the 780,000 restored to work under the Conciliation Act.

As for the relative positions of the various agencies in the settlement of all trade disputes, including both stoppage and non-stoppage of work, statistics are available only from 1907. For the seven-year period 1907-1913, when industrial relations were considerably strained, the voluntary agencies settled 11,815 cases out of a total of 12,202 trade disputes, while the agencies under the Conciliation Act settled only 387, a little over three per cent.

In all cases arbitration exceeded conciliation in so far as the number of cases was concerned, but in magnitude, as represented by the number of workers affected, conciliation played a far more important part.

As for the relative positions of the conciliation and arbitration agencies, on the one hand, and the method of direct negotiation between the parties, on the other, the former played a relatively small role in the settlement of actual stoppage of work. The total number of cases resulting in a stoppage of work in the years 1896-1913 was 11,492, involving about 6,312,000 workers; of these cases 949 were settled by conciliation and arbitration, affecting about 1,432,000 workers, the others being settled in the main by direct negotiation between the parties.

3. A General Summary

Before proceeding to an examination of the war experiment of compulsory arbitration we may well pause for a broad review of the general position of the 1896 Conciliation Act, prior to the outbreak of the Great War in 1914. When the Combination Law of 1825 was passed Secretary Peel had foreseen the futility of the prohibition of combination among the workers and advised the employers to enter into counter combinations. He was afraid that such combinations and counter combinations would only destroy "the feeling of amicability and good faith that ought to exist between employers and workmen." After half a century's industrial progress Mr. Bruce, another Home Secretary in a Liberal Government, found the situation contrarywise. With the development of trade organizations, as Sir Robert had foreseen, employers and workers came to see that their trade interests were, after all, mutual, and that the basic factors were not dumb commodities, but human beings with hearts to feel and with reason to discourse. They came to sit around a table and talk things over. The system of voluntary conciliation and arbitration had been born and had grown far and wide. Trade unionism was entitled to a Magna Charta.

Another quarter of a century rolled away to reveal industrial peace being supported upon the pillars of trade organizations which, although pitted against each other occasionally in serious disturbances, usually assembled in council rooms. Trade customs had grown strong in the well-organized industries, strong enough to govern without assistance from the law. It was high time to ban and bury obsolete measures of compulsory regulation in industrial relations. By this time democracy had reached an advanced stage and public opinion veered from the individualistic to a corporate view of society. Education had become a national obligation and codes of regulations had been nearly completed for the conduct of manufacturing and mining industries. Children and youth, the future hope of the nation, and women, the home builders, had come under the protection of the State. Industrial disputes, often destructive to industrial production, inimical to social peace, and oppressive to the poor working-class families, could not be allowed to drift along and attempts were begun, though on a "slender" voluntary basis, to look after them as a national interest. The Conciliation Act of 1896 had been passed.

Another twenty years rolled away, and after the lapse of nearly a century since 1824, the nation had undergone a complete change. Labor leaders had been called into conference with industrial captains on an equal footing to advise His Majesty's Government on matters of high national importance. Trade unionism had at last been recognized as an established institution of the country. The industrial right of peaceful strike had been freed completely from any civil or criminal liability, while on the political side labor had entered into Parliament as an independent force. In tune with this growing corporate action among industrial workers the State had also assumed the collective responsibility for social welfare, providing social services for almost the entire span of human life, from the needy infant to the aged poor. This State responsibility for social welfare, however, had apparently not gone far enough to allay labor unrest. Industrial relations had been strained to an increasing extent, partly because of the rising temper of labor quickened by the new spiritual wine of lofty socialistic views of human service, and partly because of the actual pinch caused by the increased cost of living. National stoppage of work had occurred in many basic industries of the country.

Collective action was, however, only the other side of collective responsibility. If it had been strong in disputes it had also been strong for peace. During the seven year period of serious industrial strain, 1907-1913, the various peace agencies had settled on an average more than 1,700 cases a year, and had restored to work more than 20 per cent or one sixth of the total number of workers involved in stoppages of work during the period 1896-1913. The Government agencies under the 1896 Conciliation Act alone settled cases involving about 780,000 workers, more than 10 per cent. The influence of the Government agencies could not, however, be measured wholly by statistical figures. The most important thing was the fact that the Government had assumed responsibility for industrial peace. This was another aspect of growing State responsibility for the social and economic affairs of the country.

Among the specialized organizations established by the Government was the Chief Industrial Commissioner's Department, designed to be removed as far as possible from any political influence, on the one hand, and to be used as conservatively as possible in connection with actual industrial disputes, on the other. Mr. Buxton stated before the Industrial Council of 1911 that the best method for industrial peace was to allow employers and workmen to come together and compose their differences among themselves, for, after all, it was their responsibility to work together for their mutual benefit in industrial production. But the State could not stand aloof when serious industrial disputes occurred. It should intervene "at the right moment, in the right way, by the right person." Conciliation required speed in intervention, patience in heated controversy, and deep human understanding of the difficulties with which the parties were confronted. That was the primary function of the conciliation officers of the Chief Industrial Commissioner's Department. Arbitration required other qualifications; a calm atmosphere and a judicial mind capable of estimating evidence and reaching a reasonable decision accordingly, with an intimate knowledge and actual experience of trade as a broad background. To meet these specifications the arbitration court was constituted on a tripartite basis of representation. The Industrial Council was a great factor in the forward movement, but it failed to make a clear distinction between the parliamentary government of industrial affairs in general and the judicial settlement of industrial disputes in particular. It died a quiet death.

The chief result of the activities of these State and voluntary agencies for peace was the growing realization on the part of industrial disputants that the right to engage in strikes or lockouts had also grave responsibilities and should not be used lightly. It was due to this growing conscience and training that the nation was able, with practical unanimity of opinion and popular support, to adopt the compulsory arbitration system that served it well during the greatest international hostilities history has ever witnessed.

CHAPTER III

The War Experiment of Compulsory Arbitration

I. THE MUNITIONS OF WAR ACTS, 1915-1917

A. The Industrial and Political Circumstances

THE normal procedure of voluntary settlement of trade disputes provided in the 1896 Conciliation Act broke down under the strain of the Great War and recourse was had to the old method of compulsory arbitration in so far as munitions industries were concerned. This was purely a war measure and was dropped from the national policy as soon as hostilities ceased. The pre-war measure has since been brought back and is being allowed to run its normal course. The brief episode of the war experiment is, however, of great interest as it showed both the weakness of voluntary methods at a time of great stress and the difficulty of enforcing compulsory measures in a democratic country. We shall begin with a brief examination of the conditions under which the pre-war voluntary system broke down and the compulsory measure was adopted under the Munitions of War Acts of 1915-17.

One of the basic problems facing the country during the war grew out of the urgent need for munitions. Great Britain had up to that time depended for her defence upon a great navy and a small army. But in 1914 she was obliged to assemble a great army, on the Continental scale, to be raised, organized, trained, and provided with munitions in the shortest possible time and in the quickest way. At the same time the country had also to maintain the ordinary course of trade and commerce in order to pay for her food and provide money, not only for herself, but also, if necessary, for her allies. All this required labor, which naturally became more scarce as the war progressed on a wider front and in a more intensified form. The most effective way of meeting this growing shortage of labor and the ever increasing demand for munitions appeared to be the national mobilization of the industrial resources of the country, including labor forces,[1] for war purposes. But the Government was not prepared to undertake such an adventure at the outset of the war. On the contrary it adopted a policy of "Business as Usual," which resulted in great confusion and difficulty.[2]

In the first place the Government had no clear-cut, long-range policy on the question of labor supply, with the result that the most skilled men were taken out to the front by the Army and to the dock yards by the Navy without regard to the industrial needs of war production. Naturally the engineering and shipbuilding employers were most anxious to make the best use of the skilled labor still left to them by a policy of "labor dilution". Dilution meant the saving of skilled men for skilled jobs and the bringing in of semi-skilled and unskilled labor for the less skilled work hitherto performed by skilled workmen.[3] But the trade unions objected to this principle of the "free circulation of labor" and held steadfastly to their old restrictive trade regulations for fear that the introduction of unskilled labor might adversely affect the hard-won positions of the skilled workers. This objection constituted one of the major problems of labor supply during the war period. In the second place, the Government policy of "Business as Usual" caused a rapid increase in the cost of living while wages failed to keep pace with these rising costs. Naturally there was com-

[1] *Cf.* Humbert Wolfe, *Labor Supply and Regulation*, p. 2.

[2] Prof. Henry Clay, *The Problem of Industrial Relations*, ch. 2.

[3] Dr. C. Addison, *Politics from Within*, vol. i, p. 183.

plaint that, while the workers were being asked to remain on their jobs, to do their best for patriotic reasons, and not to take full advantage of the opportunities offered by the war, the manufacturing and commercial classes were left at perfect liberty to make huge profits out of the national calamity. This feeling about profiteering was indeed one of the principal causes of labor unrest. Lord Askwith points out:

> A ship owner, who stated he had made profits, and was going to make profits, and had a right to make profits, did more harm than a great naval defeat would have done. To name "defeat" would rouse the nation to set their teeth and fight against an alien foe. The profiteer's statement would rouse class against class and only tend to disruption within the nation itself.[4]

Owing to these and other difficulties labor disputes, which had almost entirely disappeared at the beginning of the war under the great wave of patriotism, began to reappear early in 1915, at a time when the nation was in most urgent need of more munitions and war materials. Immediately after the declaration of war labor had adopted a policy of a united industrial front against the common foreign enemy by dropping many grave disputes, both existing and impending. This action was formally endorsed by the national labor conference, which, held on August 25, 1914, between the Parliamentary Committee of the Trade Union Congress, the Management Committee of the General Federation of Trade Unions, and the Executive Committee of the Labor Party, passed a resolution recommending that the trade unions should settle all existing and future disputes by peaceful means and not by recourse to strikes. This policy of industrial truce was maintained remarkably well until the beginning of January, 1915, when the number of trade disputes

[4] Lord Askwith, *Industrial Problems and Disputes*, p. 372; *cf. The History of the Ministry of Munitions*, vol. i.

was only ten, affecting less than 10,000 workers.[5] By the end of February, however, there had been a definite break in the spirit favoring industrial truce, trade disputes having increased to the number of 47. Most important of all was the general strike in the engineering trades on the Clyde side. It was important, not only as an indication of the growing impatience and defiant spirit of the Clyde workers, but also as an arrow-point to the inherent weakness of the existing negotiation machinery in the engineering trades. Under the normal procedure agreed upon between the engineering employers' federation and a large number of trade unions wage claims were first discussed at a local conference of the parties concerned, and, failing adjustment, at the central conference at York. This procedure was an excellent means of avoiding disputes in normal times, cases being dealt with in the first instance by those immediately interested and reviewed, in case of disagreement, by the national authorities of organized employers and workmen. But in a time of rapid industrial change under war conditions it was extremely slow and cumbersome. Not only would a considerable amount of time elapse between the initial presentation and the final settlement of cases, but also, in the meanwhile, fresh claims might accumulate causing a clog in the smooth flow of negotiations. Furthermore the trade unions represented in negotiation would be great in number, in many cases, with a very limited extent of cooperation among them, while the leaders of individual unions were often unable to commit themselves on any important issue before consulting with the rank and file. Another serious difficulty was the fact that the trade unions could not enforce their

[5] In the period from October to December, 1914, there were 21,128 workers involved in trade disputes with a loss of 161,437 working days. Of that number of workers only 2,241 were engaged in engineering, shipbuilding, and other metal trades. *Cf. The 12th Report of Proceedings under the Conciliation Act*, 1896, for 1914-18, vol. i, p. 5.

decisions either against those outside workers, who were reckless enough to take full advantage of the opportunities offered to them without regard to the general public consequences, or against those minority members, who were bold enough to defy the constitutional authorities of the trade unions with their own radical policies.

Conferences for the relief of labor shortage by means of dilution and peaceful settlement of disputes had been commenced as early as October, 1914, between the engineering and shipbuilding employers, on the one hand, and the trade unions, on the other, but no progress was made until January, 1915, when the whole question of labor supply was at last taken up by the Government through Sir George Askwith, then Chief Industrial Commissioner. As a result of his report a Committee on Production was appointed, on February 4, with Sir George himself as chairman, to inquire and report on the best means of ensuring that "the productive power of the employees in engineering and shipbuilding establishments working for Government purposes shall be made fully available so as to meet the needs of the nation in the present emergency." The policy of the Committee was defined in a number of reports recommending on the one hand, the removal of certain restrictive trade practices, and, on the other, the peaceful settlement of disputes by arbitration. In an Interim Report issued on February 20, four days after the outbreak of the engineering strike in the Clyde district, the Committee declared that, whatever might be the rights of employers and workmen in normal times, there would be no justification for a strike or lockout under the existing conditions, and recommended that any trade dispute arising in war production should be referred for an immediate investigation and settlement to an impartial arbitration tribunal to be appointed by the Government. This recommendation was immediately accepted by the Government, and on the following day the Committee was authorized to act as such an arbitration tribunal. The other reports with respect to the removal of restrictive trade practices were also agreed to by the engineering employers and trade-union leaders, but the process was slow and their final acceptance delayed [6] owing to the unavoidable circumstances of negotiation to which we have referred above.

The question of labor supply was most urgent and obviously required treatment of a more general nature. This requirement was met by Mr. Lloyd George, then Chancellor of the Exchequer, who summoned a national representative meeting of the trade unions for a discussion of the best means of organizing labor forces on a war basis in the light of the recent passage of the Defence of the Realm Amendment Act.[7] The meeting was held at the Treasury from March 17-19, 1915, with some 35 leading trade unions represented. Every phase of the labor situation was gone into and by 50-16 votes the principle of compulsory arbitration was adopted for the duration of the war.[8] A Memorandum, known as the Treasury Agreement, was then signed on March 19, committing the trade unions to the policy of industrial truce and the relaxation of restrictive trade regulations. It was understood that any trade practices suspended under the agreement should be restored after the war and that the customary rates of pay for the skilled men

[6] *The 12th Report of Proceedings under the Conciliation Act*, 1896, vol. ii, Appendix 1, p. 1.

[7] The defence of the Realm (Amendment) (No. 2) Act, 1915, authorized the Government to control and regulate any factory or workshop, including labor forces employed therein, for the purpose of securing the efficient production of munitions. Parl. Deb. Commons (5th Ser.) (70), 1271, March 9, 1915; *The 12th Report of Proceedings under the Conciliation Act*, 1896, vol. i, pp. 8 *et seq.*; *War Memoirs of David Lloyd George*, vol. i, pp. 293-302.

[8] Parl. Deb. Commons (5th Ser.) (72), 1564, June 28, 1915.

should be guaranteed. For the purpose of industrial truce it was agreed that any dispute arising at a munitions plant should be referred for final settlement either (1) to the Committee on Production, (2) a single arbitrator agreed upon by the parties or appointed by the Board of Trade, or (3) a court of arbitration in which labor and employers should be equally represented under an impartial chairmanship. The Amalgamated Society of Engineers, the most important of all the unions represented, did not sign the Agreement until, at a later conference, the Government had given it a written agreement that the profits of the engineering and shipbuilding firms should be controlled so that the relaxation of the trade-union practices might benefit not the private employers, but the State.

It was one thing to make an agreement with the trade union leaders and quite another to carry it with the rank and file, whose passions had been thoroughly stirred up by the war. There was inevitable suspicion directed toward the employers and central union leaders and the motives of the Government. There was also resentment at the increased cost of living, incessant physical and mental strain, and, above all, the horror of the war. In these circumstances strikes increased in the three months following the conclusion of the Treasury Agreement, affecting more than 84,000 workers and costing the country more than 525,000 working days.[9] It thus became necessary to take a further step in order to secure a peaceful continuance of work, and the Treasury Agreement was given legal effect under the Munitions of War Act, 1915. Under the new Act strikes and lockouts were made illegal under penalties and a system of compulsory arbitration was prescribed for a peaceful settlement of disputes arising in munitions plants. That the compulsory measure thus adopted was, however, essentially a

[9] H. Wolfe, *Labor Supply and Regulation*, p. 120.

measure agreed upon by organized labor and the Government[10] will become clearer as we proceed to consider the political circumstances in which the Act was passed.

In the course of time the shortage of munitions had become a burning political question involving issues far wider than that of mere labor supply. In France industry had been mobilized for war purposes at the beginning of the war, but the British War Office had adhered strictly to the old policy of carrying on munitions work through the narrow bottle-necks of the existing armament firms, which were hopelessly incapable of discharging the gigantic task imposed by the unprecedented scale of the Great War.[11] Dissatisfaction grew far and wide in the country until it was openly charged that tens of thousands of workers had been withdrawn from the industry for drill and had not been shown a single rifle for a whole six or eight months! The British youths at the front, with unsurpassed valor and fortitude, were being sacrificed by thousands for the want of munitions, while the engineering firms in the country, with adequate machinery and skilled men to produce war materials, were being kept idle by the very policy of the Government.[12] This feeling found a strong expression in Parliament on April 21, when Mr. Bonar Law, then Opposition Leader, criticised the Government as entirely inefficient in procuring the production of munitions. The Prime Minister, he said, had appointed plenty of committees to secure a sufficient supply of munitions, but committees alone would not do. The essential thing was to effect a national mobilization of the private manufacturing resources of the country

[10] *Cf. ibid.*, Appendix 8, p. 356, Report by Mr. Justice McCardie's Committee on Labor Embargoes.

[11] Dr. C. Addison, *The Manufacture of Munitions*, p. 3; *Politics from Within*, vol. i, pp. 68-73, Appendix No. 3.

[12] Parl. Deb. Commons (5th Ser.) (72), 630-32, June 15, 1915, per Sir A. Markham.

for war purposes just as the French Government had done previously.[13]

When the Asquith Administration fell and the first national coalition Government was formed toward the end of May, 1915, the first action of the new Government was the creation of a new Ministry of Munitions charged with the task of securing a sufficient supply of munitions by affecting an elaborate organization of private industries for war purposes.[14] The new Minister of Munitions, Mr. Lloyd George, at once sought wide power in the first Munitions of War Bill, which was introduced in the House of Commons on June 23, 1915. For the purpose of organizing victory, he stated, it was essential to mobilize the whole engineering and chemical resources of the country with a view to making a better use of the available materials, machinery, and labor forces. In connection with labor supply he mentioned steps that should be taken by the Government; it should first obtain an adequate supply of skilled labor; secondly, it should utilize both semi-skilled and unskilled labor, and should then insure the greatest possible efficiency of the labor forces thus increased. The quickest way of meeting these requirements would be through labor conscription, but that was out of the question, because the free British trade unions would not have it. The only alternative open to the Government was, therefore, a system of voluntary enrollment of skilled workers for Government munitions works. Subject to this limitation, however, it was absolutely necessary, the Minister was convinced, to curtail, to some extent, the rights of free enterprise, on the one hand, and the liber-

[13] Parl. Deb. Commons (5th Ser.) (71), 38-9, 277, 324-332; April 21, 1915.

[14] The Ministry of Munitions Act, 1915 (5 & 6 Geo. 5, c. 51); Parl. Deb. Commons (72), 50, 88, 199, 226, June 3, 1915, per Sir John Simon, then Home Secretary; *War Memoirs of David Lloyd George*, vol. i, chs. 8-9.

ties of trade unions, on the other. The trade union regulations tending to diminish war production should not be allowed to operate and the stoppage of work, whether by strikes or lockouts, must be avoided by means of compulsory arbitration. On the employers' side the profits should be strictly controlled by the Government so that curtailment of the trade union liberties should benefit not private employers, but the State. The chief element in disturbing the labor situation, namely, the practice of "poaching" men from one another by offering higher rates of wages, or the higgling of the market, should stop so that the Government might be able to control the movement of labor, not according to ordinary economic forces, but in accordance with the national needs of the time. These broad principles were embodied in the Munitions of War Bill, which was readily agreed to by the Labor Party and became law on July 2, 1915. Speaking in behalf of the Labor Party, Mr. John Hodge declared that it was "a sin and a crime" for any workman in a munitions plant to turn out less than the amount of which he was capable at a time when

> our brothers, our relatives, and our comrades are seeking at the front . . . to maintain that liberty, that freedom of speech, and that civil and religious freedom, which we enjoy to-day, but which we would not if the mailed fist, which has threatened Europe so long, should prevail.[15]

B. The Machinery Set Up for Compulsory Arbitration and Labor Discipline

The basic idea of the Munitions of War Act, 1915,[16] was to further the efficient production of munitions by removing

[15] Parl. Deb. Commons (72) 1183-1206; per Mr. Lloyd George; 1208-1212; per Mr. Hodge.

[16] An Act to make provisions for furthering the efficient manufacturing, transport, and supply of munitions for the present war, and purposes incidental thereto (5 & 6 Geo. 5, c. 54).

some of the chief labor difficulties, namely, the stoppage of work because of trade disputes and the failure to apply labor forces in the most effective way either owing to trade union restrictions or to lack of discipline. For the removal of these difficulties the Act devised three main sets of machinery; compulsory arbitration and legal prohibition of strikes and lockouts, the institution of what were then called the Controlled Establishments, and special Munitions Tribunals as the agency of enforcement.

The Controlled Establishments, altogether more than 6,000 in number,[17] were created primarily for the purpose of maintaining necessary labor discipline in the munitions works, which in Pt. II the Act authorized the Minister of Munitions to declare by order to be a controlled establishment at any time he thought fit. In such a controlled establishment both the employer and workers were strictly required to observe regulations to be made by the Minister governing the general ordering of work with a view to maintaining or attaining a proper standard of efficiency. No restrictive trade union practices, whether as to the limitation of working hours, method of work, demarcation, manning machineries, or the employment of semi-skilled and unskilled labor in general, should be allowed to operate, nor could changes in wage rates be made without the consent of the Minister of Munitions. In Section 7 it was further provided that for a period of six weeks, no employment should be given to a workman who had left his employment at a munitions plant without having obtained from his employer a leaving certificate. In return for these restrictions of the personal freedom of the munitions workers the employers' profits, exceeding by one fifth certain standard net profit,[18]

[17] H. Wolfe, *Labor Supply and Regulation*, p. 157.

[18] This provision was subsequently superseded by the Excessive Profits Duty.

were to be paid into the national Exchequer. Any dispute arising as to the prohibited trade practices or proposed changes in wage rates was to be referred for a final settlement to arbitration as provided in Pt. 1.

In Pt. 1 it was provided that no strike or lockout should take place in connection with any dispute arising over wages and other conditions of employment between employers and workmen, or between any two or more classes of workers, engaged on a munitions work, unless such dispute had been reported to the Board of Trade and the Board had failed to refer it to arbitration within 21 days after the date of report. Upon such a dispute's having been reported by or in behalf of either of the parties concerned the Board of Trade was required to take it under consideration and to take expedient steps for its final settlement. If thought fit the Board might refer the case to one of the arbitration tribunals set up in the Treasury Agreement or to any suitable voluntary machinery existing in the trade concerned.

Any person failing to observe an arbitration award or the prohibition on strikes and lockouts was liable to a maximum fine of £5, in the case of a workman, for each day, and, in the case of an employer, for each worker in respect of whom the offense had taken place. The Act contained no prohibition of incitement to strike, but under Regulation 42 of the Defence of the Realm Regulations as amended in November, 1915, it was an offence, punishable by penal servitude or deportation, to attempt "to impede, delay, or restrict the production, repair, or transport of war material or any other work necessary for the successful prosecution of the war." A breach of the workshop regulation applying in a controlled establishment was punishable by a maximum fine of £3, while the leaving certificate, if unreasonably withheld by an employer, could be obtained through a Munitions Tribunal, without, however, any compensation.

The reference of cases to arbitration under the Act, it will be noticed, was not mandatory, but at the option of the Board of Trade, which was also to determine the legal effect of the prohibition of strikes and lockouts. This optional power was taken away under the Munitions of War (Amendment) Act, 1916 (5 & 6 Geo. 5, c. 99), which required the Board of Trade to refer any bona-fide trade dispute to arbitration immediately after its failure to settle the case within the specified time limit of 21 days. Under the Munitions of War Act, 1917 (7 & 8 Geo. 5, c. 45), the arbitration process was further speeded up by requiring the arbitration tribunals to issue awards within two weeks, if possible, and by authorizing Government Departments to report trade disputes for the purpose of arbitration, whereas under the original Act of 1915 the power had rested solely with the parties immediately concerned. The 1917 Act also introduced a novel and important principle in its authorization of the Minister of Munitions to issue Orders extending any arbitration award to the entire trade concerned if the parties to the arbitration represented a majority of those engaged in the trade.

Just as the arbitration process was speeded up as the war progressed, so the scope of its application was extended by the wider definition of the munitions work, to which compulsory arbitration was applicable, on the one hand, and by the increased powers of the Minister of Munitions to control wages of the munition workers, on the other. Under the 1915 Act munitions work was defined as "the manufacture or repair of arms, ammunition, ships, vehicles, aircraft, or any other articles required for use in war, or of the metals, machines, or tools required for that manufacture or repair," (sec. 3). Under the 1916 Act this definition was extended so as to include, upon a Government certificate, the manufacture or repair of any class of ships, the erection of construction works, docks, harbors, the supply of light, heat, power, tramway facilities, or the repair of fire engines, or any materials necessary for such manufacture or repair work.[19] A certain number of important industries such as coal mining, cotton, railways, the manufacture of agricultural or textile machineries,[20] was not included in the scope of the Munitions Acts, but under the original Act of 1915 the Government was authorized, by Royal Proclamation, to bring under the operation of the law any trade dispute on any work of any description if such dispute appeared to be prejudicial to the manufacture, transport, or supply of munitions. This course was actually taken in a number of cases, notably in the cases of the South Wales coal miners, Lancashire card and blowing room operatives and dockers at London, Liverpool, and Glasgow.[21]

Under the original Act of 1915 wage questions were not to be dealt with directly by Government decrees, but by negotiations between the employers and workers concerned. This policy of lassez-faire was completely reversed under the amending Acts of 1916-1917, which authorized the Minister of Munitions to control the wages of the munitions workers, both skilled and unskilled, male and female. A certain balanced relationship between skilled and unskilled wage rates was a prerequisite for the successful operation of the Gov-

[19] *The 12th Report of Proceedings under the Conciliation Act*, 1896, vol. i, pp. 18-19.

[20] Pressed hard by the ever growing need for economy of labor the Government introduced an amending Bill in the House of Commons toward the end of March, 1917, proposing to extend the Munitions Acts to private industries, but the proposal provoked such strong protests from the engineering workers that the Government was forced to withdraw the proposal. Parl. Deb. Commons (92), 611, 2745-56; (97), 1118-23; 1302-1307; April 27, Aug. 15, 1917, per Messrs. Kellaway and Churchill.

[21] *The 12th Report of Proceedings under the Conciliation Act*, 1896, vol. iii, Appendix v, pp. 42, 221, 226, 414.

ernment policy of labor dilution. As we have already seen, the skilled workers objected to dilution mainly because of fear that the introduction of cheap unskilled labor might adversely affect their hard-won positions. The trade unions made it, therefore, a condition of their support of the Government policy that the substituted labor on the skilled jobs should be paid at rates which would not jeopardize the standard rates of the skilled workers and which should be legally binding.[22] The Government recognized the force of the demand, and the Munitions Act of 1916 authorized the Minister of Munitions to issue Orders in respect of the remuneration of female, semi-skilled and unskilled male workers engaged on munition works which were customarily done by skilled workers. In the course of time a number of causes, such as the excessive encouragement of piece work, the operation of the leaving certificates, and the uniform wage advances granted by arbitration awards, reversed the relative position of the skilled time workers and the comparatively unskilled piece workers, producing what was then called "the skilled men's grievances," one of the principal causes of labor unrest during the summer of 1917. With a view to removing this anomaly and restoring the normal position of the skilled and unskilled rates the 1917 Act further empowered the Minister of Munitions to issue Orders granting bonuses to the munition workers whose wages were paid on a time basis.

Should any dispute arise as to whether certain workers came under the terms of the wage orders it was to be referred for settlement to the Special Arbitration Tribunals set up for the different classes of munition workers, one for women, another for semi-skilled and unskilled male munition workers, and a third for the time workers' bonus cases.

[22] *The 12th Report of Proceedings under the Conciliation Act, 1896*, vol. i, p. 17.

Important improvements were also made in the constitution of the arbitration tribunals. Under the 1915 Act the Board of Trade was given a choice of four different kinds of tribunals, namely, the Committee on Production (see below), single arbitrators agreed upon by the parties or appointed by the Board of Trade, ad-hoc courts of arbitration consisting of representative employers and workers with an impartial chairman, or any voluntary agencies existing in the trade concerned. Under the Acts of 1916 and 1917 three more special arbitration tribunals were added to deal with those special cases that might arise over the interpretation of wage orders issued by the Minister of Munitions. The provision for the last alternative in the 1915 Act was a clear indication of the desire on the part of the Government not to enforce compulsory arbitration if the dispute was capable of a settlement by the parties concerned. As in fact, however, differences reported to the Board of Trade had in most cases already gone through such voluntary procedure and had failed of settlement very few cases were referred in this manner. Ad-hoc courts of arbitration, another piece of the pre-war machinery, were also resorted to in only a few cases since it was often impossible to get a quick appointment of such a court, owing to the fact that the panel members were busy on other important work during the war time. The majority of cases settled by arbitration were, therefore, dealt with either by single arbitrators [23] or by the Committee on Production.[24] In most cases the single arbitrators were appointed from the chairmen's panel constituted for ad-hoc courts of arbitration and dealt with cases of relatively small importance, while the Committee on Production settled general claims and questions of principle, its decisions

[23] For a summary of decisions by single arbitrators see *The 12th Report of Proceedings under the Conciliation Act*, 1896, vol. iii, Appendix v.

[24] *Ibid.*, vol. ii, Appendix I.

constituting leading cases for the guidance of single arbitrators and other wage-controlling authorities.

The Committee on Production was originally composed of Sir George Askwith (now Lord Askwith) Chairman, Sir Francis Hopwood (now Lord Southborough), and Sir George Gibb, representing the Board of Trade, the Admiralty, and the War Office respectively. Later, in 1915, Sir David Harrell and Lord Balfour were appointed as additional members in order to cope with the increasing number of cases brought before the Committee. In May, 1917, the Committee was reconstituted on the basis of a tripartite representation, with Sir David Harrell and Sir George Bibb as chairmen and four representative members, two employers and two workmen. As this form became popular additional divisions were created in the course of 1917 and 1918 until, at the end of the war, it consisted of five chairmen and eight representative members.[25]

The Committee as reconstituted in May 1917 had the advantage, according to the nature of particular cases referred, of sitting in divisions with the representative members, most of whom had long served as single arbitrators and had gained wide experience in arbitration and an intimate knowledge of various trades. This enabled the Committee to settle cases more expeditiously and to command

[25] Chairmen:

Sir David Harrel (appointment, 1915)
Sir William Mackenzie (1917)
Judge Walworth H. Roberts (1918)
Mr. E. C. K. Gonner (1918)
Sir Cyril Jackson (1918)

Workers' Representatives:

Mr. F. S. Button (1917)
Mr. W. Mosses (1917)
Mr. John Barker (1918)
Mr. James Gavin (1918)

Employers' Representatives:

Col. J. M. Denny (1917)
Mr. J. Duncan-Elliot (1917)
Mr. J. Fullerton (1917)
Mr. J. W. White (1917)

fuller confidence of the parties appearing before it. This is well attested by the fact that cases were referred to it in an increasing number after its reconstruction and that the personnel was retained in arbitration service long after the Committee had ceased to exist.[26]

The creation of the Special Arbitration Tribunals under the amending Acts of 1916 and 1917 was based upon the principle that special cases should be dealt with by special agencies well versed in the subject matter and that these agencies should represent both employers and workmen under an impartial chairmanship. In fact, however, the members of the Special Arbitration Tribunal for the time workers' bonus cases, created early in 1918, were identical with those of the Committee on Production, while the Special Arbitration Tribunal for semi-skilled and unskilled men, established early in 1916,[27] was allowed to lapse after having dealt with very few cases. The Special Arbitration Tribunal for women munition workers, also created in the spring of 1916,[28] had a two-fold function to discharge. As an advisory committee it was to advise the Ministry of Munitions on its wage policy, while as an arbitration court it was entitled to decide the differences that might arise out of the wage orders issued by the Ministry.

[26] Most of the members were retained on the Interim Court of Arbitration when, under the Wages (Temporary Regulation) Act, 1918, this Court took the place of the Committee on Production, and, when the Interim Court was in turn superseded by the Industrial Court set up under the Industrial Courts Act, 1919, Sir William Mackenzie, one of the original members of the Committee on Production, was appointed as president of the new court.

[27] The tribunal consisted of Mr. (now Sir) Lynden Macassey, chairman, Mr. Charles Duncan, Mr. Hutchinson, Mr. (now Sir) Allan Smith, and Mr. J. C. Ward.

[28] The tribunal consisted of Mr. Lynden Macassey, chairman, Mr. Ernest Aves, Mr. F. S. Button, Miss Susan Lawrence, Mr. Allan Smith and Mrs. Streatfield.

The principal arbitration tribunals during the war were, therefore, three in number, the single arbitrators, the Committee on Production, and the Special Arbitration Tribunal for women. Among these tribunals a fair unity of decisions was maintained, primarily because special cases were referred to special agencies and because the Committee on Production occupied such an eminent position that its decisions became the guide for other arbitration tribunals.

It is interesting to note that, while the arbitration process was made more expeditious and its scope extended, the punitive parts of the Munitions Acts were either greatly mitigated or altogether abolished as the war drew near to its end. In the first place the liability to imprisonment for the non-payment of fines imposed for strike offences under the Act of 1915 was removed under the Amending Act of 1916. The new Act also repealed the power of private owners of the controlled establishment to prosecute offences against the workshop regulations, and entrusted such power solely to the Government representatives. In the second place the leaving certificate system was considerably modified in 1916, and was finally abolished under the Act of 1917. As originally provided under the 1915 Act the system was complained of as tying the workman to his position while leaving his employer at perfect liberty to dismiss him at any time for whatever reason. The 1916 Act accordingly provided that any employer dismissing a workman without giving him a week's notice or a leaving certificate should be liable to the payment of compensation, unless he had reasonable cause for the dismissal or the workman discharged was guilty of misconduct. In cases, moreover, where the workman desired to change his position in order to be paid at the full rates of his trade upon his completion of apprenticeship or to apply his skill to greater advantage to the national interest, or in case the employer had failed to observe the fair wages resolution of the House of Commons on March 10, 1909,[29] the leaving certificate was not to be withheld. These improvements could not, however, arrest the complaints of the engineering workers and the Government was forced to abolish the system altogether under the Munitions of War Act, 1917, with some guarantees which also failed of practical application.

In the third place important improvements were made in the constitution of the Munitions Tribunals, which were set up for the special purpose of enforcing the Munitions Act, apart from the ordinary courts of law. The number of the Tribunals was about 60 in all and consisted of two classes, both of which had a summary jurisdiction.[30] The first class or General Munitions Tribunal was empowered to deal with all offences under the Acts except those falling within the jurisdiction of the second class, or Local Munitions Tribunal. The second class Tribunal had power to deal with cases concerning leaving certificates and the workshop regulations applying in the controlled establishments. The courts of both types consisted of a chairman and two or more assessors representing employers and workmen. The chairmen were usually chosen from those who had served as chairmen of the Courts of Referees under the National Insurance Act of 1911, while the assessors were

[29] The Fair Wages Resolution passed by the House of Commons on March 10, 1909, required Government contractors and subcontractors to pay rates of wages and observe conditions of labor not less favorable than those commonly adopted by the employers in the district concerned. In Decision No. 623, issued on March 4, 1921, for the Royal Army Ordnance Corps Depot at York, the Industrial Court ruled that the Army Council was not obliged under the fair wages resolution "to pay the highest rate which is being paid in the district for any given class of labor which they may employ," but "to pay rates which are generally regarded as fair wages by good employers in the district."

[30] The Munitions Tribunals Rules, 1915 (348); Munitions Tribunals Amendment (No. 2) Rules, 1917 (CMD. 8716).

appointed from certain panels of representative employers and workers constituted for the purpose by the Ministry of Munitions. As operated under the 1915 Act it was complained that in many cases the chairman ignored the assessors and took too legalistic a view of offences that in normal times would not be regarded as offences at all,[31] and that different local and general Munitions Tribunals had no principle of unity, pronouncing different punishments for one and the same offence.[32] The basis of some of these complaints was removed under the Act of 1916, which added a woman assessor in cases involving women workers and directed the chairmen to consult the assessors and, except on points of law, to give effect to their agreed opinion. All offences for which the maximum fine did not exceed £5 were transferred to the jurisdiction of the second class Tribunal and appeal was granted from a Munitions Tribunal to a judge of the High Court of Justice.

Even under war conditions the free British workers would not submit to too strict governmental regulation and regimentation, and the Government showed its ready appreciation of the difficult situation by making concessions, trusting more in the good sense of the workers than in the mere force of the law,[33] another instance of the British "muddling through" by compromise and common sense.

2. COMPULSORY ARBITRATION IN OPERATION

A. The Efficacy of Compulsory Arbitration

It is impossible to measure with any mathematical accuracy the exact results and difficulties, and to define the causes either of success or failure of the war experiment in compulsory arbitration, since all social experiments deal with

[31] Parl. Deb. Commons (76), 2081; per Mr. John Hodge, Dec. 15, 1915.

[32] The Report of the Balfour Committee, 1915 (CD. 8136), par. 10.

[33] Parl. Deb. Commons (97) 1307; Aug. 15, 1917, per Mr. W. Churchill.

largely intangible things. Only certain broad outstanding facts, which have more or less direct bearing on the subject under discussion, may be mentioned and analyzed. The first thing to note is the fact that eminent authorities have admitted that the Ministry of Munitions achieved in fullest measure its great task of supplying munitions to meet war needs, and that this was done, at any rate on the labor side, on the basis of arbitration and conciliation adapted to war conditions under the Munitions Acts.[34] The efficacy of compulsory arbitration may then be illustrated by the relatively small number of actual stoppages of work and the comparatively large number of cases settled by arbitration during the war period.

The figures of strikes and lockouts for the war period, as compared with those for the pre-war and post-war years, are given below:

Year	No. of Strikes and Lockouts	Workers Affected (in thousands)	Working Days Lost (in thousands)
1911	872	952	10,155
1912	834	1,462	40,890
1913	1,459	664	9,804
1914	972	447	9,878
1915	672	448	2,953
1916	532	276	2,446
1917	730	872	5,647
1918	1,165	1,116	5,875
1919	1,352	2,591	34,969
1920	1,607	1,932	26,568
1921	763	1,801	85,872[35]

The total number of strikes and lockouts occurring during the four-year period from 1915 to 1918 was, it will be noticed, only 3,099, involving about 2,712,000 workers with

[34] Report by Mr. Justice McCardie's Committee on Labor Embargoes, cited in Wolfe, *Labor Supply and Regulation*, pp. 147, 360.

[35] *The 21st Abstract of Labor Statistics issued by the Ministry of Labor in 1934*, p. 125.

a total loss of about 16,921,000 working days, while the total numbers of working days lost in the single post-war year 1919 and the three years immediately preceding the outbreak of the war, 1911-1913, were respectively 34,969,000 and 60,849,000. This is remarkable when we take into consideration the fact that causes for stoppage of work are more numerous during a war than in peace times. Conditions were changing rapidly, requiring quick adjustments of wages, not only to the rapid increase in the cost of living, but also as between the different classes of wage earners whose relative positions were profoundly changed by the different requirements of war. Authoritative allocation and control of labor supply meant of necessity interference with personal freedom and existing trade practices with the inevitable results of misunderstanding, suspicion, irritation, resentment, and grievances. Long hours of work naturally produced fatigue, while the sudden expansion of the munition factories caused in many localities bad housing conditions. These war privations told heavily on the workmen's psychology, straining their temper and capacity of endurance as the war dragged on. Furthermore there was the inevitable shortsightedness of human nature evident in the wide spread of profiteering, which in many cases added fuel to the smouldering flame of labor unrest.[86]

It should not be imagined, however, that the comparatively small number of stoppages of work during the war was attributable solely to the existence of compulsory arbitration, which itself was made possible only by the war conditions. If there were numerous causes for stoppages of work there were also strong forces working in the cause of

[86] *Cf.* A Summary of the Reports of the Inquiry Commission on Industrial Unrest by Mr. G. N, Barnes, 1917 (CD. 8696); *The 12th Report of Proceedings under the Conciliation Act, 1896*, vol. i, pp. 6-7.

industrial peace. The vast majority of workers were patriotic and determined to win the war at any price. The trade-union leaders generally did their best to secure a continuance of work, while the employers' motive to fight wage claims was largely removed by the fact that any increased cost of war production due to wage advances could be recovered from the Government, the real employer of the munition workers in the last analysis.[37]

However that may be, the fact remains that a great number of awards were issued by arbitration tribunals during the war period covering millions of workers, most of whom accepted the decisions without a cessation of work. It will be noticed in the following table that, while the number of cases settled by arbitration and conciliation in 1914 was approximately the same as in the immediately preceding years, the number of cases settled in the ensuing years showed a very large increase.

Year	No. of Cases Settled by Conciliation and Arbitration
1911	92
1912	73
1913	99
1914	81
1915	397
1916	1,412
1917	2,474
1918	3,583 [38]

[37] Prof. Henry Clay, *The Problem of Industrial Relations*, pp. 47-8, 50.

[38] The figures for the pre-war years include cases both settled and dealt with under the Conciliation Act, 1896, while those for the war period include cases settled under the Conciliation Act as well as under the Munitions Acts. *The 12th Report of Proceedings under the Conciliation Act*, 1896, vol. i, pp. 45 *et seq.*

The Number of Cases as Classified by Arbitration Agencies

Agencies Year	1914	1915	1916	1917	1918	Total
Committee on Production	—	141	500	815	2298	3,754
Tribunal for Time Workers' Bonus Cases .	—	—	—	—	64	64
Tribunal for Women's Cases	—	—	35	107	204	346
Single Arbitrators, Ad-hoc Courts of Arbitration, and Conciliation	81	256	877	1552	898	3,664
Interim Court of Arbitration *	—	—	—	—	119	119
Total	81	397	1412	2474	3583	7,947

* The Court was instituted under the Wages (Temporary Regulation) Act, 1918 (8 & 9 Geo. 5, c. 61); see *Post*, p. 125.

Apart from the remarkable increase in the total number of cases, which amounted to about 8,000, one of the outstanding features of the table is the steady increase shown in the number of cases referred to the Committee on Production, the premier arbitration tribunal during the war period. Up to 1917 the cases referred to single arbitrators were about twice as numerous as those referred to the Committee, but in 1918 the position was reversed and the Committee dealt with far more cases than did single arbitrators. The change may be accounted for by three facts. In the first place a large proportion of the claims made in 1918 was in connection with the 12½ per cent and 7½ per cent bonuses or their equivalent, granted to skilled and unskilled time workers under the Act of 1917,[89] and, in order to secure co-ordination of decisions the cases were referred for determination mainly to the Committee on Production. In the second place, certain improvement was made early in 1917 in the recognized procedure of negotiation in the engineering trades which materially assisted the expedition and regularity of the arbitration process of the Committee on Production. Under a new National Wages Agreement, negotiated by Sir George Askwith, Chairman of the Com-

[89] *Post*, pp. 91, 114.

mittee on Production, and agreed upon by the Engineering Employers' Federation and a large number of engineering trade unions, the ordinary conference method of negotiation[40] was suspended for the duration of the war or any further period to be agreed upon between the parties. The Committee on Production was authorized to determine general wage claims as well as, in certain exceptional cases, district claims, at its four-monthly regular hearings, the awards of the Committee to have a legally binding effect on all the federated engineering firms throughout the country. Subsequently similar agreements were entered into by a large number of trades, including shipbuilding, building, Scottish iron and steel, chemicals, and dockers, all of which considerably enhanced the position of the Committee and augmented the number of cases brought before it for settlement. In the third place it is probable that, after the Committee was reconstructed in 1917, its value as a judicial body was more fully tested and that more confidence was placed in it.

The Committee on Production issued altogether 3,754 awards[41] dealing in the majority of cases with wage claims made by trade unions on behalf of their members and granting advances, at first sporadically, but since March, 1917, at regular four-monthly hearings, with a view to assisting the workers in meeting the rapid increase in the cost of living. It was thought inadvisable for the Committee to start any "philanthropic reconstruction" of industry in the middle of the war or to embark upon any "unknown contingencies," and therefore the Committee adopted as the basis of its decisions the principle of "equal suffering and equal relief" under existing industrial arrangements, with

[40] *Ante*, p. 66; *cf. The 12th Report of Proceedings under the Conciliation Act*, 1896, vol. i, pp. 37, 50.

[41] During the first few months of its existence the Committee on Production acted as a voluntary arbitration court and issued 39 awards, all of which were of a district character and were accepted by the parties.

some bias in favor of "the under dog".[42] Generally speaking wages had been frozen from August, 1914, to January, 1915, and, although from February on unprecedented wage advances were secured by those workers whose labor was urgently required for the purposes of war, the advances did not keep in pace with the increase in the cost of living. And it was to maintain the balance between wages and the cost of living that the Committee on Production issued a series of general and district wage awards mainly for the engineering, shipbuilding, and other metal trades. The wage awards issued for the engineering trades may be summarized as follows:

Date of Awards	Nature of Awards
March, 1915	4s. per week on time rates, and 10 per cent on piece rates
July, 1916	3s. per week on time rates only
March, 1917	5s. per week both to time and piece workers
July, 1917	3s. " " " "
Nov., 1917	5s. " " " "
July, 1918	3s. 6d. " " " "
Nov., 1918	5s. " " " "
Total	28s. 6d. plus 12½ per cent to time workers 21s. 6d. plus 17½ per cent to piece workers[43]

[42] Lord Askwith, *Industrial Problems and Disputes*, p. 385; *Memorandum on the Proeedings of the Committee on Production from May, 1917 to April, 1918*, 1918 (CD. 9126), p. 4.

[43] The average weekly time rates in the engineering and shipbuilding trades in August, 1914 were 38s. 11d. for fitters and turners, and 40s. 4d. for the platers. The percentage increases in the time rates, granted during the war period, compared with those in the cost of living are as follows:

July	Fitters & Turners	Laborers	Platers	Food	General Cost of Living
1914	100	100	100	100	100
1915	110	—	—	132½	125
1916	111	—	—	161	145-150
1917	134	154	130	204	180
1918	173	213	169	210	200-205

See Arthur L. Bowley, *Prices and Wages in the United Kingdom, 1914-1920*, pp. 70, 128, 131.

The first award of a district character was issued for the shipyards in the Clyde district on March 1, 1915, granting an advance which was to be regarded "as a war advance and recognized as due to and dependent upon the existence of the abnormal conditions prevailing in consequence of the war." This form of wording was slightly changed in the first general award of March, 1917, which stated that the amounts awarded were to be regarded "as war advances, intended to assist the workers in meeting the increased cost of living, and are to be recognized as due to and dependent on the existence of the abnormal conditions now prevailing in consequence of the war."

Between the first award of March, 1915 and the second cycle of wage advances in July 1916, the Committee on Production dealt with a large number of district claims and generally granted an advance of 4s. per week on time rates and 10 per cent on piece rates with a view to bringing the lower district rates up to the new national standard achieved by the first award. A new cycle of demand for general wage advances had begun about August, 1915, but the Committee, by an apparent acquiescence in what was then called the Cabinet embargo on wage increases,[44] refused to grant any new advance. This position was untenable and in July, 1916, the Committee commenced its second cycle of advances by granting 3s. per week to the time workers alone, for the reason that the piece workers had had an opportunity of making extra money by extra exertion, an opportunity that was not open to the time workers. On March 1, 1917, the first general award under the National Wages Agreement in the engineering trades was issued and was followed by four awards in the course of 1917 and 1918. These awards altogether granted 21s. 6d. per week both to time and piece workers, bringing the war advances to a total of 28s. 6d.

[44] *Post*, p. 110.

per week, in the case of time workers, and 21s. 6d. plus 10 per cent in the case of piece workers.

The uniform advances granted by the Committee on Production, the encouragement of piece work, and the operation of the leaving certificates system combined to produce "the skilled men's grievances." In order to allay these complaints a bonus of 12½ per cent on earnings was granted to all time workers engaged on munitions work in the course of October and December, 1917. These general advances to the time workers, however, disturbed the relative position between time and piece earnings, and the Committee on Production advised the War Cabinet to authorize an advance of 7½ per cent to piece workers. This advance was granted in January, 1918, only to evoke further complaints from the time workers.[45]

It is important to note that a large proportion of the cases settled by arbitration during the war period fell in the engineering and shipbuilding trades which were the "munitions" trades proper. In the aggregate this group accounted for about 35 per cent of the total number of cases, with other trade groups in the following order: other metal trades, iron and steel manufacture, public utility, building, transport, chemical, and textile trades.[46]

Generally speaking, trade unions found compulsory arbitration more expeditious in settling disputes than the ordinary conciliation board procedure. It was much quicker to report differences under the Munitions Acts at an early stage and get an award which was legally enforceable for a definite period of time, usually four months, than to spend much time with employers in negotiations which might result in a deadlock leading to a stoppage of work. On the

[45] *Post*, p. 114.

[46] Compiled from government reports on conciliation and arbitration for 1914-19.

employers' side it was also to their advantage to have wage matters settled quickly by compulsory arbitration, in the result of which they had no longer the same keen financial interest that they had in normal times when the reimbursement of wage increases could be recovered only from private consumers.

In a general summary it may therefore be said that the war experiment of compulsory arbitration was a fair success. It saved time and temper at a time when the country needed complete unity and quick action. By the substitution of an authoritative and impartial method of settlement of disputes for the old process of protracted negotiation the system of compulsory arbitration effected expedition in the place of delay and created unity among the diverse and conflicting interests of private employers and workers. At any rate it made an orderly and fairly quick adjustment of wages to the rapidly changing industrial conditions due to the emergency of war. That this process was generally approved of is amply demonstrated by the fact that a considerable number of cases was referred to the Committee on Production and to single arbitrators, not under the Munitions Acts, but by agreements between the parties immediately concerned.

B. Some of the Difficulties of Compulsory Arbitration

A. The Illegal Stoppage of Work

The broad cause of the difficulties that faced compulsory arbitration during the war period was, of course, government control of labor supply, or the imposition of labor discipline in the broader sense of the term. Discipline was essential to the national policy of industrial mobilization, and compulsory arbitration, together with legal prohibition of stoppage of work and authoritative maintenance of workshop discipline, constituted a trio-code of regulation. It would be as futile to prescribe a system of compulsory arbitration for the purpose of industrial peace, while freely permitting strikes and lockouts, as to prohibit stoppage of work, for the sake of efficiency, without checking actual sabotage at individual workshops. Likewise any difficulties arising in connection with either the legal prohibition of strikes and lockouts or the authoritative maintenance of workshop discipline would vitally affect the course of arbitration, since, after all, it was dependent upon the good will and good temper of the workers for its effectiveness.

That compulsory arbitration during the war was not a complete success is best illustrated by the fact that the majority of strikes and lockouts occurred, in spite of their legal prohibition, in connection with the munitions and other allied trades, as is shown below:

NUMBER OF STRIKES AND LOCKOUTS IN MUNITIONS AND OTHER ALLIED TRADES

Year	Building	Metal, Engineering, Shipbuilding	Mining	Textile	Transport	Total
1914*	34	48	50	16	20	168
1915	63	189	85	67	75	479
1916	73	105	75	74	44	371
1917	51	225	148	70	32	526
1918	107	420	173	75	48	823
Total	294	987	531	302	219	2,367
Total of All Cases						3,099
		Workers Involved (in thousands)				
1914*	1	6	22	3	1	33
1915	16	46	298	33	25	418
1916	6	75	64	61	28	234
1917	7	429	281	65	26	808
1918	36	242	383	268	59	988
Total	66	798	1,048	430	129	2,481
Total of All Cases						2,712

Working Days Lost (in thousands)

1914*	51	362	27	284	25	749
1915	130	357	1,657	369	152	2,665
1916	103	305	326	1,161	103	1,998
1917	68	3,063	1,183	710	184	5,208
1918	186	1,499	1,263	1,704	277	4,929
Total	1,088	5,586	4,656	4,228	741	15,549
Total of All Cases						16,921 [47]

* From August to December of the year.

A further analysis of the figures reveals the fact that, out of a total of 2,481,000 workers involved, the coal miners accounted for about 962,000, the engineers and other metal workers for 671,000, and the cotton textile workers for 268,000, making altogether a total of 1,901,000, or more than 70 per cent. In other words, there were in the well-organized industries a few important strikes which were of such extent and duration as to account for a very large proportion of the working days lost in the entire period and against which legal prohibition was practically of no avail.

The failure of compulsory arbitration as reflected in the great number of stoppages of work in the munitions and other allied trades calls for some explanation. It may be sought in (1) the inadequateness or clumsiness of the arbitration tribunals, (2) the nature of the enforcement technique, (3) some of the more fundamental problems involved in Government control of the labor supply, such as the restriction of freedom of movement, discipline and labor dilution, the slow realization on the part of the Government that labor control and wage adjustment should go together under a well thought out co-ordinating policy, and (4) the general effect of war privation and weariness.

[47] Compiled from the Abstracts of Labor Statistics covering the years.

B. War Privation

From the psychological point of view the general effect of war privation and weariness would seem to have been the greatest cause since a detailed study of the strike movements during the war period shows that as the war drew near to its end, with the inevitable accumulation of privation, strain, and weariness, industrial unrest also increased. The number of disputes in August, 1914, was less than 20, went up to 70 in March, 1915, and dropped to less than 20 in December, 1915. It rose to more than 50 in April, 1916 returning to the level of less than 20 in December, 1916. After January, 1917, however, the number of disputes continued in an upward direction until it reached the peak of 100 in September, 1918, and involved more than 230,000 workers. In other words trade disputes varied in number at a comparatively low level in the first two years of the war, but in the last two war years they continued in an upward direction, thereby indicating a correspondingly increasing strain on the workmen's psychology.[48] From this angle it is perhaps true that the efficacy of compulsory arbitration was after all a matter of human endurance and temper and that nothing short of the cessation of war would have materially assisted the cause of industrial peace.

C. The Inadequacy of Arbitration Methods

From the technical point of view it is of greater interest to note some of the difficulties inherent in the nature of compulsory arbitration and the technique of legal enforcement as provided under the Munitions Acts. Generally speaking compulsory arbitration was found inadequate in two directions. It was of no avail in cases where a large number of workers was resolved, for one reason or another,

[48] *The 12th Report of Proceedings under the Conciliation Act, 1896*, vol. i, a chart opposite to p. 62.

not to countenance any authoritative determination of their claims. On the other hand, small individual workshop questions, such, for instance, as the relationship between foremen and workmen, the system of payments, and other trade practices were more adapted to settlement by conciliation than by arbitration. As an illustration of the first point we may take the strike case of the South Wales coal miners in July, 1915. The coal mining industry had been placed outside the scope of the Munitions of War Act, 1915, on the plea that the miners had already an adequate machinery for peaceful settlement of trade disputes. A serious wage dispute took place, however, in the South Wales coal fields in the summer of 1915, resulting in an actual strike. Negotiations had been carried on since March between the South Wales Miners' Federation and the Coal Owners' Association, with the help of the Board of Trade. Toward the end of June certain proposals were accepted by the Miners' Executive, but disputes arose on certain points in the proposed terms of settlement. On July 12 a special conference of the miners' delegates rejected the interpretation by the President of the Board of Trade of the points at issue and passed a resolution declaring that the miners would cease work unless their original demands were granted by the employers. On the following day a Royal Proclamation was issued under the Munitions Act of the year, making it an offence to take part in a strike in the coal fields, and a General Munitions Tribunal was set up for the whole area. In response to a request from the Miners' Executive the President of the Board of Trade consented to reopen negotiations, and a special conference was summoned for July 15. But on that very day about 200,000 miners went out on strike, the miners' delegates conference having rejected the Executive's proposal that work should be continued on day to day contracts, pending a final settlement. Shortly afterward Mr. Lloyd

George, the Minister of Munitions, and Mr. W. Runciman, President of the Board of Trade, went down to Cardiff and settled the case by granting practically all the claims of the strikers, leaving to arbitration only small technical matters.[49]

As for the competence of arbitration in the settlement of small individual workshop questions it is well to note some of the recommendations made by the Balfour Committee, appointed in October, 1915, to inquire into the causes of unrest among the Clyde district munition workers. The Committee stated in its interim report that many of the differences brought before it were "not so illustrative of disputes on definite matters of principle . . . as indicative of local friction surrounding the relationship of particular employers and employed," and asserted that such friction, if left long uncontrolled, would lead "to a state of irritation among organized workers which quickly spreads beyond the boundaries of the establishment where the trouble first arose to other works, and frequently for adventitious causes wholly unconnected with the origin or merits of the dispute it becomes elevated into a matter of principle affecting all employers and munition workers generally throughout the district." To deal quickly with the trouble at its source was the only effective way of eradicating industrial differences, and for this purpose the Committee recommended that a mediation or conciliation officer should be appointed for the district with ample powers to settle such disagreements with the least delay.[50]

The charge of delay in the settlement of disputes was one of the major criticisms directed against the arbitration tribunals. The "dilatory" process of arbitration, according to

[49] *The 12th Report of Proceedings under the Conciliation Act*, 1896, vol. iii, p. 43; *cf.* Lord Askwith, *Industrial Problems and Disputes*, pp. 391-5.

[50] The Interim Report, pars. 2-4, 17, cited in Wolfe, *op. cit.*, pp. 344 *et seq.*

Mr. Kellaway, Parliamentary Secretary to the Ministry of Munitions, often caused more "irritation" among the workers than did the differences at issue.[51] The arbitration process was accordingly considerably speeded up under the amending Acts of 1916-17 as well as by the reconstruction of the Committee on Production in May 1917, to which we have already referred, but the question was not satisfactorily disposed of until the end of the war. It was perhaps inevitable that complaints should be made of the slowness of arbitration at a time when industrial conditions were changing rapidly owing to the emergency of war. Writing in December, 1918, Mr. Justice McCardie's Committee on Labor Embargoes points out that, while Government Departments should remember that great irritation might be caused to those who sought redress if they formed the impression that their complaints were not examined with sufficient promptitude, the workers failed "to appreciate the unavoidable period required for the ascertainment of the facts, the hearing of both sides, and the well considered determination of the points at issue. Hasty decisions do not create confidence." [52]

D. The Technique of Legal Enforcement

The technique of legal enforcement, as distinct from moral pressure, presented the same problems as those that had been found by various pre-war commissions and committees as almost insurmountable and had finally led to the passage of the Conciliation Act, 1896. The question of legal enforcement of industrial agreements, including arbitration awards, was taken up and considered by the Whitley Committee, appointed in 1916. This Committee came to the old conclusion that moral pressure would be more effective in the

[51] Parl. Deb. Commons (92), 2747; per Mr. Kellaway, April 27, 1917.

[52] *The 12th Report of Proceedings under the Conciliation Act,* 1896, vol. i, p. 32.

long run than would any system of legal enforcement.[53] This opinion is instructive in the light of the fact that, while the vast majority of arbitration awards issued during the war period were loyally accepted without a cessation of work, the technique of legal enforcement was of no use in cases of determined opposition by a large number of workers. Legal enforcement meant imprisonment in the last analysis, and it was impossible to imprison great multitudes of workmen whose service was urgently required for the purposes of war. The imprisonment of individual strike leaders would also create an impression of martyrdom which would cause high feelings among the workers and make matters worse. In fact many strike leaders, notably in the Clyde district, preferred imprisonment to the payment of fines imposed for strike offences, causing additional friction and ill feeling between employers and workmen. It was because of this difficulty that the Balfour Committee recommended the repeal of the power to imprison for strike offenses, a recommendation that was adopted in the amending Act of 1916.

It would be interesting to make a complete study of the experiment of legal prohibition of strikes during the war period, but no published material is available except in the Returns made by the Munitions Tribunals to the Ministry of Munitions. These reports cover only the first year, from July, 1915, to July, 1916. According to the returns the total number of prosecutions for illegal strikes was 56, involving 1,612 workers, of whom 1,006 were convicted. From the strikers convicted £1,365 in fines was collected.[54]

[53] *The 12th Report of Proceedings under the Conciliation Act*, 1896, vol. i, p. 27; *cf.* Report by the Industrial Council on Industrial Agreements, 1913 (CD. 6952); *U. S. Department of Labor, Bureau of Labor Statistics Bulletin, No. 133*, p. 22.

[54] There was only one prosecution for illegal lock-out, but no conviction resulted; see Returns made to the Ministry of Munitions, 1915 (CD. 8143), 1916 (CD. 8360).

In the same period there occurred 22 serious strikes in the vital war industries, namely, 12 in the coal-mining industry, 8 in the engineering and shipbuildng trade, and 2 in the textile trade and the docks. The number of workers involved in the strikes was about 300,000, with an approximate loss of 1,700,000 working days.[55] From the comparison of these two sets of figures it becomes apparent that the number of workers convicted of illegal strikes was a little over one-third of one per cent of those who had actually taken part in the strikes, while the amount of fines actually paid amounted to less than one-sixtieth of one per cent of the maximum penalty imposed under the Munitions Acts. That the legal prohibition of strikes was therefore intended more as a warning than for actual application in every case with the full force of law is a safe inference. In fact it was applied only in extreme cases to the strike leaders and left untouched the rank and file who merely ceased work following their leaders in the illegal stoppage of work.

The difficulty of enforcement may be illustrated by citing the experiences in a few illegal strikes. The South Wales coal strike of 1915, which cost the country about £1,500,000 and 1,200,000 working days, was settled by negotiation and no punishment was imposed on the strikers. This settlement was followed by a shipwright's strike which took place in Glasgow, in August, 1915. This time seventeen strike leaders were brought to trial and fined each £10 with 21 days in which to pay, and, in the event of failure to pay, 30 days' imprisonment. On September 23, 14 of the men concerned paid their fines, but 3 refused to pay and were arrested and imprisoned. Thereupon some 97,000 organized workers threatened to cripple all the factories in the Clyde district if their leaders were not released. The payment of the fines

[55] Milton Moses, "Compulsory Arbitration in Great Britain during the War," *26 Journal of Political Economy*, 1918, pp. 890-891.

was eventually arranged somehow and the men were released. Another strike took place at a munitions plant at Dalmuir toward the end of December, 1915. Twenty-eight men were brought to trial on January 8, 1916, and were fined £5 each. The Ministry of Munitions thereafter suggested the possibility of remission of the fines if the men would express regret. Although they refused the fines were never paid nor pressed for.[56]

The high feeling among the Clyde district munitions workers resulting from these strikes and other causes found expression in March, 1916, when various strikes were organized by the Clyde Workers' Committee, a committee of shop stewards that was opposed to the passage of the Military Service Act of 1916 and generally to the compulsory measures taken under the Munitions Acts. The Ministry of Munitions felt that the case was not one which could be suitably dealt with by the comparatively mild penalties provided under the Munitions Acts, and, accordingly, under Regulation 14 of the Defense of the Realm Regulations, the Ministry requested the military authorities to remove six leading members of the Clyde Workers' Committee to other parts of the country. This was done, a protest meeting followed, three further arrests were made and the workers arrested were deported from the area on the charge that they had delayed the production of munitions at certain controlled establishments, a serious offence under Regulation 42 of the Defence of the Realm Regulations. In addition thirty of the strikers were fined £5 each to be deducted from their wages. The strikes came to an end in the first week of April, 1916.[57]

In June, 1916, some 5,000 engineers went out on strike at Barrow over the issue of labor dilution. The strike was

[56] H. Wolfe, *Labor Supply and Regulation*, pp. 127 *et seq.*

[57] *Ibid.*, p. 133; *Annual Register*, 1916, pp. 94-96.

a violation of the Treasury Agreement and a breach of the Munitions Acts. A notice was published by the Government giving the strikers 48 hours in which to return to work. It was intimated that upon their failure to do so, proceedings would be taken under the Defense of the Realm Act against those who had instigated the strike and under the Munitions Acts against those who had taken part in the stoppage of work. All picketing was prevented and all public houses were closed. The threat of the Government was successful in ending the strike.

The same method was used in the case of a strike of the Liverpool boiler-makers in December, 1916, with the same result.[58]

In May, 1917, engineering strikes broke out in various parts of the country over the questions of recognition of shop stewards and the extension of dilution to private industries. The Government issued a notice calling the attention of the strikers to the unconstitutional nature of the strikes and to the provisions of the Defence of the Realm Regulations. Seven of the strike leaders were arrested on the charge of having impeded the production of war materials. The Prime Minister himself then intervened for a peaceful settlement of the disputes, giving an understanding that no further intimidation and arrest would take place. The men resumed work, and the strike leaders were released on the condition that they would adhere to the terms of the settlement arranged by the Government.[59]

In July, 1918, engineering strikes took place at Coventry, Leeds, Birmingham, Manchester, and other districts over the question of labor embargoes. This time the Government brought in the Military Service Acts declaring that

[58] Milton Moses, "Compulsory Arbitration," *26 Journal of Political Economy*, 1918, p. 896; *Annual Register*, 1916, pp. 202-3.

[59] *The Annual Register*, 1917, pp. 96-7, 130-2.

the strikers had ceased work "not in pursuance of a trade dispute, but in an endeavor to force the Government to change the national policy essential to the prosecution of the war." The men on strike had been granted exemption from military service for the sole reason that their services were considered of more value to the State in the workshops than in the army. Should they fail to return to work immediately their protective certificate would cease to have effect, and they would become liable to the provisions of the Military Services Acts. This manifesto had the desired effect and at the end of the month the Minister of Munitions was able to announce that work had been resumed in Birmingham and Coventry and that a committee was to be appointed to investigate the causes of the trouble, with Mr. Justice McCardie as chairman.[60]

In brief, the enforcement technique as provided under the Munitions Acts broke down in cases of serious strikes, and the heavier weapons, devised primarily for the purpose of the defence of the country and not for the settlement of ordinary trade disputes, were brought into use.

E. Restriction on Individual Freedom

Some restrictions on freedom of movement were unavoidable under a policy of Government control of labor supply. These restrictions were imposed through the leaving certificate system, which provoked almost from the outset to the end of the war bitter opposition from the workers.[61] This system removed the rights of the workers to choose their market and to leave employment when they were the victims

[60] *Cf.* Report by Mr. Justice McCardie's Committee on Labor Embargoes, cited in Wolfe, pp. 146, 350; *Annual Register*, 1918, pp. 121-23; Parl. Deb. Lords (57), 167, April 8, 1924, per Lord Askwith.

[61] In the first year from July, 1915, to July, 1916, the Munitions Tribunals dealt with 15,210 complaints in connection with the leaving certificate system.

of oppression by their employers. Furthermore it subjected workers to the danger of unemployment for a certain period of time and, after the appearance of the Military Services Acts, to call by the recruiting officers. When these points are considered it is not surprising that the Balfour Committee, appointed only a few months after the passage of the Munitions of War Act, 1915, devoted more than half of its report to the difficulties arising from the operation of the leaving certificate. It was pointed out that the system tended to create unemployment in two ways. The employers dared not engage workmen without a leaving certificate, while the workers, ignorant of this condition, often left their work without having obtained certificates. The appeal to the Munitions Tribunals was of no use, because several days of unemployment must elapse before a certificate could be granted. The system had also been taken advantage of by many employers for the purpose of petty tyrannies. Changes in the methods of work, a long-standing issue, had been forced through, and certificates were refused to those who were out of work because of a strike or the breakdown of machinery. Men from distant places were not allowed to return home or to change their positions for the better. As the cost of living rose rapidly and continuously the workmen came to feel more and more the effect of these restrictions, and their grievances grew. This was especially true of the skilled time workers who could not change their work or earn extra money by working on a piece-work basis. These skilled men's grievances found expression in the summer of 1917 in the cloudbursts of the engineering strikes which finally brought the entire system of leaving certificate to an end.

It was soon proved that the removal of the system had in fact demolished the only effective basis of government control of labor supply. For it was only within the shelter afforded by the system that employers could press the unpopular policy of dilution, enforce discipline at individual workshops, and above all control wages to some extent. With the withdrawal of the scheme the foundation of all these things had gone, because labor, with the employers at its mercy, was now free to move wherever it liked. With a view to checking the rapid rise of wages and the continual change in labor personnel the Government decided, in July, 1918, to adopt what was then popularly known as the Labor Embargo system, under which a certain number of munitions firms were required to obtain licenses from the Ministry of Munitions before engaging any skilled workmen. This scheme, which was objected to as an attempt to reintroduce, by the side windows, the old scheme of leaving certificates, led to the serious strikes at Coventry and other districts. These strikes effectively killed the last attempt to check the free movements of workers in search of better wages.

The general feeling about the limitation of freedom of movement was well expressed by a Member of Parliament, who, in referring to an aggrieved workman, said:

> A man looks around and sees that sort of thing and says: "To blazes with all your Munitions Acts and Regulations! Is it not absurd that here am I, qualified for an electrician's job, but not qualified for the other job, and the electrician's job having 10s. more a week attached to it, and some foreman, or some Act of Parliament, or some Tribunal says that I, a free British workman, may not walk a hundred yards and get the new job?" [62]

Considerable difficulty was also found in the maintenance of labor discipline at the controlled establishments. According to the Munitions Tribunals Returns the total number of workers convicted of offences against the workshop regu-

[62] Parl. Deb. Commons (92), 2786; per Mr. J. M. Hogge, April 27, 1917.

lations during the first year from July 1915 to July 1916 was 10,645, the fines collected from these workers amounting to £9,766.[63] The great majority of the offenders were women, whose general offence, loss of time due mostly to illness or other circumstances, was deserving of sympathy and understanding rather than criminal treatment. The female workers did not wish to talk much about their illnesses before the public court. They also had the old difficulty of getting witnesses in support of their case against the employers. The criminal treatment of these trivial offences in itself was felt to be a cause of grievance and brought forth strong protests in Parliament.[64]

It should not be imagined, however, that the government or the individual employer always was a hard taskmaster, with the government regulations in hand as a cracking whip. From the outset the employers were rather reluctant to use the Munitions Tribunals for the purpose of enforcing the workshop rules. They believed that the friction likely to be engendered by lodging complaints before the court would more than outweigh the advantages resulting from the fines to be imposed. On the part of the government it was also recognized that appeal should be made to the Tribunals only as a last resort. In the ordinary course the timekeeping officers, appointed by the Ministry of Munitions for each area, would visit individual workmen charged with serious faults in time-keeping, and talk things over with them. These visits were important both as a means of ascertaining the underlying causes of bad time-keeping and of curing it. In many cases the good work of the time-keeping officers was facilitated by the establishment of Joint Workshop Committees, consisting of an equal number of representatives of

[63] Returns, 1915 (CD. 8143), 1916 (CD. 8360).

[64] Parl. Deb. Commons (92), 2769-2773, April 27, 1917, per Mr. Anderson.

the workers and of the management. The general function of these Committees was to settle complaints and supervise welfare work. An authoritative opinion holds that the persuasion of the time-keeping officers and the Joint Workshop Committees did more to improve time-keeping than did all the complaints brought before the Munitions Tribunals.[65] It was indeed partially because of their success during the war period that the Whitley Committee proposed in its scheme of Joint Industrial Councils the formation of efficient Workshop Joint Committees as an essential part of the whole structure of industrial peace.

F. Labor Dilution

Labor dilution was another of the principal causes of industrial unrest during the war, yet it was essential to the replacement of the labor forces which were depleted by military recruiting. By the end of the war nearly five million workers out of a total of about 14,350,000 of the employed male population had gone to the Colours. This tremendous loss to the industrial forces was made up by new recruits, chiefly women workers under the Government policy of labor dilution in so far as munitions industries were concerned.[66] Most of the women workers were new in industry and in the way of their introduction to industrial work stood what was then called trade-union restrictions. For a clear understanding of the difficulties that the policy of dilution faced it is therefore necessary to know what these restrictions were. They might be classified under five headings: (1) practices requiring that only skilled men with certain definite qualifications, such for instance as due apprenticeship,

[65] H. Wolfe, *Labor Supply and Regulation*, p. 178.

[66] The total number of women workers introduced to industrial work during the war period was about 1,659,000, of whom about 414,000 were engaged in the metal trades. Wolfe, *Labor Supply and Regulation*, pp. 77-78.

approved experience, membership in a skilled trade union, could be permitted to perform certain classes of work; (2) practices assigning to various classes of skilled men the type of work appropriate to each; (3) regulations regarding the ratio of skilled to unskilled workers, particularly with regard to the number of apprentices admissible to the trade; (4) practices prescribing the number of hours of labor, the methods of work including over-time, piece or time work; (5) embargo on the employment of any but trade unionists in certain classes of work.

These restrictions, it will be noticed, were really a bulwark of protection for the skilled workers against capital as well as against unskilled labor. In fact they were the objective for which trade unionism had toiled for many years. It is not surprising, therefore, that these restrictions were relaxed with great reluctance and amid much misunderstanding, suspicion, and turmoil, even after the trade union leaders had given their pledge, in the Treasury Agreement of 1915, to approve dilution. Dilution was one of the principal causes of the engineering strikes in the Clyde district in the winter of 1915-1916, and the proposal of its extension to private industries resulted in the outbreak of the engineering strikes in the summer of 1917. In the course of Parliamentary debates it was admitted that dilution could not be carried out unless accompanied by agreements between those immediately concerned even in the controlled establishments where the trade union leaders had given their pledge to introduce dilution. It was therefore useless to try to extend the system to private industries without labor's consent.[67]

[67] Parl. Deb. Commons (97), 1304; Aug. 15, 1917, per Mr. W. S. Churchill, then Minister of Munitions.

G. Lack of Co-ordination in Wage Control

The slow realization on the part of the Government that labor control and wage adjustment should go hand in hand under a well thought out and co-ordinated policy caused considerable trouble during the war period and left a mass of problems for settlement in the post-war years. We have seen that at the outbreak of the war the Government adopted the policy of "Business as Usual", leaving the wage issue, the root of all labor unrest, to the ordinary process of negotiation between the employers and employed concerned. Through the inevitable sequence of events the Government was drawn deeper and deeper into the field of wage control until at the end of the war it found itself directing the wages of a vast majority of the entire working population of the country. Such control had not been planned, however, nor were the powers conferred by piece-meal legislation to meet successive emergencies broad enough to tackle the wage question as a whole. In the first place the Munitions Acts did not cover the entire industrial field, since they did not include such important industries as the coal mining, railways, shipping, textile, and agriculture. Secondly, wage control was not placed in a central co-ordinating department but was divided between different Ministries, namely, the Ministry of Munitions, the War Office, the Admiralty, the Coal Controller, the Railways Executive Committee, the Maritime Board, the Agricultural Wages Boards, the Ministry of Labor, and the Committee on Production. The policies of these various departments were not always in perfect harmony.

The lack of co-ordination and the slow bestowal of wage control through piecemeal legislation resulted in the rise of diverse wage movements in different industries, and in delay in the settlement of disputes. Under the system of divided powers it was the practice of the trade unions to petition the separate executive Departments. These Departments, hard pressed by the incessant need of an increased supply of labor, were unable in many cases to resist the demands of labor for special treatment, especially when the demands came from those in a strong strategic position, because their trade was of special importance to the State. They were likewise frequently unable to refuse petitions for equal treatment submitted by those in a weaker position, because the Departments felt discrimination to be unjustifiable under public control of the industries. Should the trade unions pleadings fail in these quarters they would appeal to the War Cabinet which, although always ready to listen, was more interested in broad political expediency than in any well informed and detailed wage settlements. This constant wrangling over wages between the trade unions and the different Government Departments was in itself responsible for delays in the settlement of disputes. The settlements more often resulted in forced concessions which created further conflicts between Government Departments, embarrassed the arbitration tribunals, and provoked further demands from other trades.

An example of the difficulties is furnished by the Cabinet embargo on wage increases, the coal controller's awards, and the skilled men's grievances. On November 18, 1915, Mr. Bonar Law, then Leader of the House of Commons, stressed the great need for national economy, stating that "those representing the working classes, as well as the commercial classes, should set their forces resolutely against any increased pay by the Government in any shape or form for anything that had to be got in connection with the war." This suggestion was formally incorporated in a Government Memorandum to the Committee on Production and other persons acting as single arbitrators issued toward the end of the month. In this Memorandum it was stated that the

Government had given earnest attention to the financial position of the country and had come to the conclusion that "any further advances of wages, other than following automatically from existing agreements, should be strictly confined to the adjustments of local conditions where such adjustments are proved to be necessary." [68] The Committee on Production did not express any opinion on this suggestion, but implicitly obeyed it by refusing to grant any new general advances in wages for several months.[69] This position was hotly criticised by trade unions on the ground that the Government had no authority to direct the independent statutory arbitration tribunals, upon whose integrity labor had relied when it abandoned its right to strike. These tribunals, the unions maintained, should in the matter of wage determination concern themselves solely with industrial conditions and not with directions from the Government. The prestige of the Committee would have been seriously damaged, had it not, in July, 1916, begun its second cycle of wage advances in order to meet the increased cost of living.

The coal controller responsible for the coal-mining industry issued an award on September 28, 1917, granting a special war wage of 1s. 6d. a day for colliery workers of 16 years and over, and 9d. a day for those under 16. This immediately provoked a demand for an extension of this wage scale to the mines and work relating to mining with which the Ministry of Munitions was concerned. The Ministry of Munitions proposed that the question should be referred to the Committee on Production but, as it was likely to lead to strikes, the proposal was ruled out. The Ministry was therefore compelled to negotiate with the Miners' Federation, and an agreement was eventually reached which amounted to a 12s. award, inclusive of all advances up to

[68] Lord Amulree, *Industrial Arbitration*, p. 140.

[69] *Ante*, p. 90.

date. When the agreement came to be administered it was found that among the groups of workers involved conditions varied from firm to firm and from district to district in respect of the basis of wages, and that the ability to pay was not equal as between firms working for the government, since they could be compensated for the increased labor charges, and those not so employed, because they could not look for such compensation. This latter difficulty was so acute that in the case of lead mines the award was not paid until the Ministry had undertaken to reimburse the employers for the estimated additional labor cost of £150,000. Similarly the difficulties as between varying wage bases could be settled only when a separate agreement was reached with the Iron and Steel Confederation. Under this agreement either the bonus of 12½ per cent or the coal controller's award might be extended to the trade to be merged in the sliding scale in future. In June, 1918, the coal controller made a further award of the same amount as in the previous year. This award again caused the Ministry of Munitions to carry on protracted negotiations with the object of making elaborate arrangements for handling situations arising from its extension to other industries.[70]

The protests made by the Ministries of Labor and Munitions against the coal controller's award of 1917 were referred to an inter-departmental committee for investigation and report. In its report the Committee stated that the strong pressure by powerful trade unions could be resisted only by a single central authority representing all Government Departments dealing with wage questions, and added that there was no justification in principle for treating the coal-mining industry by a separate authority. The coal controller asserted that both the mine owners and miners were in strong opposition to any interference by the Ministry

[70] Wolfe, *Labor Supply and Regulation*, pp. 261-2.

of Labor because the people in the mining industry believed that the industry, by virtue of its strength and peculiar character, should occupy a privileged position. The Committee, however, could not support the claim, because the State was the real employer and the natural authority to deal with wages on behalf of the State resided in the Chief Industrial Commissioner's Office in the Ministry of Labor, with the Committee on Production as the final arbitration authority. The report was approved by the War Cabinet, but it bore no practical fruits.[71]

Toward the end of 1917 another inter-departmental Committee, known as the War Cabinet Labor Committee, was appointed, with Mr. G. N. Barnes as chairman, " to co-ordinate the acts of Government Departments on matters connected with industrial wages and disputes by laying down general principles for their guidance and settling questions of policy affecting more than one department." The Committee did not fulfill its function aside from laying down the principles that the Government Departments should (1) confine concessions within the general limits set by the Committee on Production, (2) deal with inequalities within an industry or class of workers, and (3) observe the general principle that no advance should be made that was likely to disturb existing working conditions or district rates.[72] It was perhaps too much to expect any single Department to carry the whole burden of settling wage questions with a consistent policy at a time when the various supply departments were all hard pressed by the incessant need of labor supply, and, therefore, labor had the State at its mercy.

During 1916 automatic machines, manned largely by both male and female unskilled labor, were introduced and widely

[71] Prof. Henry Clay, *The Problem of Industrial Relations*, pp. 50-60.

[72] *The 12th Report of Proceedings under the Conciliation Act*, 1896, vol. i, p. 31.

installed. With this innovation the system of payment by results was also widely extended. An inquiry early in 1917 disclosed the fact that at least one-third of the engineering firms of the country were working on a piece-work basis. As the earnings of the unskilled new comers on piece work began to approach and then even surpass those of the skilled workers—supervisors, tool room hands, setters-up, and mill-wrights—the nature of whose duties made it difficult for them to do piece work, grievances grew and difficulties were experienced in all the great engineering centers. Sheffield, for example, sent to the Ministry of Munitions a deputation of skilled men who demonstrated that their earnings were about half of those of the unskilled machine tenders. The Government had promised to prevent cutting of piece prices; the situation could therefore not be remedied by reducing the earnings of the unskilled. At the same time it was thought economically impossible to meet the situation by raising the skilled men's earnings to those of the unskilled. The position was further aggravated by the granting of flat war advances to both classes under arbitration awards, which obscured the position of the skilled and the unskilled. The grievances grew to such proportions and intensity throughout 1916 and 1917 that the Commissioners on Industrial Unrest were unanimous in recommending that skilled supervisors and others on day rates should receive a bonus. This recommendation was accepted by the Government and a flat bonus of 12½ per cent was granted as from October 13, 1917, to certain limited classes of skilled engineers. Within a week demands to be included in the bonus were received from all classes of skilled and semi-skilled time workers. The unskilled and finally the piece workers followed with demands to which the Government was compelled to bow. Bonuses were granted to practically all adult male munition workers, whether on a time or a piece-work basis.

When this was accomplished the position as between skilled and unskilled remained unaltered except for a general addition to wages all around, a situation which led to the strikes in July, 1918. After a thorough investigation of the causes of the labor trouble Mr. Justice McCardie's Committee on Labor Embargoes stated that the relative position of the skilled time workers and the unskilled piece workers was a question that was almost insoluble.[73]

The unbalanced wage movements were thus one of the principal causes of industrial unrest during the war period and left difficult questions for the post-war years. Divergency in wages was not, however, a new thing. Even before the war wages were as various in amount, in the method of determination, and in the areas to which they were applied as it is possible to conceive. In the first place trade unionism, the basic operative force in collective bargaining, had grown up on different bases in different trades. At the bottom of the whole social structure there were the agricultural workers and the casual laborers at the docks. The dock workers were being rapidly organized, but the nature of their occupation made it almost impossible to fix a satisfactory wage base. The agricultural workers were very poorly organized, and wages of 14s. a week were paid to adult males in certain of the poorer districts. Above them came the vast volume of the unorganized trades, in some of which wages varying from 2½ d. to 3⅓d. per hour, were regulated by the Trade Boards. At the top there was a small number of well-organized industries such as the coal mining, steel, engineering, shipbuilding, textile, railways, and building trades, in which national unions had grown up but in which wages varied from district to district, with different methods of determination. The coal mining

[73] Wolfe, *Labor Supply and Regulation*, pp. 266 *et seq.*; Appendix 8, p. 353-4.

trades, for instance, fixed their rates, subject to the minimum set by the Coal Mines (Minimum Wages) Act, 1912, upon the weekly output of the districts concerned, while the steel trades fixed theirs on a sliding scale based on the selling price of certain standard products. The rates for the textile trades, cotton and wool, might be described as national because the bulk of the trade in each case was strictly localized. In the shipbuilding and engineering trades collective bargaining had been developed to a high point, but district rates varied from a minimum of 24s. a week for a skilled fitter in Cornwall to a maximum of 46s. for the same class of workmen in London. Nor was there uniformity between districts as to the methods of payment. In the engineering trade piece work was permitted, but more than 80 per cent of the workers were employed on time work. In the same way piece work, which was the rule in the shipbuilding trade on the northeast coast, was absolutely forbidden at Liverpool. In the engineering trades there was for a piece worker a time-work minimum below which his earnings were not to be permitted to fall, but there was no such minimum in the shipbuilding trades. Again, in the general engineering trades women were not employed, except to a limited extent on the northeast coast, but in the light engineering trade of the Birmingham area they were commonly employed at rates varying from 6s. a week at 14 years of age to 12s. for an adult of 21. There was moreover a further important difference between the shipbuilding and the engineering trades. In the former the number of unions was limited in so far as craft work was concerned to a comparatively small number, but in the engineering trades an employer in a single establishment might have to negotiate with as many as twenty unions, with no common mind and no policy in view.

Although wages were in a confused state even before the war, the tendency to divergency was vastly accelerated by the war. While firms engaged in civilian work either lost contracts or took orders at lower prices in order to keep the works going, those engaged in munitions work could not carry out their rapidly accumulating contracts because of the lack of labor; they were compelled therefore to raise wage rates in order to attract more workers. These advances took the form of bonuses of all types: sometimes the same for skilled and unskilled, sometimes more to one group than to the other, sometimes the same for time and piece workers, sometimes flat rates for time workers and percentage rates for piece workers. In all cases, however, there was a tendency to vary from district to district. A return prepared for the Ministry of Munitions showed that, by September, 1915 the average percentage increases in the weekly earnings in the districts of Belfast, Lincoln, and Weymouth varied from 25 to 70, while in the Clyde shipbuilding trades the wage increases for different classes of workers differed from 2 per cent in the case of painters to 43 per cent in the case of fitters, over the pre-war level. Even in a single large establishment wages differed among different classes of workers. At a Birmingham plant employing 212 tool makers, for instance, 57 earned over £5 a week, 34 over £7, and 5 over £10.[74] Such divergencies in earnings were bound to produce industrial unrest, for after all it is characteristic of human nature that the spectacle of the more fortunate should excite envy in the less fortunate and should provoke agitation for betterment. The principle of equal suffering and equal relief prescribed by the arbitration tribunals would probably have saved a world of trouble, if it had been uniformly applied from the outset of the war. But the policy of drifting had produced a mountain of inequalities

[74] Lord Amulree, *Industrial Arbitration*, p. 195, Appendix 2; *cf.* the *History of the Ministry of Munitions*, vol. v.

and an attempt to mete out equal treatment upon the basis of inequalities resulted only in further inequalities and grievances.

3. CONCLUSION

The brief episode of the war experiment throws a new light on a few old situations. As in the days of Edward III, it was found during the world war that the maximum utilization of labor supply for a national emergency could not be effected without an encroachment upon personal freedom of movement, on the one hand, and a restriction of the free course of commodity prices and wages, on the other. Secondly, it was essential to have a central executive Department with a comprehensive and consistent policy for the well balanced regulation of the diverse movements of wages. Thirdly, however, it was established that even under war conditions the interplay of economic forces could not be entirely superseded by an authoritative determination of the national or social needs of the country. For, although it was admitted on all sides that the war could not be won without the co-operation of "the hewers of wood and the drawers of water," such co-operation could not be demanded of the modern British workers whose free spirit would not countenance a blind allegiance to the State. Their co-operation could be won only through persuasion and understanding and by measures that would satisfy their sense of fair play and justice. It was definitely proved that no amount of machinery, whatever its power and however well devised, could prevent disputes if the fundamental issues about which the workers cared greatly were either unsettled or settled only partially. This lesson prompted the Whitley Committee to recommend the granting of a fuller measure of self-government to the workers for the purpose of industrial peace; it also motivated the post-war Government when it passed legislation for unemployment insurance and other measures to insure social security.

Within these broad limits we may say that the war experiment showed some methods of industrial peace to be more effective than others. In the matter of workshop regulation conciliation was more effective than arbitration, and in arbitration a permanent court on a representative basis of employers and workmen was more effective than ad-hoc courts on non-representative basis. Recognition of the effectiveness of these measures in the settlement of industrial disputes led to the adoption of the Industrial Courts Act, 1919, to which we shall refer in the following chapter.

CHAPTER IV

The Government Agencies for Industrial Peace; with Special Reference to the Industrial Courts Act, 1919

I. INTRODUCTION

A. The Circumstances Leading to the Passage of the Industrial Courts Act, 1919

It is proposed in this chapter to examine the actual operation of the Government agencies for industrial peace with special reference to the Industrial Courts Act, 1919, which was passed after considerable amount of industrial disturbance following the war, an act which brought back the pre-war procedure of voluntary conciliation and arbitration with some important improvements.

During the war it had become clear that the great national struggle could not be won without the active cooperation of workers who had become conscious of their immense power as a national productive force and were organized in strong trade unions,[1] and their claim for a higher status and a better standard of living, with a voice in the control of industry, became irresistible, not only in the light of the exalted war idealism but also in view of the services they had rendered to the national cause.[2] It had also become clear that the termination of hostilities would raise many difficulties, which, if mismanaged, might create serious labor unrest and

[1] See the *21st Abstract of Labor Statistics*, p. 135.

[2] Parl. Deb. Commons (5th ser.) (85), 363; Aug. 2, 1916, per Mr. G. J. Wardle.

plunge the nation into social chaos at a time when she would barely have emerged from the greatest struggle in her history and would require unity and every bit of energy for the purpose of peace reconstruction. The Government was fully aware of these circumstances and attempts were made to form a long range plan of peace by appointing various Reconstruction Committees, including the Whitley Committee on Relations between Employers and Employees, appointed in October 1916,[3] and by creating a new Ministry of Labor early in 1917.

In presenting toward the end of 1916 the New Ministries and Secretaries Bill, which proposed to set up a Ministry of Labor, in the House of Commons, Sir George Cave, then Home Secretary, stated that the misunderstanding between employers and workmen should not be allowed to interfere with the prosecution of the war and that, for this purpose, there must be a strong central authority "to note the rocks ahead, and, when trouble arises, to conciliate if possible, and if need be to control, those concerned." Mr. Lloyd George, then Prime Minister, added that the Ministry of Labor would not confine its task to the settlement of industrial disputes, after all a small part of the industrial problem, but that it would become in the real sense of the term a Ministry of Labor having for its chief function the promotion of the welfare of labor. The new Ministry would take charge of the administration of the Conciliation Act, 1896, the Labor Exchanges Act, 1909, the Trade Boards Act, 1909, the National Insurance (Unemployment) Acts, 1911-1916, and Part 1 of the Munitions of War Act, 1915. These Acts had been administered by the Board of Trade.[4] The Bill

[3] The Work of these committees was coordinated by the creation of a new Ministry of Reconstruction in August, 1917. *Report on the Work of the Ministry of Reconstruction*, 1919 (CD. 9231), p. 2, appendix 1-3.

[4] See ch. 2, p. 48, footnote 28.

passed smoothly,[5] and the new Ministry of Labor was duly constituted early in 1917, with Mr. John Hodge as its first Minister.

The Whitley Committee published five Reports [6] and recognized labor's claim for a better social order in their chief contention that industrial peace could not be secured on a mere cash basis [7] but that it required the granting of a greater measure of self-government to the industrial workers through a scheme of joint industrial councils. The Whitley Reports were accepted by the Government and Joint Industrial Councils were established in a number of industries. No piece of social machinery, however well devised and well meant, could, however, get rid of industrial disputes altogether, any more than any human agency could calm the angry seas in a storm. As an essential part of its reconstruction program for post-war industrial relations, therefore, the Committee recommended that a standing court of arbitration and ad-hoc courts of inquiry should be established as the regular means of peaceful settlement of the industrial disputes that were bound to arise under any form of social organization. These institutions should, however, be on an entirely voluntary basis as "the experience of compulsory arbitration during the war period has shown that it is not a successful method of avoiding disputes and in normal times it would undoubtedly prove even less successful." The voluntary means for the peaceful settlement of disputes in the most important industries was one of the marked features of the industrial organization of the coun-

[5] Parl. Deb. Commons (5th Ser.) (88), 1006, 1141-3, 1159, 1169, 1179, 1344, 1394, 1505. Lords (23), 1065.

[6] Fully discussed in the following chapter.

[7] S. J. Chapman, *Labor and Capital After the War*, Introduction by J. H. Whitley; J. H. Whitley, "Works Committees and Industrial Councils," in *Labor and Industry*.

try, and there was no reason why these voluntary agencies should not work effectively after the war. They would indeed achieve an even greater success under the proposed system of joint industrial councils which would meet regularly for the discussion of common interests and thus promote a better atmosphere for an amicable settlement of disputes by voluntary conciliation machinery.

In the case of grave disputes, however, the Committee believed that the Ministry of Labor should be authorized to appoint a court of inquiry for the purpose of making an impartial and authoritative inquiry into the facts in dispute. The Ministry might publish any reports to be made by the court of inquiry for the information of those immediately concerned as well as of the public at large. Such inquiries should not, however, carry any compulsory power of prohibiting strikes or lockouts. As for the expediency of settling disputes by arbitration the Committee thought that a useful distinction might be made between methods dealing with those minor cases in which the parties might desire a local hearing, where the matters in question were of relatively small importance, and methods of treating cases affecting comparatively large sections of industries or involving general principles. Cases in the first category might conveniently be decided by single arbitrators, but those in the second might more properly be referred to a standing court of arbitration. Such a standing court would have the advantage of being in a position to issue uniform and well correlated wage awards because of its receipt of regular appeals from different trades. It could also give systematic treatment to trade disputes, treatment that could not be expected under the system of ad-hoc courts of arbitration which existed before the war.[8]

[8] The Whitley Committee, the Fourth Report on Conciliation and Arbitration, 1918 (CD. 9099).

The war ended on November 11, 1918, and the twelve months immediately following the Armistice presented features that were without parallel in the industrial history of the country. Millions of men were returning from the trenches and the munition factories to be reabsorbed into civil life, while the immense concentration on war production during the previous four years, the wear and tear on industrial and financial equipment, the shortage of raw material and shipping facilities, the exhaustion of the nation's man power and industrial skill, and the general disorganization of economic conditions throughout the world made it difficult for industry immediately to return to peace production without causing serious industrial dislocations and social unrest. The outstanding problem facing the country during this period was that of working out special measures to secure a comparatively peaceful and speedy transition from war to peace conditions.

There was a consensus of opinion among both the employers' and workers' organizations in favor of early relaxation of Government control over wages and other conditions of employment and of the resumption of the pre-war practice of leaving matters of industrial agreement to the decision of private employers and workmen.[9] No one knew, however, what serious social and political complications might arise as a result of premature removal of control, especially in view of the uncertain future of business and of price movements, on the one hand, and the high tension of labor inspired by war idealism, on the other. It was generally feared that a sharp decline in wages, which might follow military demobilization and Government relaxation of control, would cause serious industrial disturbances. Such a result should be avoided as far as possible, not only to protect from disappointment and disgrace the men returning

[9] *Report on Conciliation and Arbitration for 1919, 1921* (221), pp. 4, 9.

from the front, but also in order to give the country a breathing spell before its return to the normal task of peace reconstruction. Furthermore the pre-war machinery of negotiation between employers and workmen had lain idle for several years, most of the important industries having regular recourse to arbitration for wage regulation. In these circumstances very few industries were ready to resume independent discussion of wages and other important issues.

On the other hand the only adequate machinery for compulsory wage regulation was provided in the Munitions of War Acts and these Acts would not be required after the cessation of munitions production for war purposes. The question of post-war labor conditions and the future position of wage awards granted by the arbitration tribunals during the war period had, for some time prior to the Armistice, been under consideration by a Committee appointed by the Ministry of Reconstruction and presided over by Sir John Simon. Following the presentation of its Report Mr. G. H. Roberts, then Minister of Labor, called a national conference of representative employers and workmen, on November 13, 1918, at which Mr. Lloyd George, Prime Minister, proposed that "as a first step towards the restoration of general confidence the rates of wages prevailing in each industry or branch of industry in any district at the date of the Armistice should be maintained and enforced by statutes as the minimum rates of wages payable for a limited period." [10] This proposal was eventually agreed to by the conference, and the Wages (Temporary Regulation) Act, 1918, was passed on November 21, (8 & 9 Geo. 5, c. 61).

As indicated in its title, the Act was a purely temporary measure to tide over current difficulties. Broadly speaking,

[10] *The Report on Conciliation and Arbitration for 1919*, p. 4; Parl. Deb. Commons (110), 3105, 3309-11; Nov. 15, 18, 1918; Lords (32), 286-292.

it achieved three main objects: (1) it continued for six months the standard rates existing at the time of the Armistice as minimum rates, which might be enforced by Government inspection and punishment through a Munitions Tribunal; (2) it repealed the clauses of the Munitions of War Acts relative to the prohibition of strikes and lockouts, thus removing the legal obstacles in the way of strikes for wage increases over and above the prescribed rates; (3) it retained compulsory arbitration only for the purpose of determining cases arising from or in respect of the minimum rates, that might be changed by an agreement between the employers and workers concerned with the approval of the Minister of Labor or by an award of the Interim Court of Arbitration.

The Interim Court of Arbitration, which superseded the arbitration tribunals set up under the Munitions of War Acts, was in fact a continuation of the Committee on Production both in its composition,[11] procedure,[12] and principles of wage determination.[13] In all, the Court issued 932 awards[14] dealing mostly with disputes that involved small groups of private concerns or single municipal corporations or other semi-public bodies. The general awards, numbering only 64, covered engineering, shipbuilding, chemicals,

[11] The Interim Court of Arbitration was instituted on November 22, 1918, and continued in service until the following November when it was superseded by the Industrial Court established under the Industrial Courts Act, 1919. It had a chairman, Sir David Harrel, and four divisional chairmen, including Sir William Mackenzie who became the first President of the Industrial Court. *Report on Conciliation and Arbitration for 1919*, p. 29.

[12] *Ibid.*, Appendix II, p. 44.

[13] A. G. B. Fisher, *Some Problems of Wages and Their Regulation in Great Britain since 1918*, p. 29.

[14] For a summary of the decisions see the *12th Report of Proceedings under the Conciliation Act*, 1896, vol. ii, Appendix IV, p. 791, and the *Report on Conciliation and Arbitration for 1919*, Appendix V, p. 51.

explosives, building, railway shopmen, cement, flour milling, and other less important industries, most of which during the war had followed the practice of regulating wages by arbitration. The fear of unemployment and wage collapse immediately following the cessation of the war was proved groundless by the subsequent development of the industrial situation. The peace requirements for reconstruction and repair after the four years' waste of the Great War created such great demands for goods in most trades that the country soon passed from temporary unemployment to a boom condition, in which both prices and wages rose sharply. In many cases the supply of labor was found inadequate. In such circumstances the imposition of general minimum rates under the Wages (Temporary Regulation) Act constituted no substantial burden on the industry, and very few complaints were made of the Interim Court awards, which granted in the majority of cases claims for wage increases and other improvements in working conditions.[15]

The Interim Court thus proved a successful means of advancing wages in an orderly and peaceful manner in a period of considerable difficulty, but, like the Committee on Production during the war period, it was unable to secure complete industrial peace in the turbulent year 1919. During that year there occurred serious stoppages of work in many important industries, notably, the coal mining, engineering, shipbuilding, railways, and the Lancashire cotton trades. The number of trade disputes during the year had

[15] The Court concerned itself with the interpretation of the prescribed rates under the Act and other awards already made in more than 200 cases. There were only three occasions on which the Court's awards were rejected and followed by strikes; of the strikes the most important was that of the iron founders in the late part of 1919; see *Post*, p. 170; the *Report on Conciliation and Arbitration for 1919*, p. 16; A. G. B. Fisher, *Some Problems of Wages and Their Regulation in Great Britain since 1918*, pp. 24-25.

been exceeded only once in the entire period 1888-1919, while the number of workers affected, the highest recorded, nearly equaled the combined total for the four war years, 1915-1918.[16] The principal causes of unrest were of course the widespread demand for a higher standard of living with a higher status for labor and a share in the control of industry, benefits that had been profusely promised by statesmen during the war period. There were also many contributory causes, such as the removal of patriotic motives for keeping at work, the withdrawal of the legal prohibition on strikes and lockouts, and the desire, after four years' strenuous labor, for a rest and for the long overdue settlement of grievances. In such circumstances it was perhaps inevitable that the country should go through considerable labor unrest, no matter what well devised peace machinery it might have had for the settlement of industrial disputes.

Another national conference of employers and workers was held in February, 1919, to consider the disturbed state of industry. Following the recommendations of this conference the Wages (Temporary Regulation) Act, 1918, was extended from May to November, 1919, under the Wages (Temporary Regulation) Act, 1919 (9 & 10 Geo. 5, c. 18). Before the expiration of the second period the trade unions requested a further extension of the Act for 12 months in view of the still unsettled economic condition of the country. The employers raised no serious objection to the continuance of the minimum rates prescribed under the Act. They were, however, opposed to the continuance of compulsory arbitration on wage issues, although they favored the interpretation of the prescribed rates, thus barring any variation, through arbitration, in the existing rates. This opposition of the employers which made it necessary for the Government to review the whole position of the existing arbitration

[16] *Ante*, p. 84.

scheme, led to the introduction of the Industrial Courts Bill on November 3, 1919, extending the Wages (Temporary Regulation) Act until the end of September, 1920, and providing for the establishment of a standing industrial court and ad-hoc courts of inquiry, which had been recommended by the Whitley Committee.

In the course of Parliamentary debate Sir Robert Horne, Minister of Labor in charge of the Bill, explained that representation had been made by individual trade unions and certain Joint Industrial Councils that the award of the proposed arbitration court should have legally binding power on all employers engaged in the industry concerned. This had been the case during the war period. Sir Robert, recognizing the soundness of the principle, inserted a clause in the draft Bill to achieve the desired object. It was thought only fair that, if the arbitration award was to be binding on those who were not parties to it, the parties themselves should also be bound by the award. Another clause was accordingly inserted in the Bill, making it illegal for any trade union to pay strike pay in case of an illegal strike against the award. When the labor representatives read this clause they objected most strenuously to its compulsory nature, holding it to be an infringement of the rights that they had obtained under the Trade Disputes Act, 1906. The Minister of Labor was placed in a decided dilemma. If he inserted the clause favored by the trade unions the other clause would be necessary in order to secure uniformity, but to include the latter clause was practically to wreck the whole scheme of arbitration, for the probable result was that the unions would never come to arbitration at all. Under these circumstances the Minister decided to drop both clauses and make the Bill another measure of voluntary conciliation and arbitration, pure and simple, except in respect of the court of inquiry which the Minister proposed to invest with certain legal powers. Speaking on behalf of the Labor Party Mr. Clynes readily agreed to the principle of the proposed permanent industrial court, but strongly objected to the compulsory powers of the court of inquiry, which he described as a novel and untried method in the country. In Committee the compulsory powers of the court of inquiry were cut out entirely.

Labor difficulties were embedded in the very foundation of human society, said Sir Robert, and their roots went down to its very beginning. No one could be foolish enough to suppose that a single measure or any series of measures would furnish a solution of the difficulties. The Bill would bring "a better atmosphere and a happier spirit" in industrial relations, however, by enabling trade disputes in many cases to be settled in a peaceful and impartial way through public agencies. The proposed standing industrial court was a distinct improvement on the existing system of ad-hoc courts of arbitration inasmuch as it would secure well co-ordinated wage judgments in closely related industrial disputes. Such coordination which it was almost futile to expect from ad-hoc courts was essential in view of the interdependent nature of wage scales in modern industries.[17]

The Industrial Courts Act, 1919, (9 & 10 Geo. 5, c. 69), as a permanent piece of legislation, is notable for three main reasons. In the first place, by establishing a standing Industrial Court, it gave a more or less logical conclusion to the long process of growth of industrial conciliation and arbitration under the Conciliation Act, 1896. Secondly, it gave statutory effect to the suggestions made long before that the Government should have power to set up an impartial court of inquiry in case of grave industrial disputes. Thirdly, the scope of the Act is very wide and the methods adopted

[17] Parl. Deb. Commons (120), 1131, 1707, 1897; (121), 87, 92-122, 123-206, 411-464, 667-680, 1208; Nov. 6, 10, 1919.

are extremely flexible. For the purpose of the Act a trade dispute is defined as any dispute arising between employers and workmen or between workmen in connection with the terms of employment of any workman employed, or to be employed, under a contract of service or apprenticeship, whether manual labor, clerical work, or otherwise, excepting those who are engaged in the naval, military, and air forces under the Crown.

The flexibility of the methods provided under the Act is shown in Section 2, which reads as follows: "Any trade dispute defined in this Act, whether existing or apprehended, may be reported to the Minister by or on behalf of the parties to the dispute, and the Minister shall thereupon take the matter into his consideration and take such steps as seem to him expedient for promoting a settlement thereof." Under this section the Minister of Labor may appoint a conciliator either from within or outside his Ministry or may make arrangements for the parties to meet under an impartial chairmanship. He may also, with the consent of both parties, refer the case (1) to the standing Industrial Court, (2) to a single arbitrator appointed by him, or (3) to a special board of arbitration consisting of an impartial chairman appointed by the Minister and members representing employers and workmen. In case of any arrangement for the peaceful settlement of disputes being in existence in the trade concerned, the Minister may not, except with the consent of the parties, refer a dispute in accordance with the provisions of the Act until the conciliation machinery has been tried and has failed in securing a settlement.

The standing Industrial Court consists of three groups, namely, representatives of employers, of workmen, and of the public, all appointed by the Minister of Labor for such terms as may be fixed at the time of their appointments. The President of the Court and the chairman of a division of the Court must be chosen from among the independent members. The Minister of Labor is also authorized to make or to authorize the Industrial Court to make rules regulating the procedure of the Court.[18] Subject to such rules the Court may sit in divisions with or without assessors; determine cases by a single member court, as the President may direct; with the consent of the parties act notwithstanding any vacancy that may occur in its membership, and interpret any previous award without a fresh report or reference. Where the members are not able to agree on an award the chairman may decide with the full power of an umpire. The Court is expressly prohibited from making an award that is inconsistent with any Act of Parliament regulating wages and other conditions of labor. The reference of cases to the Court is made, not by the parties concerned, but by the Minister of Labor, to whom a trade dispute may be reported by either party to the dispute, directly or through the local conciliation officers maintained by the Ministry in various industrial centers. Once referred to the Court the terms of reference can be changed only by a further agreement between the parties. No person may be represented before the Court by counsel or solicitor except with the permission of the Court. The Minister of Labor may also refer cases to the Industrial Court for advice on any matter he may think fit.

In the case of grave dispute existing or apprehended the Minister of Labor may, without application from the parties concerned, inquire into the causes and circumstances of the dispute, and, if he thinks fit, may appoint a court of inquiry which may, without any compulsory power, require any person to furnish necessary information or give evidence upon oath. The court may consist of one or more persons and

[18] The Industrial Court (Procedure) Rules, 1920, *The Ministry of Labor Gazette*, April, 1920, p. 207.

may make inquiries either in private or public sittings as it may desire. Any report to be made by the court to the Minister should be laid before both Houses of Parliament as soon as possible. The Minister may cause it to be published at any time. No information, obtained through court evidence, affecting any trade union or individual business concern should be made public without the consent of those immediately concerned.

It is clear from this brief review of the circumstances leading to the passage of the Industrial Courts Act, 1919, that a study of the British Government agencies for industrial peace in the post-war period involves an examination of the working of (1) the emergency measures adopted immediately after the Armistice, (2) the Industrial Courts Act, 1919, (3) the machinery under the Conciliation Act, 1896, (4) the Whitley Councils. We have already briefly discussed the emergency measures under the heading of the Wages (Temporary Regulation) Acts. The Conciliation Act, 1896, which, although it still exists on the Statute Books, has for practical purposes been superseded by the Industrial Courts Act, 1919. The Whitley Councils we shall discuss in a subsequent chapter. In this chapter we are mainly concerned with the Industrial Courts Act, of which the standing Industrial Court and Courts of Inquiry are two distinct features while the Ministry of Labor is the executive and conciliation agency.

B. The Ministry of Labor in Relation to Industrial Disputes

The existing organization of the Ministry of Labor consists of six Departments, of which the Unemployment Insurance Department, the Employment and Training Department, and the General Department are most important.[19]

[19] Mr. F. L. C. Floud, Secretary of the Ministry of Labor, kindly caused his staff in 1932 to prepare a note on the history and organization

It is the General Department that is responsible, among other things, for the administration of the Conciliation Act, 1896, and the Industrial Courts Act, 1919, as well as for the betterment of industrial relations generally. The Ministry also maintains six outstation offices in the principal industrial centers, each of which has a staff of conciliation officers.

The Ministry watches over the progress of trade disputes and at the proper time gets in touch with the employers and workers concerned, placing its conciliation service at their disposal. If conciliation fails it tries to get the issue referred to arbitration, whether by the Industrial Court, a single arbitrator, or an ad-hoc court of arbitration. In the case of grave dispute the Ministry may upon its own initiative appoint a court of inquiry. In many cases it fails to prevent a stoppage of work, but its intervention exerts a restraining influence, reminding the parties of their grave responsibility to the community at large and thus making it possible for them to listen to reason at a time of heated controversy over questions of great importance. No major industrial dispute breaks out into the open without having first received the careful study and skillful intervention of the Ministry, which may be invoked by the parties at any time without a loss of dignity. The conciliation work of the Ministry is mentioned in the summary of Government intervention in trade disputes during the post-war period as a whole.[20]

A detailed study of the operation of the Courts of Inquiry and of the Industrial Court follows.

of the Ministry of Labor for the personal use of the author. An exhaustive description of the various phases of the Ministry's activities may be found in the Evidence submitted in 1930 by the Ministry to the Royal Commission on Unemployment, particularly the Minutes of Evidence by Messrs. Eady and Barlow on the 1st-7th, 11th-12th days; see also the *Annual Reports of the Ministry; ante*, p. 48, footnote 28.

[20] See *Post*, p. 171.

2. THE COURTS OF INQUIRY

A. The Courts in Operation

The power to appoint a court of inquiry has been used with great reserve [21] and only in cases of grave disputes on matters of exceptional importance. In the entire 16-year period from 1920 to 1935, only 18 courts have been appointed to deal with disputes affecting such important industries as coal mining, transport, building, engineering, and the woollen textile trades. The conservative use of this power is due primarily to the grave responsibility falling upon the Minister in appointing a court that on two points is quite distinct from an arbitration court. While in the case of arbitration the reference may be made only with the consent of the parties, who are therefore bound, morally if not legally, to take part in the proceedings and to accept the findings of the court, without much public discussion, the court of inquiry, in view of the gravity of the questions at issue, may be appointed by the Minister of Labor on his own initiative. The parties may refuse to participate in the inquiry, which is conducted often in an open public session, and may refuse to accept its results which may be published by the Minister and are required to be laid before both Houses of Parliament. In other words the primary function of the court of inquiry is not so much to settle the case by direct contact with the parties as to elucidate the facts and enlist public sympathy for a speedy and peaceful settlement of disputes affecting the vital interests of the community at large.

In a majority of the cases the court consisted of three members, but, sometimes, of one, five, seven or more. The court would sit in public, with the representatives of each side presenting their cases and with witnesses called to give

[21] *The Report of the Ministry of Labor for 1923-24*, p. 13.

evidence. After a careful consideration of the facts and arguments presented by the parties the court issued its report, describing in clear and terse language the historical circumstances of the disputes, summing up the contentions of each side, placing various considerations in their right proportion, and setting forth its own findings with considerable force of persuasion and with moderation. The setting up of a court of inquiry did not always prevent a strike or lockout, nor did it suspend one already in progress,[22] but its report usually served as a basis for compromise and settlement. In two cases the court acted as a mediator and the disputes were settled amicably in private conversations. On two occasions representatives of the workers concerned declined to take part in the inquiry and the court failed to settle the cases.

A brief summary of the operation of the courts of inquiry from 1920 through 1935 is given in the following table.

Case: Date of Appointment	Court Constitution	Pending Inquiry	Nature of Dispute	Date of Report: Result
Coal Tippers: (Transport) Dec. 31, 1919	Members, 5	No Stoppage of Work	Wage Rates & conditions of Service	June 4, 1920: Amicable Settlement Reached
Dock-Workers: (Transport) Jan. 22, 1920	Members, 9	"	"	Mar. 31, 1920: Amicable Settlement Reached
Electrical Trades: Sept. 11, 1920	Members, 7	Strike & Lock-Out	Union Membership	Joint Industrial Council Intervened, Resulting in Settlement; Court Adjourned

[22] On March 25, 1924 Lord Askwith introduced an Industrial Courts Amendment Bill in the House of Lords. The Bill proposed that any strike or lockout taking place within 30 days, pending a public inquiry, should be subjected to penalty. The Bill passed the House of Lords, but the Labor Government declined to proceed with the Bill in the House of Commons on the ground that an automatic penalization of a strike taking place in spite of the law might cause hostile feelings among the strikers and might arouse sympathy among outside workers. This might have the result of prolonging the strike itself. Parl. Deb. Lords (56), 980; (57), 159, 182; Commons (173), 1854, May 19, 1924.

Case: Date of Appointment	Court Constitution	Pending Inquiry	Nature of Dispute	Date of Report: Result
Tramway Industry: Jan. 5, 1921	Members, 5	No Stoppage of Work	Wage Rates	Feb. 25, 1921: Amicable Settlement Reached
Engineers' Disputes: Apr. 27, 1922	Member, 1	General Lock-Out	Over-Time, Managerial Functions	May 10, 1922: Settlement on Lines of Report Reached After 13 Weeks' Stoppage of Work
Coal Tippers: (Transport) Mar. 20, 1923	Members, 5	No Stoppage of Work	Shift System	Court Acted as Mediators; Secured Settlement
Dock-Workers: (Transport) Feb. 18, 1924	Members, 3	National Strike	Rates & Guaranteed Work	Agreement Reached Between Parties
Railway Shopmen (Engineers) Mar. 7, 1924	"	No Stoppage of Work	Standardization of Rates & Conditions	Craft Unions Refused to Attend Court: Report was Ignored
London Tramway (Transport) Mar. 21, 1924	"	Strike & Sympathetic Strikes	Wage Rates	Interim Report on Mar. 24: Settlement Reached upon Introduction of London Traffic Bill at Suggestion of Report
Coal Mining: April 15, 1924	"	No Stoppage of Work	Wage Rates	May 8, 1924: on Basis of Report Agreement was Reached
Coal Exporting Ports: (Transport) May 17, 1924	"	Local Strike; National Stoppage Threatened	Strike-Breakers' Question	May 26, 1924: Compromise Reached on Lines of Report
Building Industry: July 3, 1924	Members, 3	National Strike & Lock-Out	Wages & National Affiliation	July 15, 1924: Agreement was Reached on Lines of Report
Covent Garden Market Porters: (Transport) Sept. 1, 1924	"	Strike	Wage & Unionism	Sept. 11, 1924: Work was Resumed on Employers' Terms
Steel House: (Building) Mar. 14, 1925	"	No Stoppage of Work	Demarcation	Apr. 23, 1925: Result Unknown

Coal Mining: July 13, 1925	"	No Stoppage of Work	Wage Rates	July 28, 1925: Miners refused to take part in Inquiry. Report being ignored, Royal Commission was Appointed
Railway shopmen (engineers) Dec. 24, 1925	"	"	National Standardization of Rates and Conditions	Feb. 8, 1926: Compromise reached on lines of suggestion in Report
Woollen Textile: Jan. 7, 1930	Member, 1	"	Wage Rates	Feb. 28, 1930: Report failed of Settlement, Strike Followed
Fishing Industry: Apr. 15, 1935 *	Members, 3	Stoppage of Work	"	Court acted as Mediators, Settlement Reached

* For a detailed description of the cases see the *Ministry of Labor Gazette*: Feb., April, June, Sept., Oct., 1920, pp. 60, 168, 291, 482, 542-3; Jan., March, 1921 pp. 10, 124; May, 1922, p. 200; April, Sept., 1923; pp. 153, 323; March, April, May, June, Sept., 1924, pp. 81, 112, 121, 156-7; 194-5, 237-8, 278, 319; May, July, Aug., 1925, pp. 153, 227, 266; Jan., Feb., 1926, pp. 9, 41; Jan., March, May, June, 1930, pp. 9, 47, 84, 163, 202; April, May, June, 1935, pp. 132, 172, 211. Reports by Courts of Inquiry: Reports on Dock Labor, 1920 (55); Electrical Trades, 1920 (CMD. 990); Tramway, 1921 (37); Engineering Disputes, 1922 (CMD. 1653); Coal Tippers, 1923 (CMD. 1948); Railway Shopmen, 1924 (CMD. 2113); London Tramway, 1924 (CMD. 2101); Coal Mining, 1924 (CMD. 2129); Leith Coal Trimming, 1924 (CMD. 2149); Building, 1924 (CMD. 2192); Covent Garden Market Porters, 1924 (CMD. 2244); Coal Mining, 1925 (CMD. 2478); Railway Shopmen, 1926 (CMD. 2583); Woollen Textile, 1930 (CMD. 3505); Fishing Industry, 1935 (CMD. 4913).

B. The Five Vital Issues of Industrial Peace

No social machinery can secure industrial peace without facing squarely certain fundamental issues of human rights and duties, any more than a piece of mechanical machinery can procure the production of goods without reference to human needs and desires. It is not primarily social machinery but social justice based upon the recognition of such rights and duties that settles the question of peace. Such issues become more insistent as civilization reaches a higher state and Government responsibility for their solution increases with the march of democracy. The courts of inquiry have expressed their considered opinion on a number of issues that may be taken as a good example of the types of issues on which the British Government must sooner or later take a definite stand if its responsibility for industrial peace is to be discharged without faltering.

They involve the questions as to (1) whether wages should be a first charge on industry, (2) how far workers should be consulted on matters of management, (3) how the corporate power of trade unionism may be made consistent with the right to individual freedom, (4) how far working conditions within an industry should be standardized with a view to securing equal treatment for equal work, and (5) how public utility services should be made efficient and inexpensive and at the same time responsible for the welfare of those engaged in them. The importance of the first question is clear when we take into consideration the increasing responsibility of the Government for securing a decent livelihood to every member of the community. The second question is an essential part of the larger demands of labor for the joint control of industry so that the workers' actual experience may be combined with managerial responsibility for more efficient production and their voice be heard in the determination of the conditions under which their work is to be done. The third question touches the basic British faith in democracy itself, while the fourth raises the difficult question of human equality and unequal economic conditions. The fifth indicates the public responsibility of certain industries, responsibilities that cannot be properly discharged without some degree of Government co-ordination and control.

A brief description of cases follows under separate headings. (1) *Whether wages should be a first charge on industry.* This issue was presented by the coal mining disputes in 1924 and 1925. In the coal mining dispute of 1924, which arose in connection with a revision of the National

Agreement of 1921, the miners maintained that a minimum wage should be the first charge on the net proceeds of the coal-mining industry, the actual amount to be decided in the light of the increased cost of living, on the one hand, and the improved general standard of living, on the other. The court, in principle, conceded the miners' contention by stating that "the provision of a minimum wage should have precedence over distribution of profits," although it could not "specify conditions as to the basis on which that minimum should be fixed."[23] A similar view was expressed in the report of another coal-mining inquiry court appointed in the following year. This Report stated: "We do not think that a method of fixing wages which allows of their indefinite diminution can be regarded as satisfactory. . . . The claim that wages must be a first charge on the proceeds of industry is a contentious and ambiguous one. If the meaning be that wages at some agreed minimum rate in practice be a charge before profits are taken, we concur in that view." What that minimum should be was to be a matter for negotiation between the parties. The conflict between "the economic wages," which the coal mining industry could afford to pay under existing conditions, and "the social wages," which the miners demanded as necessary for a decent standard of living, was, in the view of the court, closely related to the question of efficiency and organization of the coal-mining industry as a whole, and the court indicated certain directions in which necessary reconstruction might be carried out.[24]

(2) *How far workers should be consulted on matters of management.* This question was raised in an acute form in the engineering trade disputes which led finally to a stoppage

[23] 1924 (CMD. 2129); *The Ministry of Labor Gazette*, May, 1924, p. 156.

[24] 1925 (CMD. 2478); *cf.* "The Industrial Court's Decisions on the Standard of Living," *Post*, p. 155.

of work on March 11, 1922. On April 27 Sir William Mackenzie (now Lord Amulree), then President of the Industrial Court, was appointed as a court of inquiry, and, on May 10, he issued his report setting forth that the real cause of the stoppage of work was doubt as to whether any change in the recognized working conditions should be carried out by management without a previous consultation with the workers concerned. The Report further stated that, in the case of the Amalgamated Engineering Union, the specific mention of the employers' right to determine the necessity of overtime was also involved. With regard to the second point the court pointed out that the question of overtime was a matter of urgency and ruled that the most competent person to decide it was the employer. As for the first point the court made a distinction between prior consent and prior consultation with the workers concerned in carrying out the instructions of management, and recommended that full opportunities should be given for prior consultation, if not for prior consent, when any change was proposed in the recognized working conditions. The employers accepted these suggestions with the modification that the unions should be consulted beforehand, not in all cases but in those cases in which the proposed change might result in a general displacement of one class of workers by another in the establishment concerned. The unions accepted this proposal and the dispute was settled in the first part of June, 1922.[25]

(3) *Trade Unionism v. Individual Freedom.* In March, 1924 during a local strike among the coal trimmers at Leith, the employers engaged a number of workers with a guarantee of permanent employment. The Transport and General Workers' Union strongly objected to the employment of strike breakers as a violation of the cardinal principle of

[25] 1922 (CMD. 1653); *The Ministry of Labor Gazette*, March-July, 1922, pp. 156, 200, 246, 287.

trade unionism and threatened a national strike throughout the coal-exporting ports to enforce their contention. The Minister of Labor appointed a court of inquiry, which reported that the workers whose employment was in question were not experienced coal trimmers, but miners imported from somewhere else. The court recommended that no hindrance should be placed in the way of their return to their usual vocation. The dispute was settled on June 12 on the basis of this suggestion.[26]

In the following August some three thousand porters employed at the Covent Garden Market went out on strike over wage questions, but a deadlock was reached on the question of open versus closed shops. The employers insisted that they were entitled to employ any man they desired while the workers were free to join whatever unions they liked. The Transport and General Workers' Union again threatened a national strike to maintain their contention of a closed shop. The court of inquiry that was appointed recommended that the right of employers to employ such men as they desired and the right of men to join whatever unions they liked were not inconsistent with the right of the trade unions to approach non-union men with a view to persuading them to become members. A compromise was reached on this basis and the dispute was settled on September 24, 1924.[27]

(4) *National Standardization of Working Conditions.* This issue was presented by the building dispute in 1924 and the railway shopmen cases in 1924 and 1925. In April, 1924, the National Wages and Conditions Council for the building industry classified the Liverpool district as Grade A, in accordance with the national grading system of wages existing in the industry. To this decision of the National

[26] 1924 (CMD. 2149).

[27] *The Ministry of Labor Gazette*, Sept.-Oct., 1924, pp. 319, 370.

Council the Liverpool operatives objected, threatening a strike unless the Liverpool employers should enter into a separate district agreement with them as had previously been done. At a full conference of the building employers held on June 20 a national lockout was decided upon to enforce the decision of the Council, and a national strike was declared as a counter movement by the national organizations of the building operatives. The Minister of Labor appointed a court of inquiry. In its report issued on July 15 this court stated that the main cause of the dispute was the refusal of the Liverpool operatives to submit to the authority of the National Wages and Conditions Council on which both the employers' and operatives' national organizations were represented and asserted that much misunderstanding had ensued in the resulting issues. The court therefore recommended that, on the recognition of their mutual misunderstandings, negotiation should be resumed between the two sides of the National Council with a view to jointly settling the Liverpool difficulties. Negotiations followed on the line of this suggestion and the dispute was settled on August 22, the Liverpool operatives having consented to accept "agreed national machinery for fixing wages and conditions of service" with regional wages committees to deal with questions of regional importance.[28]

Under the Industrial Court's Decision No. 728, issued on July 8, 1922 the conditions of employment of railway shopmen were standardized to a great extent. Early in 1924 the National Union of Railwaymen, which had previously repeated the request that Decision No. 728 should be applied to the Great Northern Railway now amalgamated in the London and North Eastern Railway under the Railways Act, 1921, declared that unless their request was granted by the railway company their members employed on the Great

[28] 1924 (CMD. 2192).

Northern Section of the railway would go out on strike. A court of inquiry was appointed on March 7, but the representatives of the craft unions, the Amalgamated Engineering Union, the Boilermakers' Society, and the National Union of Foundry Workers, refused to participate in the inquiry for the reason that their craft principle of wage determination was diametrically opposed to the industrial principle adopted in Decision No. 728.[29] The court proceeded with the inquiry without their help and found it to be an established fact that Decision No. 728 was in operation on all railways except the Great Northern and Great Central Sections of the L. N. E. Railway. The Court therefore recommended that "it would be to the advantage of the railway, the trade unions, and the shopmen, if, so far as possible, the terms and conditions of service of railway shopmen were uniform throughout Great Britain."[30] A similar view was expressed by another court of inquiry which was appointed toward the end of 1925 to consider the question of the application of Decision No. 728 to the Great Central Section of the L. N. E. Railway.[31] The discussion dragged on until 1927 when the various unions having members in the railway shops came to an agreement on the question of memberships and decided to set up a national joint negotiation machinery for the shopmen, with the Industrial Court as the final court should they decide to refer cases to arbitration.[32]

(5) *Government Co-ordination and Control of Public Utility Services.* The London tramwaymen, more than 16,000 in number, went out on strike over a wage question

[29] See *Post*, p. 162.

[30] 1924 (CMD. 2113); *The Ministry of Labor Gazette*, Mar., May, 1924, pp. 112, 156-7.

[31] 1926 (CMD. 2583).

[32] See *Post*, p. 248.

on March 22, 1924, and about 23,000 omnibus workers struck in sympathy. A court of inquiry appointed the preceding day issued on March 24 an interim report stating that the claim of the tramwaymen for an increase in wages was not seriously questioned by the tramway undertakings; the companies, however, were not in a financial position to meet the claim owing to competition from the omnibuses and to other heavy expenditure incurred under certain Acts of Parliament. There was a consensus of opinion among the witnesses appearing before the court that no increase in the fare would meet the situation and that some co-ordination and control of passenger traffic in the metropolitan area, essential to the future prosperity of the tramway industry, would alone offer a basis for a satisfactory settlement of the dispute. The Government accepted this suggestion by introducing the London Traffic Bill which received a Second Reading in the House of Commons on March 28. In the meantime a provisional agreement was reached between the parties and work was resumed on April 1.[83]

The public responsibility in the tramway industry was further stressed in the court's final report, which stated that, in those industries seriously affecting public services, prompt and sustained effort should be made, in case of dispute, to reach a settlement by means of established negotiation machinery, and that, failing this, arbitration should be the mutually recognized procedure for a final and peaceful settlement of disputes.[84] The National Joint Industrial Council for the tramway industry accepted this suggestion and in July, 1924, instituted an Arbitration and Conciliation Tribunal, with Sir William Mackenzie, then President of the Industrial Court, as chairman.[85]

[83] The *Labor Gazette*, April, 1924, pp. 121-2; see *Post*, p. 175.

[84] 1924 (CMD. 2101).

[85] *The Annual Report of the Ministry of Labor for 1923-4*, p. 44.

3. THE INDUSTRIAL COURT

A. The Court in Operation

From the reported decisions of the Court it appears that the President of the Industrial Court has established the practice of constituting a court according to the nature of each case or group of cases referred for settlement. In one case after another, with a view to securing a speedy as well as co-ordinated judgment in closely related cases, he appoints members who are well acquainted with the subject matter. These courts consist of one, four, five or more members, but usually of three, in cases affecting women a woman member forming part of the court. Assessors are seldom required as the trade knowledge of the court members is sufficient to enable them to follow and appreciate the points presented by the parties. The court sits usually at the court house at Old Palace Yard, Westminster, but local hearings take place in important industrial centers. No fee is charged and the parties appearing before the court incur no cost except their own travelling and clerical expenses. In cases where the dispute is accompanied by a strike or lockout the Minister of Labor usually requires work to be resumed before he refers the case to the Industrial Court.

If both parties are agreed upon the terms of reference the matters can be remitted to the Court and disposed of within a few days, save in cases of exceptional difficulty. The parties who are notified by the secretary of the Court of the date and place of hearing, may appear before the Court through counsel or solicitor with the permission of the court, (thus far invariably granted) through representatives of their trade organizations, or in person. In general the party seeking a change in the status quo presents the case first, supporting it with due evidence; the opposite side then states its case, commenting, if it so desires, upon the case presented by the other side. The proceeding of the Court is privileged, and anything said at the hearing is not actionable. There is no statutory requirement that the hearing be private, but in deference to the wish of the parties the Court has followed the policy of sitting in private. A copy of the shorthand notes generally taken of the proceedings may be obtained by the parties at the usual expense. When a decision is made by the Court it is announced in writing, signed by the arbitrators and the secretary of the Court, and an advance copy is sent to the parties.

The award of the Court is well received by both parties in the majority of cases. So far there have been a few cases, not more than four, in which one or the other party has refused to accept the awards.[36] In the case of rejected awards it has been decided by local law courts that the aggrieved party might be entitled to a civil remedy on the ground that, by consenting to arbitration, both parties had contracted an obligation to abide by the findings.[37] This legal position taken by the law courts may be sound, though it has never reached a higher court for final decision. "Unless willingness to abide by the decision of the Arbitration Court be a prior assumption in all cases, arbitration is useless as a method of settling industrial disputes." [38] As a matter of practical importance, however, this position is entirely contrary to the general policy of British trade unions, whose strong objection to compulsory arbitration, it will be recalled,[39] forced the framer of the Industrial Courts Act to withdraw his original compulsory provisions. Their gen-

[36] See *Post*, p. 170.

[37] A. G. B. Fisher, *Some Problems of Wages and Their Regulation in Great Britain since 1918*, pp. 150-151.

[38] Parl. Deb. Commons (157), 439-441, July 26, 1922, per Dr. Macnamara, then Minister of Labor.

[39] See *ante*, pp. 129-30.

eral practice of accepting strict moral obligations, while declining to assume legal responsibility for their industrial agreements still remains the same as it was in 1919. It is important to note in this respect that in at least one case the local law court's decision in favor of compulsory enforcement of the arbitration award is reported to have made the trade unionists in question less willing subsequently to take advantage of the facilities offered by the Industrial Court.[40]

B. The Position of the Industrial Court as an Industrial Peace Agency

We have seen that the Industrial Court was established for the discharge of a double function. It was intended as an agency for the peaceful and judicial settlement of industrial disputes affecting comparatively large sections of the industry or involving general principles; and, secondly, as a court to systematize wages to some extent by rendering well co-ordinated judgments in related cases. In other words the Court was intended to be not only an agency for industrial peace but the wage co-ordinating authority of the country as well. It was hoped that through continuity in its personnel the Court would gain so much trade knowledge and arbitration skill that the industries would repose full confidence in it and would regularly submit their differences to it for settlement. By regular and systematic treatment of these differences it was believed that it might be able to co-ordinate wage movements in the different industries.

There has been a notable continuity in the personnel of the Court as originally appointed in November, 1919. Its first President, Sir William Mackenzie (now Lord Amulree), for instance, who had served both on the Committee on Production as reconstituted in 1917 and on the Interim Court of Arbitration, continued his service until 1926, when he was

[40] Fisher, *op. cit.*, p. 151.

succeeded by the present incumbent, Sir Harold Morris. It has also been the general practice of the Minister of Labor to appoint the president of the Court as an arbitrator in as many different cases as possible. He takes the position of referee in the determination of compensation under the Electricity (Supply) Acts, 1919-1928,[41] of chairman of the Railways National Wages Board,[42] and of chairman of the National Industrial Board under the Coal Mines Act, 1930.[43] Under the British Sugar (Subsidy) Act, 1925, and the Road Traffic Act, 1930, disputes on questions of fair wages are required to be referred to the Industrial Court for final settlement. Furthermore the Civil Service National Whitley Council agreed in February, 1925, that any difference arising in the service collectively and failing of settlement by the Council should be referred to the Court. Agreements of a similar character have been entered into by a wide variety of trades and industries, notably by the building trade, the railway shopmen, and the iron and steel workers.[44]

These attempts have been made with a view to enabling the Court to discharge with success its double function. It

[41] Reference under the Acts is not a trade dispute and the procedure of the court is regulated by the Arbitration Act, 1889, which grants the court certain compulsory powers with regard both to its proceeding and its findings.

[42] *The National Wages Board has Ceased to Exist*, see ch. vi, pp. 245-46.

[43] See *Post*, p. 233.

[44] The agreements cover railway shopmen, railway power house staffs, craftsmen employed at the Billingham on Tyne factory of the Synthetic Ammonia Company, Ltd., in the chemical firms of Runcorn and Northwich areas, roller-turners in the North of England and Scotland, semi-skilled and unskilled workers in steel works, the Sheffield saw-mill industry, the London cabinet and upholstery trades, the national building industry, engine and crane drivers, carmen, motor and wagon drivers in the London building trades, and road transport workers in the London distributive trades. Mr. W. H. Reynolds, secretary of the Industrial Court, kindly prepared a note on the organization and procedure of the court in 1932 at the request of the author.

has, however, proved difficult to combine these duties in a single function under the Industrial Court as at present constituted. They require separate treatment upon different principles. It is essential that the Court should command the confidence of the parties, not by imposing upon them its official views, however well advised and justified on the ground of the public interest, but by adjusting the conflicting interests of the parties to their own satisfaction; it is equally essential that the Court, as a wage co-ordinating authority, should cover as wide an area of industrial disputes as possible with a consistent and coherent wage policy of its own, even though this policy may not meet the requirements of the particular trades appearing before it in its capacity as an agency for industrial peace. These difficulties may be made clear by a careful study of the actual cases dealt with by the Court and a clear understanding of the actual operation of the Court may help us make a correct appraisal of its position in the British industrial peace scheme as a whole.

We shall first examine the position of the Industrial Court as a peace agency. Its success in this role is really a prerequisite to the successful discharge of its function as a wage co-ordinating authority. A general summary of the Court's operation in 1920-1932 is given in later tables.[45] The total number of cases dealt with was 1,503, of which 540, nearly 36 per cent, were handled in the single year 1920; 684, or nearly 45 per cent in the six years 1921-1926; and 279, or about 19 per cent in the six years 1927-1932. In 1920 the economic condition of the country was still abnormal and unsettled. This condition gave rise to numerous applications for wage alterations, while both workers and employers, having been accustomed to arbitration during the war period, readily resorted to it for wage regulation. Further-

[45] Pp. 152-3; compiled from the reported decisions of the Court as well as from the Annual Reports of the Ministry of Labor.

more the Industrial Courts Act had extended the Wages (Temporary Regulation) Acts, 1918-1919, to the end of September, while the National Wage Agreements in the engineering and other trades continued in force until about the same time. After 1920, it will be noticed, the figures fell rapidly, with some upward trends in 1924 and 1925, until they again reached, in 1929, the pre-war level. Out of the total of 1,503 settlements the engineering, shipbuilding, and other metal trades accounted for 504, or nearly 34 per cent; the railway shopmen 195, or about 13 per cent; the civil service, 186, or about 12 per cent; the public utilities 182, or about 12 per cent. This made a total among the four industries of about 71 per cent. The majority of the cases concerning the engineering and other metal trades took place in 1920 and in the ensuing four years, while those affecting the civil service and railway shopmen occurred in 1925 and thereafter. The inference is that after 1925 the Industrial Court was mainly concerned with cases affecting the civil service[46] and railway shopmen. These cases accounted in all for 381, or nearly 70 per cent out of a total of 548 cases settled in the period.

Another important point to note is that the major staple industries of the country, such as coal mining, railway traffic, iron and steel, engineering after 1920, and the cotton textile industries, which are well provided with their own negotiation machineries, have seldom appeared before the Court for the general settlement of wage questions.

It will be noticed in Table 11 following that wage questions were the most important item dealt with by the Court. They accounted for nearly one-half, while disputes over working conditions and hours of labor constituted only a little over one-tenth of the total number of cases dealt with

[46] For a detailed study see L. D. White, *Whitley Councils in the British Civil Service*, ch. v.

TABLE I

ARBITRATION SETTLEMENT BY THE INDUSTRIAL COURT

Trades	1920	1921	1922	1923	1924	1925	1926	1927	1928	1929	1930	1931	1932	Total
Building	36	6	3	1	—	—	1	1	2	—	—	—	—	50
Mining	7	2	—	—	1	—	—	—	—	—	—	—	—	10
Iron & Steel	18	4	2	—	2	1	—	—	—	1	—	—	—	28
Engineering and Shipbuilding	151	28	11	94	93	17	8	3	4	2	5	2	—	418
Other Metals	73	1	2	2	2	1	—	—	—	2	—	2	1	86
Textile	31	4	3	—	4	—	1	—	—	—	—	—	—	43
Clothing	3	—	—	—	3	2	—	—	—	—	—	—	1	9
Boots and Shoes	—	1	—	—	—	—	—	—	1	—	1	—	—	3
Railway	—	—	—	—	—	101	41	17	7	6	13	7	3	195
Transport	19	15	2	2	6	3	4	1	1	2	7	—	10	72
Paper Making and Printing	4	1	1	2	2	—	1	—	—	—	—	—	—	11
Woodworking	23	1	—	—	2	1	1	—	—	—	—	—	—	28
Bricks and etc.	6	2	—	—	2	—	—	—	—	—	—	—	—	10
Glass	3	1	1	—	—	—	—	—	—	—	—	—	—	5
Oil, Chemical, and etc.	13	7	—	1	3	3	—	1	—	2	—	—	—	30
Food, Drink, and etc.	21	4	2	—	4	4	1	—	—	—	—	—	—	36
Leather	2	—	—	—	—	—	—	—	—	—	—	—	—	2
Public Utility	101	28	4	8	9	8	1	13	3	1	2	4	—	182
Civil Service	—	—	—	—	—	20	43	44	29	17	13	12	8	186
Miscellaneous	29	17	6	3	10	4	2	2	5	6	2	8	5	99
Total	540*	122	37	113	143	165	104	82	52	39	43	35	28	1,503

* Includes Decision No. 180A.

TABLE II

NUMBER OF CASES DEALT WITH BY THE INDUSTRIAL COURT AS CLASSIFIED BY SUBJECTS

Year	Wages Inc.	Wages Dec.	Wages Total	Hours of Work	Working Conditions	Interpretation of Awards	Others	Total
1919	40	—	40	—	2	—	7	49
1920	345	—	345	6 [a]	32 [b]	63	115	561 [c]
1921	41	23	64	1	31 [d]	16	11	123 [e]
1922	3	13	16	—	13 [f]	8	—	37 [g]
1923	3	13	16	—	11 [h]	84	—	111 [i]
1924	44	2	46	—	15	61	17	139 [j]
1925	29	1	30	—	8 [k]	99	28	165 [l]
1926	48	2	50	—	8 [m]	39	9	106
1927	45	—	45	—	16 [n]	19	6	86
1928	19	3	22	1	15	9	5	52
1929	16	3	19	1	5	7	7	39
1930	23	1	24	—	3	13	3	43
1931	20	3	23	—	5	6	—	34 [o]
1932	7	4	11	—	5	2	10	28
Total	683	68	751	9	169	426	218	1,573 [p]

[a] This includes one case that is also counted under the heading of wages.

[b] This includes 17 cases that are also counted under the heading of wages.

[c] This includes 4 cases of interpretation that do not carry the Decision number, such as No. 180A and others.

[d] This includes 8 cases that also are counted under the heading of wages.

[e] This is exclusive of Decisions Nos. 704-710, given towards the end of the year but not reported.

[f] This includes 2 cases that are also counted under wages heading.

[g] This is exclusive of Decisions Nos. 712 and 722, not reported.

[h] This includes one case also listed under wages heading.

[i] This is exclusive of Decisions Nos. 770, 771, 772, which were not printed.

[j] This is exclusive of Decisions Nos. 965, 976, 977, 995, which were not printed.

[k] This includes 2 cases also counted under the wages heading.

[l] This is exclusive of Decisions Nos. 1042 and 1099 which were not printed.

[m] This includes 2 cases counted also under other headings.

[n] This includes 4 cases also counted under other headings.

[o] This is exclusive of Decision No. 1519, which was not printed.

[p] This includes 37 cases counted twice, 4 cases carrying no Decision Nos., and excludes 19 decisions that were not printed. Since its establishment in November, 1919, up to the end of 1932, the court issued 1,551 awards that carried regular decision numbers.

by the Industrial Court. Wage claims covered sometimes an entire industry, as for instance, in the railway shopmen case (Decision No. 728), and the engineering trades case (Decision No. 180). Sometimes, however, they involved only a handful of workers or even a single workmen, as for instance, in the cases of railway shopmen gradings. In other words there has been no differentiation between big and small cases, even though, according to the Whitley Committee, these different cases require different types of arbitration courts. The large number of interpretations required was due to the difficulties arising under the Wages (Temporary Regulation) Acts as extended by the Industrial Courts Act and under Decision No. 728, applying to railway shopmen.

C. The Position of the Industrial Court as a Wage Co-ordinating Authority

As a wage co-ordinating authority the Industrial Court is required to do two things: to cover as wide an area of wage movements in different industries as possible and to apply its wage policy with consistency to the particular cases brought before it under different circumstances. In the preceding section it has been made clear that the Court has failed to meet the first requirement. In this section we shall examine the extent to which the Court has been able to fulfill the second requirement.

Before proceeding to a careful study of the principles enunciated by the Court in a number of leading cases it may be well to consider first the limitations of the Court. The Court has no right, as we have seen, to issue awards that are inconsistent with the principles laid down by Parliament; principles embodied in such legislation as the Factory, Truck, Mines, Education, Trade Boards, and the Agricultural Wages Boards Acts. These Acts of Parliament, which prescribe the national standard of security, below which no workman, under the stress of private economic competition, is to be allowed to fall, constitute the background against which free enterprise may test its abilities, with freedom of choice in the matter of appealing to the Industrial Court as an arbitrator. The Court may interpret, but may not change the national standard, nor may it enforce its decisions against the will of the parties appearing before it for wage settlement. In other words, Parliament has outlined for the Court no principle to guide it in its decisions, except by setting up a national minimum standard of decency, nor has it conferred on the Court compulsory power to enforce its own ideas of justice or fairness.

The principal grounds on which wage issues have been debated and decided by the Industrial Court may be summarized in the four principles involving: the standard of living, the cost of living, ability to pay, and fair wages, all of which allow different combinations under different circumstances.

(1). The Standard of Living. We have seen that the principle of minimum wages as a first charge on industry has been recognized by the courts of inquiry. The Industrial Court has also approved the principle in a slightly different form. In Decision No. 61, for the gas industry, issued on January 12, 1920, the Court stated: "Where the wages paid in an industry are so low as to leave the workers without the means of an adequate and decent livelihood, the financial position of the employers is a matter of secondary importance." A similar view was expressed in Decision No. 853, for the canal boatmen, issued on November 23, 1923. The Industrial Court, like the courts of inquiry, did not define the exact meaning of the expression "adequate and decent livelihood," nor did it specify the exact conditions upon which a definite minimum rate should be fixed. From

Decisions Nos. 305 and 594, issued respectively on May 11, 1920 and January 11, 1921, it appears that the Court instead of establishing principles of its own, followed the actual practice of the Trade Boards. The Trade Boards determine minimum rates "by reference to the capacity of the trades as carried on in the less remunerative sections and the less well favored districts." It has been pointed out in criticism that the Industrial Court has thus failed to make clear its own idea as to what a "fair" standard of minimum wage should be in the light, not of the financial position of any particular firm or industry in question, but of the general economic conditions of the country at large, an idea that would have given "some coherency to the activities of the various Trade Boards and to the whole arbitration system" of the country.[47]

At any rate it is evident from these decisions that, where the Trade Board minima as determined by independent statutory authorities were concerned, the Court had no choice but to decree rates to be observed at any cost. Above the minima, however, the Court had no fixed idea as to an absolute standard of living. Decision No. 48, issued on December 31, 1919, is a good illustration. It dealt with the demands made by the National Amalgamated Union of Shop Assistants against the Army and Navy Co-operative Society for a general advance of 35 per cent in wages of all employees and for minimum rates varying from 45s. to 74s. for a week of 44 hours for adult male workers. The Court, after having considered "the importance to the shareholders, the employers, and the public, of maintaining the Society on a satisfactory financial basis and securing for the employees rates of wages in conformity with the new standards established and necessitated by the general economic

[47] Dr. Mary Theresa Rankin, *Arbitration Principles and the Industrial Court*, p 171.

conditions now prevailing," awarded a general wage advance of 35 per cent in some cases, and of 20 per cent in others, with minimum rates varying from 45s. to 68s. for a week of 48 hours for adult male employees. The Court did not define the meaning of "satisfactory financial basis", or of "the new standards" of living, the two general grounds of the award. Nor did the Court explain the exact relationship, measurable in figures, between the two general grounds of its consideration and the particular wages and hours of labor finally prescribed. In other words the general grounds enunciated by the Court were too general and broad to cover the specific ground of the particular decision. The decision was really more in the nature of a compromise or a rough guess as to the bargaining powers of the parties than a strict adjustment of their just claims.

This position is perfectly understandable. While it is possible in theory to calculate a certain rate of interest or dividend that would suffice to maintain capital at the existing level and even to provide an increase, it is practically impossible for the Industrial Court to lay down definite conditions as a satisfactory financial basis for a particular private concern. For under the existing industrial system of private ownership it is upon the responsibility of private employers that the risks of business are taken, each employer trying to get whatever he can out of the total industrial production of the country. From the human needs [48] point of view it may be argued that from certain existing demands, such as poor relief, unemployment benefit, old age pensions, and workmen's compensation, it is possible to define a minimum standard of living that would provide a broad basis upon which to award a fair minimum wage in any given case, according to skill, the nature of the work, or any other relevant circumstances. Such definition of a minimum

[48] *Cf.* J. A. Hobson, *The Conditions of Industrial Peace*, pp. 36-39.

standard of living would, however, as a decent living standard for the modern family, obviously be inadequate to provide, not only a sufficient quantity and variety of pure and wholesome food, decent clothing for all weathers, proper housing conditions with sufficient room and conveniences, but also sufficient leisure, reasonable recreation, and a hundred other things necessary for its cultural refinement. These things may be termed luxuries, but they are nevertheless essential to the efficient functioning of modern democratic citizenship. It would, of course, have been clearly beyond the power of the Industrial Court to define such things in a precise term, even if it had not wisely avoided the attempt to do so.

(2) The Cost of Living. So closely related to the standard of living is the cost of living that, during the war, the Committee on Production awarded general wage increases in order to assist workers in meeting the increased cost of living. After the war the Industrial Court took the position that the cost of living is only one of the many factors that enter into wage determination and that its importance should be given different weight under different circumstances.[49] This position was made clear in Decision No. 180 (Engineering Trades, March 10, 1920), in which the Court states:

> An alteration in the cost of living does not in itself necessarily warrant any corresponding alteration in wages. The remuneration of the various classes of workpeople should, in ordinary circumstances, depend on the value of the work done, and the value of the work done depends on the state of the market and demand for the products of the workshop (par. 14).

The Court then pointed out that there was no justification for a further increase in wages in the engineering industry

[49] With this in view the Court declined to concede the proposals for an automatic regulation of wages on a cost of living sliding scale in Decisions Nos. 688 and 728.

on the ground of the costing of living alone, but that the prosperous position of the industry warranted a certain amount of wage increases. In the next general award No. 395, issued on July 14, 1920, the Court ruled that, although there had been some advance in the cost of living, the industrial position of the engineering industry did not justify any change in existing wage rates.[50]

The cost of living was thus relegated to a secondary position of importance in wage determination, while the ability to pay was given first place. Subsequent decisions show, however, that this position could not be consistently maintained under all circumstances.

In Decisions Nos. 516-518, issued in November, 1920, for the pit prop trade in Scotland, it was shown that the trade was not prosperous, but since the cost of living had advanced, the Court compromised by advancing wages, but not to the full extent demanded by the workers. This attitude of compromise was more fully expressed in Decision No. 521, issued on November 8, 1920, for the Scottish textile trade. In this Decision the Court stated that at a time of transition from abnormal war conditions to ordinary peace production there must be some compromise between "the mechanical regulation of wages on the basis of the cost of living and the regulation of wages solely by reference to the state of the market in the particular industry" under consideration. In this decision it was shown that although

[50] The engineering unions were not satisfied with this decision and withdrew from the National Wages Agreement, maintaining that, if the cost of living was not a good argument in support of wage claims, the only possible alternative justification was an increase in productive power, and asserting that, if this was true, the workers should secure for themselves all the benefits that might arise from such an increased productive power instead of allowing any more millionaires to be created. *The British Trade Union Review*, Oct., 1920; *cf. Report on Conciliation and Arbitration for 1920*, pp. 23-35.

the cost of living had advanced and the particular trade was fairly prosperous, the general industrial situation of the country as a whole showed signs of falling off. The Court therefore compromised, awarding an increase of 3s. instead of the original claim of 15s. a week.

Decisions Nos. 524 and 589 reveal a different set of discrepancies in the policy of the Industrial Court. We have seen that in Decision No. 395 the engineers were denied an increase in wages, not on the ground of the increased cost of living, but because of the financial position of the industry. In Decision No. 524, however, the Admiralty engineering employees were granted an increase of 5s. a week on the precise ground of the increased cost of living, and not because of increased prosperity. In Decision No. 589, dealing with the chemical trade, issued in January, 1921, the Court admitted that the future of the industry was uncertain, but nevertheless ruled that the claim for an advance in wages was warranted on other grounds, among them "the unduly low rates which prevailed prior to the war." Three months later an extension of this award to the chemical workers in London was asked for but the request was refused in Decision No. 636 on the ground that the state of the trade did not justify it.

By April, 1921, the cost of living had fallen and applications for wage reductions were submitted to the Court. Here again the Court considered the question in the light of different circumstances. In Decision No. 643 the Court ruled that, since there was a fall in the cost of living, wages should be reduced by at least the amount of the last advances. In Decision No. 684, however, the Court declared that wage reductions did not proceed invariably "upon exactly the same basis and according to the same measure as were adopted in granting increases. . . . Other considerations need to be taken into account." The "other considerations" were not disclosed in the case, but Decision No. 717 showed that the principal one was the state of the trade or "the capacity of the industry to pay rates without restricting the demand for the product or imposing an undue burden on the employers." This point was made clearer in Decision No. 925, in the chemical trade, issued in June, 1924. In this decision it was shown that although the cost of living had declined the trade was recovering from the depression. The Court therefore compromised by granting half of the workers' original claim for wage increases.

A general conclusion from this brief review of the decisions is that the general principles enunciated by the Court were interpreted and applied in a number of different combinations under the varying circumstances of each particular case.

(3). The Ability to Pay. This principle was defined in three ways under Decision No. 180. In the first place the remuneration of the various classes of workers engaged in a particular industry was to be determined or limited [51] by the market value of their work. Secondly, no industry was a complete unit in itself, but part and parcel of the organized activities of the whole community; wage questions should therefore be considered as a rule, not from a purely separatist view, but from a national point of view, although the special circumstances of the particular industry involved must be taken into due account. Thirdly, the proper combination of the two points of view might be obtained by carefully following wage movements in the different industries in the country as a whole. Each of the three points had difficulties that have not fully been met by the Industrial Court.

The market value of the work done by certain classes of workers engaged in a particular trade or industry may

[51] Lord Amulree, *Industrial Arbitration*, p. 185.

answer the question as to the possible wage limit, but it supplies no precise principle for the actual determination of a particular rate within that broad limit. This defect was clearly shown in Decisions Nos. 181, 191, 192, 261, 379, and 380. These decisions extended Decision No. 180, and granted to the workers employed in the shipbuilding, railwayshops, Irish engineering, explosives, shipbreaking, and waste metal trades,[52] the same wage increase as that awarded to the engineers. It is obvious, however, that under no circumstances could such widely different trades as those under discussion have been equally prosperous and therefore have warranted exactly the same increases in the wage awards. The Irish engineering employers had indeed protested that their production costs were much higher than those prevailing in England, while the explosives and shipbuilding trades pleaded for special treatment on the ground that they had special difficulties. But the Court treated them all alike without apparently making any serious effort to arrive at an accurate estimate of the abilities of the different trades to pay.

The questions as to whether wage rates should be determined on an industrial or on a craft basis of trade organization cuts cross the principle of the ability to pay and opens up the whole issue of a national versus a separatist view in wage determination for a particular industry. The Industrial Court decided in favor of the industrial principle in Decision No. 728, issued on July 8, 1922, for the railway shopmen, and determined their wages and other conditions of service, not upon broad consideration of "the rates of wages agreed upon or recognized by employers and work-

[52] Similarly Decision No. 395, which refused to grant a wage advance in the engineering industry, was extended to the shipbuilding, railway shops, and explosives trades under Decisions Nos. 396, 424 and 474, respectively. It is interesting to note that the railway shopmen were given a separate footing in Decision No. 728.

men in other industries employing similar classes of labor," but upon the basis of "the special conditions attaching to the railway service" as a distinct industry." [53] This decision, which was quite a departure, it will be noticed, from the second rule laid down in Decision No. 180, was followed by a number of decisions that reveal the fundamental difficulty of using the industrial principle as a guide in wage coordination. For the Court in Decisions Nos. 742, 785, 808, 1228, and 1369, which applied that principle under varying circumstances, showed a tendency to recognize, on the one hand, separatist wage movements in particular industries such as the railway and electricity supply industries (which may occupy special positions in the industrial system of the country as a whole), and to create, on the other, an artificial division of wage rates among certain classes of workers who may be employed by many different industries.[54]

[53] The craft unions contended that "in so far as the railway companies employ men who are members of a particular craft or calling, they should pay the rates of wages which are recognized by other employers in that trade" in the country, while the National Union of Railwaymen maintained that the manufacturing and maintenance work carried on by the railway companies was an essential part of the railway transport business, and that therefore the wages and other conditions of employment of the shopmen should be determined in accordance with the conditions obtaining in the railway industry as such. The Court pointed out that, in many instances, there were no generally recognized craft district rates properly applicable to the railway shopmen, and that, where such rates existed, they did not move in all trades simultaneously or by the same amount, and, therefore, if paid at such rates, some railwaymen might suffer a reduction or enjoy an advance, which would not necessarily apply to their fellow workers employed in the same establishment. On these and other grounds the Court decided for the industrial principle.

[54] In Decision No. 742, issued in November, 1922, the Master Boilermakers' Federation claimed wage reductions on the ground of the falling prosperity of the boilermaking trade, but the workers rejected the employers' demand on the ground of the prosperous state of the domestic engineering industry as a whole, of which the trade in question was a branch. The Court decided that, while the boilermaking trade was a

(4) The Principle of Fair Wages. In view of these difficulties it has been suggested that the industrial principle should be displaced by what is called the craft principle which demands that wages be "regulated by the general value of the type of labor in question and not by its value in any particular industry."[55] In other words wage rates in any particular industry should be determined in comparison and in

branch of the domestic engineering industry, rather than a separate industry in itself, the financial position of the particular trade should be taken into account in order to determine the extent to which changes of a general nature should be applied in its special case. In Decision No. 808, issued in May, 1923, for the Manchester newspaper industry, the employers requested a reduction in wages of the engineers employed in the printing departments on the ground of reduction in the cost of living and in the general engineering rates outside, but the workers rejected the demand on the ground that the low rate in the outside engineering industry was due to special conditions which did not apply to the newspaper industry and that the argument of the cost of living was equally unacceptable because the industry in question was in a prosperous condition. The Court decided that a case had been made out for a reduction of wages from the point of view of the newspaper industry as a separate industry, but not to the full extent of the employers' claim because of the special position of the engineers. In Decision No. 785, issued in April, 1923, the Court granted an independent status to the electricity supply industry in the northwestern district mainly on the ground that the industry was "a self contained industry," to which the economic conditions of the general engineering industry did not apply. When the electricity supply workers employed at certain Government and railway power houses applied to the Court to have the wages and other conditions of service obtaining in the outside electricity supply industry extended to them the Court refused the request on the ground that their circumstances were different from those in the outside industry.

[55] "The craft principle," writes Dr. Rankin, "in itself is a special interpretation of the fair wage principle (as that principle is stated in the Resolution of the House of Commons of 1909). It is an endeavor to substitute 'must', which may mean here either moral coercion or economic advisability, for 'should' in the principle of fairness. . . . It means at least that the basic wages rise or fall with movements of industry in general." Rankin, *Arbitration Principles and the Industrial Court*, pp. 88, 114; *cf.* Hobson, *The Conditions of Industrial Peace*, pp. 46-47.

consonance with the different wage movements in the country as a whole, and not by reference to the special conditions of a particular industry. In fact this principle, hinted at in the third rule of Decision No. 180, had long been in practice to a limited extent under the Fair Wages Resolution of the House of Commons of 1909, which required the Government contractors to pay wages and observe conditions of labor not less favorable than those generally adopted by the good employers in the district concerned.

From the point of view of wage co-ordination this principle has two points of great importance. In the first place different wage movements are often the cause of industrial disputes, because it is only human nature to think it fair to have wages advanced or reduced in a particular industry in conformity with wage movements in other similar industries. Secondly, the general level of wages in the last analysis must be based on the ability of the industry in general to pay. In a number of actual cases, however, the Industrial Court has shown that the idea of fairness is not absolute but relative to the ability to meet the wages bill. This ability differs from one section to another even within a single industry, and varies according to the conditions of service obtaining in different industries. It is therefore difficult to compare different wage movements with absolute fairness.

In Decisions Nos. 61 and 281, for instance, the Industrial Court allowed wage variations in the gas and cotton textile industries in view of the fact that different gas concerns had varying abilities to meet wages bills while there were special conditions to be considered in the cotton trade in the particular locality concerned. In Decision No. 915, however, the Court refused to grant such differentiation to the Scottish sugar-refining industry on the ground that the wages and conditions of service in the industry at large should be as uniform as practicable. In Decision No. 665 the Court ruled that wage adjustments in the Government dock-yards should be made "in accordance with and as influenced by the general movement" of wages in the outside shipbuilding industry, but in Decision No. 743 the Court added that because of the special conditions obtaining in the Government establishments, such general similarity did not necessarily mean that wages in this industry should follow "faithfully and minutely every change of wages either upwards or downwards that occurs in private employment." In Decision No. 1324, for the postal service, issued in July, 1924, the Court finally came to the conclusion that:

no hard and fast rule can be laid down which would be capable of automatic application. Changes in either an upward or downward direction may be necessary in order to maintain a due consonance with general national or industrial considerations, but any such changes fall to be made after a careful review of the various issues involved in a manysided problem (par. 25).

D. Summary

In conclusion we may fairly say that in the particular cases brought before it the Industrial Court has failed to apply its general principles with the consistency required for the successful discharge of its function as a wage co-ordinating authority. Lord Amulree expressed the opinion that, in disclosing the general grounds of its decisions, the Court has taken a tentative step toward the formation of a body of industrial case laws.[56] Our review of the Court's decisions seems hardly to warrant this conclusion. For the general principles enunciated by the Court have often served as a cloak, and have borne no real organic relationship to the point actually made in a particular decision. A direct relationship between general principles and a particular case is really the essence of the "precedent" that is the key-note

[56] Lord Amulree, *Industrial Arbitration*, pp. 190-2.

of any system of case laws. The actual result of the Court's decisions has been more in the nature of compromise or conciliation than of a strict award of justice as is shown in the following tables. It is interesting to note that in instances both of arbitration by the Industrial Court and of direct industrial action a large number of disputes were settled by compromise, with the percentage figures running practically as follows: 42-43 per cent. compromise, 35 per cent in favor of the employers, and 22-23 per cent in favor of the workers.

TABLE I

RESULTS OF THE INDUSTRIAL COURT'S DECISIONS AS CLASSIFIED [a]

Year	In Favor of Employers	In Favor of Workpeople	Compromise	Total
1919	11	22	16	49
1920	159	145	239	543 [b]
1921	44	19	52	115 [c]
1922	17	7	11	35 [d]
1923	37	25	48	110 [e]
1924	56	27	56	139 [f]
1925	72	25	66	163 [g]
1926	48	17	39	104
1927	22	17	43	82
1928	17	8	27	52
1929	12	7	20	39
1930	21	6	16	43
1931	13	5	16	34 [h]
1932	11	7	10	28 [i]
Total	540	337	650	1,536
Percentage	35	22	43	100

[a] Analysed from the reported Decisions of the Court annually published by H. M. Stationery Office in London.

[b] This includes 4 interpretation cases without bearing Decisions Nos.

[c] 7 cases from Decision No. 704 to No. 710 are excluded.

[d] 2 cases Decisions Nos. 712 and 722 are excluded.

[e] 3 Decisions Nos. 770-772 are excluded.

[f] 4 Decisions Nos. 965, 976-977, 995 are excluded.

[g] 2 Decisions Nos. 1042 and 1099 are excluded.

[h] Decision No. 1519 is excluded.

[i] The total number of the decisions issued by the Industrial Court up to the end of 1932 was 1,551, without counting the four interpretation cases of 1920.

TABLE II

RESULTS OF STRIKES AND LOCKOUTS AS CLASSIFIED BY SETTLEMENT[a]

Year	In Favor of Employers	In Favor of Workers	Compromise	Total
1920	507	390	710	1,607
1921	315	152	296	763
1922	222	111	243	576
1923	183	187	258	628
1924	235	163	312	710
1925	189	154	260	603
1926	126	67	129	322[b]
1927	118	61	129	308
1928	144	42	116	302
1929	164	89	178	431
1930	155	71	196	422
1931	166	108	146	420
1932	168	88	133	389
Total	2,692	1,683	3,106	7,481
Percentage	35	23	42	100

[a] See the 21st Abstract of Labor Statistics issued by the Ministry of Labor in 1934, p. 132.

[b] Exclusive of the General Strike of 1926.

From these percentage figures it may be argued that in practical results there is not much difference between arbitration and direct action, and that therefore it is in the interest both of the community at large and of the parties immediately concerned that the waste and ill-feeling resulting from direct industrial action should be avoided by submission of all disputes to arbitration for a peaceful settlement. From the psychological point of view, however, the trouble is that when they are in a strong position, the industrial parties may feel that, since arbitration so often ends in compromise or the splitting of differences, they might as well take the chance of an actual trial of strength rather than resort to argument before a court of arbitration in order to gain all their points.

The fundamental difficulties confronting the Industrial Court arise then from two primary facts, namely, the industrial situation and the position of the Court under the existing system of industrial organization. Wages in different trades are variously affected by the unequal forces of the market, and no effective means can be found to secure their co-ordination on a national basis unless the social needs of the country are interpreted and enforced by public authorities under a social system of compulsory industrial regimentation, a development hardly to be expected from the general outlook of British democracy.[57] Secondly, the Industrial Court may have its own idea of justice or fairness in accordance with which industrial disputes ought to be adjusted. But the Court's official position does not entitle it to rule according to such standards because the Court has no power to enforce its decision against the will of the parties appearing before it. A few examples may illustrate this point.

In July 1919 the Interim Court of Arbitration refused the engineering unions' demand for an increase of 15s. per week in wages on the ground that the cost of living had been

[57] "A socialist society," writes Mr. Cole, "is not merely a society in which the means of production have passed into a social ownership: it is a society in which what is to be produced, at what prices the products are to be distributed, what incomes the individual citizens are to have, how much of its income the community is to save and how much to spend on current consumption, are all matters to be collectively determined in accordance with the ends which the collective wisdom of the community sets up as the guiding principles of its economic policy." A similar note was struck by Sir Henry Betterton when, referring to public assistance to the unemployed workmen as a right, he said: "If the State were to pay compensation for loss of employment, the State must, for its own protection, determine what kind of employment the worker should be willing to take and upon what terms. In its own interests the State would have to impose strict discipline and control over the private actions of unemployed persons. I am satisfied that the workers themselves would never agree to the regimentation involved in such a policy." G. D. H. Cole, *Studies in World Economics*, p. 252; Parl. Deb. Commons (283), 1087-8, Nov. 30, 1933.

reduced (Award 588). In the following month the Iron-founders gave notice to the engineering employers concerned to terminate the Engineering National Wages Agreement, in accordance with which they had submitted their claim to the Interim Court, and in September ceased work to enforce their demand. In July 1920 the Industrial Court refused the engineering unions' claim for a wage increase on the ground that, although there had been some advance in the cost of living, the industrial position of the industry did not justify a change in the existing rates. The unions dissatisfied with the decision followed the example of the Iron-founders by withdrawing from the National Wage Agreement in September. In Award No. 422 the Court granted an advance of 5s. a week to the hosiery workers in Scotland, but the employers in Kilmarnock refused to accept it. In Award No. 727 the Court granted a considerable reduction in wages in the printing industry, but the printers in Newcastle struck against the reductions. The last two cases were brought before local law courts, which decided that the findings of the Industrial Court were binding upon the parties. This decision, however, was without much practical result.[58]

Another point to note is that the Industrial Court is a judicial court constituted for the specific purpose of adjusting industrial disputes, and not for the purpose of forming industrial policies. Such policies may be determined either by the existing Imperial Parliament or by a new Industrial Parliament. Thus those who represent the actual forces operative in the industrial fields may settle industrial issues more directly and on a broader basis than that on which the decisions in the Industrial Court are founded.

This is not to depreciate the work of the Industrial Court, but to appreciate its position more accurately. In its limited field the Court offers a rational, expedient, and cheap means for the settlement of industrial disputes.

[58] See *ante*, pp. 147-8.

4. A GENERAL SUMMARY OF GOVERNMENT INTERVENTION IN TRADE DISPUTES FROM 1920–1932

We are now in a position to make a general summary of the broad results of Government intervention in trade disputes through various agencies during the years 1920–1932.[59] The total number of cases settled was 2,625, of which 1,503 were dealt with by the Industrial Court, 183 by single arbitrators, 81 by ad-hoc courts of arbitration, 20 by courts of inquiry, and 838 by the conciliation efforts of the Ministry of Labor. As in the pre-war years arbitration exceeded conciliation, the pre-eminent position being taken by the Industrial Court, while in conciliation the agreements reached through efforts of the conciliation officers of the Ministry greatly outnumbered the settlements secured through conferences presided over by an independent chairman. In arbitration the group of engineering trades occupied a leading position with the public utility, railway, civil service, other metal, transport, and building trades following in order, while in settlement by conciliation the transport trade led the food, building, engineering, and textile trades.

The figures for Government intervention include those cases in which a stoppage of work took place as well as those which did not lead to such an occurrence. No record has been kept of the progress of trade disputes settled by voluntary means without leading to a cessation of work. An exact estimate of the position of Government intervention in trade disputes occurring in the country as a whole is, therefore, impossible, but the following tables may give us some idea as to the relative position of Government intervention and direct negotiation between the parties immediately concerned so far as the settlement of actual strikes

[59] For details see Appendix, Tables nos. 1-2, compiled from the annual reports of the Ministry of Labor and the *Labor Gazette*, unless otherwise specified.

METHODS OF SETTLEMENT OF STRIKES AND LOCK-OUTS[a]

	Number of Disputes which were Settled by						
Year	Direct Negotiations	Conciliation	Arbitration	Return to Work on Employer's Terms	Replacement of Workers	Closing of Works	Other Methods
1920	1,184	128	62	122	89	9	13
1921	573	48	20	62	38	5	17
1922	408	54	9	59	33	3	10
1923	478	49	22	51	17	2	9
1924	500	76	19	64	37	5	9
1925	432	44	13	68	29	3	14
1926	222	20	6	45	22	5	3
1927	227	15	5	30	19	3	9
1928	199	14	5	55	21	2	6
1929	279	26	11	80	24	4	7
1930	265	39	9	68	32	2	7
1931	274	34	3	62	33	6	8
1932	228	37	3	74	39	3	5
Total	5,269	584	187	840	433	52	117

	Percentages of Total Number of Disputes						
	%	%	%	%	%	%	%
1920	73.7	8.0	3.8	7.6	5.5	0.6	0.8
1921	75.1	6.3	2.6	8.1	5.0	0.7	2.2
1922	70.8	9.4	1.6	10.3	5.7	0.5	1.7
1923	76.1	7.8	3.5	8.1	2.7	0.3	1.5
1924	70.4	10.7	2.7	9.0	5.2	0.7	1.3
1925	71.6	7.3	2.2	11.3	4.8	0.5	2.3
1926	68.7	6.2	1.9	13.9	6.8	1.6	0.9
1927	73.7	4.9	1.6	9.7	6.2	1.0	2.9
1928	65.9	4.6	1.7	18.2	6.9	0.7	2.0
1929	64.7	5.8	2.8	18.6	5.6	0.9	1.6
1930	62.8	9.2	2.1	16.1	7.6	0.5	1.7
1931	65.2	8.1	0.7	14.8	7.9	1.4	1.9
1932	58.6	9.5	0.8	19.0	10.0	0.8	1.3
Total	897.3	97.8	28.0	164.7	79.9	10.2	22.1

Number of Workers Directly Involved
(in thousands)

Year	Direct Negotiations	Conciliation	Arbitration	Return to Work on Employer's Terms	Replacement of Workers	Closing of Works	Other Methods	Total
1920	1,593	89	34	57	4	1	1	1,779
1921	1,719	14	7	28	1	—	1	1,770
1922	476		1	24	1	—	1	512
1923	229	38	20	54	1	—	1	343
1924	316	188	19	53	1	1	—	558
1925	183	26	174	10	6	1	—	400
1926	1,127	5	1	10	1	—	1,580	2,724
1927	69	7	5	5	—	—	3	89
1928	55	4	1	19	—	—	—	79
1929	79	5	391	16	1	—	1	493
1930	174	88	3	20	1	—	—	286
1931	206	163	4	48	1	1	1	424
1932	52	135	—	146	4	—	—	337
Total	6,278	771	660	470	22	4	1,589	9,794

[a] See the 20th and 21st Abstracts of Labor Statistics issued by the Ministry of Labor in 1931 and 1934, pp. 126, 133. The cases in which less than 500 workers were involved are not counted in the table.

and lockouts is concerned. During the 13-year period 1920-1932 direct negotiation settled 5,269 cases out of a total of 7,482, or an average of 69 per cent, while conciliation and arbitration by Government agencies settled 771, or only 9.6 per cent. Out of a total of 9,794,000 workers involved in the disputes direct negotiation dealt with 6,278,000 workers, or more than 64 per cent, while conciliation and arbitration settled cases involving 1,431,000 workers, or less than 15 per cent.

It is evident from this brief review of government intervention in trade disputes that the various industries, which have different habits and customs in dealing with disputes, have utilized the different methods provided under the Industrial Courts Act. These varied schemes are wide and flexible enough to meet the individual requirements of different industries. The engineering, railway (shopmen), public utility trades, and the civil service, for instance, have made use chiefly of the Industrial Court, while the iron and steel manufacturing trades have preferred single and ad-hoc courts of arbitration. The building, textile, clothing, woodworking, food and allied trades have regularly resorted to the method of conciliation through the officers of the Ministry of Labor, while the transport industry has availed itself of the facilities offered by the Industrial Court, the conciliation officers, and the courts of inquiry.

This diverse procedure for the attainment of industrial peace is of course a direct result of the Government's policy in industrial disputes, of remaining in the background as far as possible in order to allow employers and workmen to compose their differences among themselves according to their own best abilities. It is important to note, however, that this traditional policy of laissez-faire is becoming increasingly untenable as the Government assumes more responsibility for social welfare and as labor's claim for a decent living standard becomes more insistent.

We have seen that the courts of inquiry concerning the coal mining disputes in 1924 and 1925 reported that minimum wages should be a first charge on industrial proceeds and that the court of 1925 made the further statement that the conflict between "the economic wages" that the coal-mining industry could afford to pay under existing conditions and "the social wages" that the workers demanded as necessary for decent living could be met only by an increase in productive efficiency through the reorganization of the coal-mining industry as a whole. The question of reorganization had been taken up in 1919 by the Sankey Commission, which reported in favor of nationalization and joint control.[60] It was again taken up in 1925 by another royal commission under the chairmanship of Sir Herbert Samuel. This Commission rejected the proposal for nationalization, but recommended State ownership of minerals, amalgamation of the mining undertakings, combination of allied industries, and better organization of distribution.[61] In 1925 the Government, recognizing that the coal-mining industry as a whole was, under existing conditions, financially unable to continue either to give employment or to produce coal on the scale demanded by the interests of the country, had decided to grant a subsidy amounting to about £23,350,000 for a period of nine months in order to fill the gap between the minimum wage provisions of the national wages agreement of 1924 and the lower level of wages that would result from the coal owners' proposals for a new agreement. As a result of the recommendations of the Samuel Commission there have been passed the Mining Industry Act, 1926, and the Coal Mining Acts 1930 and 1932. These Acts were designed to promote the reorganization of the coal industry by means of amalgamation of the undertakings and by regulation of the production, supply, and sale of coal on a more or less compulsory basis.[62]

Another instance of the breakdown of the laissez-faire policy led to the passage of the London Traffic Act, 1924. Passed as a result of the London Tramwaymen's strike, it provided for the control and regulation of passenger traffic in the metropolitan area so that the trams, tubes, and omni-

[60] *The Reports of the Coal Industry Commission* issued in July, 1919, CMD. 210; the *Labor Gazette*, March, July, 1919, pp. 125, 270.

[61] *The Report of the Royal Commission on the Coal Industry* issued in 1926, CMD. 2600; the *Labor Gazette*, March, 1926, p. 80.

[62] *The Ministry of Labor Gazette*, April, 1927, p. 49; August, 1930, p. 281; June, 1932, p. 208.

buses "may be able to earn a living and pay their wages." [63] Trade unionism has also been given a new status under the Cotton Manufacturing (Temporary Provisions) Act, 1934. This Act enables the trade unions to enter into legally binding wage agreements with the organized employers engaged in the weaving section of the cotton industry.[64] These general tendencies we shall discuss more fully in chapter 7.

[63] Parl. Deb. Commons (171), 1697, March 28, 1924, per Mr. H. Gosling, then Minister of Transport. The London Traffic Act, 1924, was followed up by the passage of the London Passenger Transport Act, 1933, which transferred all the existing passenger transport undertakings in the metropolis to a public authority, the London Passenger Transport Board.

[64] *The Ministry of Labor Gazette*, June-July, 1934, pp. 157, 231.

CHAPTER V

The Joint Industrial Councils

I. THE ESTABLISHMENT OF THE COUNCILS

A. The Basic Principles of the Whitley Reports

THE Committee on Relations between Employers and Employed, generally known as the Whitley Committee after its chairman's name, was appointed, as we have seen, in October, 1916, as a sub-committee of the Cabinet Committee on Reconstruction set up by Mr. Asquith in the previous March. The terms of reference were: "(1) to make and consider suggestions for securing a permanent improvement in the relations between employers and workmen, and (2) to recommend means for securing that industrial conditions affecting the relations between employers and workmen shall be systematically reviewed by those concerned, with a view to improving conditions in future." The Committee was composed of officials of leading employers' associations, trade unions, and prominent economists and social workers.[1] The

[1] J. H. Whitley, Chairman (Chairman of Committees, House of Commons); F. S. Button (formerly member of Executive Council, Amalgamated Society of Engineers); G. J. Carter (Chairman, Shipbuilding Employers' Federation); S. J. Chapman (Professor of Political Economy, University of Manchester); Gilbert Claughton (Chairman, London and North Western Railway Company); J. R. Clynes (President, National Union of General Workers); J. A. Hobson (Professor of Political Economy, London School of Economics); Susan Lawrence (Member of the Executive Committee of the Women's Trade Union League); J. J. Mallon (Secretary, National Anti-Sweating League); T. R. Ratcliffe-Ellis (Secretary Mining Association of Great Britain); Robert Smillie (President, Miners' Federation of Great Britain); Allan M. Smith (Chairman, Engineering Employers' Federation); Mona Wilson (National Health Insurance Commissioner).

chairman, J. H. Whitley, then Chairman of the Committees of the House of Commons, was chosen for his known impartiality and capacity to control controversial discussions. One of the two secretaries, Mr. H. J. Wilson of the Chief Industrial Commissioner's Office, had had Board of Trade experience in dealing with industrial disputes, and the other, Mr. Arthur Greenwood, had intimate labor associations.

In the course of 1917-1918 the Committee issued altogether five reports,[2] the underlying principles of which were (1) the full and public recognition of trade unionism, (2) a large measure of industrial self-government, and (3) the traditional policy of non-compulsion in trade regulations on the part of the Government. It was the considered opinion of the Committee that "an essential condition of securing a permanent improvement in the relations between employers and employed is that there should be adequate organization on the part of both employers and workpeople." The Committee took this principle of trade organization as the starting point of their entire policy for joint co-operation, and devised different methods according to the degree of organization existing in various industries. For the well organized industries the Committee proposed the establishment of a triple machinery, namely, a National Joint Industrial Council, District Joint Industrial Councils, and Works Committees; for the less organized industries a modified form of the National Joint Industrial Council, with two or more representatives of the Ministry of Labor attached to it, was recommended and for the unorganized industries the application of the Trade Boards Acts in a strengthened form.

In the proposal of the triple negotiation machinery the Committee really summed up the best practical experiences of the well organized industries and gave them a kind of

[2] 1917 (CD. 8606); 1918 (CD. 9002); CD. 9001; 9099; 9153: See J. B. Seymour, *The Whitley Councils Scheme*, ch. 2.

official approval.[8] The needs of the well organized industries were no longer served by local or individual negotiations; the machinery must be national in its scope. It was not enough, however, to secure co-operation in the national center only; active and close co-operation in the districts and in individual workshops were equally important, not only for early settlement of disputes but for proper consideration of the diverse district or sectional interests inherent in a national industry. Secondly intermittent ad-hoc negotiations were defective both because they often made it difficult to resume negotiations after a breakdown and because they also lacked the good influence that the regular meeting of a standing joint council to discuss matters of common interests, as proposed in the Whitley Reports, must exercise upon the temper and personal relations of the negotiators on both sides. Thirdly the existing joint machinery of collective bargaining, confined almost entirely to the settlement of wage disputes and closely allied questions of employment, was entirely inadequate to enlist the active and continuous co-operation of the workers whose demand for "industrial self-government" was constantly increasing. The Committee believed that "a permanent improvement in the relations between employers and employed must be founded upon something other than a cash basis." Personal relationship between a workman and his employer was out of the question under modern industrial conditions and the only possible basis other than mere cash-nexus was to grant to the work-people "a great measure of participation in the discussion about and adjustment of those parts of industry by which they are most affected." For this purpose the Committee enumerated the following topics as proper subjects of discussion by the triple machinery:

[8] The practices of the five major industries are discussed in ch. 6.

(1) the better utilization of the practical knowledge and experience of the workers;

(2) the means of securing a greater share and responsibility of the workers in the determination and the observance of their working conditions;

(3) the general principles governing the conditions of employment, especially the methods of payments, with a view to securing to the workers a share in the increased prosperity of the industry;

(4) the means of securing the greatest possible security of earnings and employment;

(5) the establishment of regular means of negotiation with a view both to prevention and better adjustment of differences;

(6) technical education and training;

(7) industrial research and utilization of its results;

(8) the provision of facilities for the full consideration and utilization of the inventions and improvements designed by workers;

(9) the close co-operation between management and workers in the improvement of processes, machinery, organization of work, and other appropriate questions;

(10) joint action on any proposed legislation affecting the industry.

These matters were regarded as of common interest to both employers and workmen, rather than as controversial subjects between them. By participation in the discussion of these matters the workers were expected to become more interested in and feel more responsible for the promotion of industrial harmony and efficiency. Perhaps it was this special emphasis on the community of interests between the two industrial partners, labor and capital, that made the Whitley Reports popular and gave the scheme a new position in the history of industrial relationships. It carved out a new domain over which the customary conciliation boards had not traveled but which was still quite a distance from the further domain of socialized industry. The socialist members of the Committee added this note to the general Reports: " while recognizing that the more amicable relations thus established between capital and labor will afford an atmosphere favorable to industrial peace and progress, we desire to express our view that a complete identity of interests between capital and labor cannot be thus effected, and that such machinery cannot be expected to furnish a settlement for the more serious conflicts of interests involved in the working of an economic system primarily governed and directed by motives of private profits."[4] This statement was to prove prophetic.

Apart from this difference as to the ultimate goal of industrial relations the capitalist and socialist members of the Committee were in complete agreement on the maintenance and continuation of the traditional policy of non-compulsion with regard to trade regulations on the part of the Government. The Committee expressed their desire strongly to emphasize " the advisability of a continuation, as far as possible, of the present system whereby industries make their own arrangements and settle their differences themselves." The Government was required to forward the proposals of the Committee to the various associations of employers and workers, recommending them to form Joint Industrial Councils, but they were advised not to go any further, either by legislation to compel those who did not choose to follow the policy or by giving the sanction of law to any agreements that might be made by such councils, although at some later stage the Government might do so if the initiative should come from the councils themselves. It had been suggested to the Committee that some means should be devised to safeguard the general interest of the commun-

[4] The members were: J. R. Clynes, J. A. Hobson, A. Susan Lawrence, J. J. Mallon and Mona Wilson, the *Final Report*, p. 4.

ity at large against any possible action of an anti-social nature on the part of the Joint Industrial Councils, but the Committee thought that the Councils would have regard for national interests in the promotion of their separate interests. "The State never parts," they said, "with its inherent overriding power, but such power may be at least needed when least obtruded." The composition of the councils was also to follow the traditional policies of the existing joint machinery for collective bargaining. They were to consist of representatives of employers' and workers' associations and not of members popularly elected. Except for this broad outline the Committee prescribed no details either for the constitution or procedure of the Councils. These matters were to be left to the trades themselves whose different circumstances required some latitude in their methods of treatment.

B. The Establishment and Collapse of the Councils

The Whitley scheme was received favorably by leading trade unions and employers' associations. The Government accepted its First Report in October, 1917, instructing the Ministry of Labor to carry the scheme into effect. Mr. Roberts, then Minister of Labor, took immediate steps by issuing a circular letter to a large number of trade unions and employers' organizations, recommending that they form Joint Industrial Councils "not as two opposing forces each bent on getting as much and giving as little as can be contrived, but as forces having a common interest in working together for the welfare of their industry, not merely for the sake of those concerned in it, but also for the sake of the nation, which depends so largely on its industries for its wellbeing." The Joint Industrial Councils would be recognized, it was announced, "as the standing official consultative committees to the Government on all future questions affecting the industries they represent." [5] In the ensuing negotiations it was soon found out that a clear cut classification of industries was possible only between those industries in which organization was sufficiently developed to justify the formation of a National Joint Industrial Council and those which did not have such an extensive organization. The Government therefore decided to recognize only one type of council, namely that which was applicable to the well organized industries and had no official representatives.[6] As for the less organized industries the Ministry of Reconstruction would promote the formation of Interim Industrial Reconstruction Committees not only for the purpose of considering the problems of reconstruction after the war, but also in the hope that improvement in organization and experience in joint action would lead the Committees to the stage of permanent Joint Industrial Councils.[7] As for the unorganized industries the Trade Boards Act of 1909 was strengthened by the passage of the Trade Boards Act of 1918.

The difficulties confronting the Ministries of Reconstruction and Labor in their efforts to establish Joint Industrial Councils and Interim Reconstruction Committees were inefficient organization, difficulty in the matter of defining the industries, rivalries between craft and general labor unions, and differences in the practices and interests of sections and districts of the industries that were to be represented on the Councils. These difficulties proved later the principal cause of the collapse of many of the Councils after a short period of existence. In some cases, however, the activities

[5] *The Ministry of Labor, Report on the Establishment and Progress of Joint Industrial Councils*, 1917-22, p. 11-2.

[6] Memorandum by the Ministries of Reconstruction and Labor, 1918 (CD. 9085).

[7] See the Ministry of Reconstruction's Memorandum of July 7, 1918, on Interim Industrial Reconstruction Committees.

of the Ministries were greatly assisted by existing machinery for collective bargaining and in others by the experience gained by the Ministries during the war on various joint bodies such as Trade Advisory Committees and Industrial Control Boards. In some cases the difficulties were overcome by war time enthusiasm and the eagerness of some of the societies to adopt the Whitley scheme which promised to confirm their war time gains, both in the matter of recognition of status and standard rates of wages. Under these influences altogether 33 Reconstruction Committees were established in 1918-1919 and 59 Joint Industrial Councils in 1918-1921 with not less than 150 District Councils and more than 1,000 Works Committees.

This was the high water mark of the movement. By the end of 1922 eleven Reconstruction Committees had ceased to function [8] and fourteen had been transformed into Joint Industrial Councils. (Of these Councils eight are no longer in existence.)[9] Since then two Reconstruction Committees have been reconstituted as Joint Industrial Councils, three have ceased to exist,[10] leaving only three Committees to function in the clay, envelope and stationery manufacturing, and the cocoa, chocolate and sugar confectionery trades.

[8] The Committees ceasing to exist covered the trades: basket making, blacksmithing and farriers, boot and shoe polishing*, brush making*, catering, cutlery*, patent fuel, railway carriage and wagon building, sugar refining*, wholesale clothing*, the making up and packing of textiles for export. The committee for the making-up and packing of textiles for export still continues to function in the London area. The trades marked with * have since been brought under the Trade Boards Acts of 1909-1918.

[9] The Councils ceasing to exist covered the industries: glass, packing case making, music trades, wire drawing, paper making, gas mantles, lead manufacture, and zinc and spelter.

[10] The Committees ceasing to exist after 1922 covered the trades: fertilizing, non-ferrous mining, and optical instrument making.

As for the Joint Industrial Councils at least 31 Councils[11] have been discontinued while only one new Council has been added to the original list. The following table gives a list of national Joint Industrial Councils at the end of 1934.[12]

	Industries	Year of Establishment
	Mining and Quarrying	
1.	China Clay*	1918
2.	Quarrying *	1919
	Pottery, Glass, Cement, Chemicals, etc.	
3.	Pottery	1918
4.	Cement *	1918
5.	Chemical Trades	1918
6.	Match Manufacturing	1918
7.	Paint, Color, and Varnish Trades	1918
8.	Soap and Candles	1920
9.	Artificial Stone Making *	1928
10.	Seed Crushing and Compound Cake	1921

[11] The Councils which have ceased to function are: baking (Scotland), bread baking and flour confectionery (England and Wales), building trade, carpets, elastic web, cord, and smallwares fabric, entertainments, furniture making, gas mantles*, gold, silver, horological, etc., glass*, hosiery (Scotland), lead manufacture*, local authorities administrative, etc. services (England and Wales), local authorities administrative, etc., services (Scotland), local authorities non-trading services (Scotland), made-up leather goods, metalic bedstead making, Ministry of Munitions, music trades*, packing case making*, paper making*, road transport, rubber, sawmilling, zinc and spelter*, surgical instruments, tin mining, vehicle building, woollen and worsted (Scotland), wire drawing*, wrought hollow ware making. In the building industry the sectional councils for plumbing and plastering are still in operation; in the local authorities administrative etc. services there are three district councils for Lancashire and Cheshire, London, and West Riding of Yorkshire; in the road transport services there are also two district councils operating for Scotland and Northmidland. The Ministry of Munitions was incorporated with the War Department. The Councils marked * had been reconstructed from the Interim Industrial Reconstruction Committees.

[12] See the Ministry of Labor, *Report on the Establishment and Progress of Joint Industrial Councils*, pp. 26-28; *Report on Collective Agreements*, 1934, vol. i, pp. 186, 213, 258, 281, 298, 312, 325; *Annual Reports*; Committee on Industry and Trade, *Survey of Industrial Relations*, pp. 300-1; *cf.* J. B. Seymour, *The Whitley Councils Scheme*, Appendix I-III.

Engineering and Metal Trades

11.	Bobbin and Shuttle Making	1918
12.	Electrical Cable Making	1919
13.	Electrical Contracting	1919
14.	Heating and Domestic Engineering	1919
15.	Needle, Fish Hooks, and Fishing Tackles	1919
16.	Welsh Tin Plate and Sheet Trade	1919
17.	Lock, Latch and Key *	1920

Printing and Allied Trades

18.	Printing and Allied Trades	1919
19.	Wallpaper Making	1919
20.	Process Engraving	1920
21.	Printing Ink and Roller Trades	1929

Woodworking

22.	Cooperage *	1920

Textile Trades

23.	Silk Industry	1918
24.	Hosiery (England)	1918
25.	Wool and Allied Textile Industry	1919
26.	Coir Mat and Matting	1919
27.	Asbestos	1919

Clothing Industries

28.	Boot and Shoe Making	1919
29.	Glove Making *	1921

Food Preparation

30.	Flour Milling	1919

Transport and Communication

31.	National Maritime Board	1919
32.	Dock Labor	1920
33.	Furniture Warehousing and Removing *	1924

Public Utilities

34.	Gas Industry	1919
35.	Electricity Supply	1919
36.	Tramways	1919
37.	Water Works Undertakings	1919

Public Administration

38.	Local Authorities Non Trading Services (Manual Workers), (England and Wales)	1919
39.	Insurance Committees Administrative, etc. Services ..	1920
40.	The Civil Service	1919
41.	The Admiralty Industrial Establishments	1919
42.	Office of Works " "	1919
43.	Stationery Office " "	1920
44.	War Office .. " "	1920
45.	Air Ministry " "	1920

* Indicates that the Councils have been reconstructed from Interim Reconstruction Committees.

Many of the well organized industries, it will be noticed, for which the Whitley Report was primarily intended, have not adopted the scheme. In the coal mining industry the union leaders have been attracted more by the proposals of nationalization and joint control of the industry, while the railways have devised a scheme of their own. The Joint Industrial Council for the building trade was disrupted by a dispute in 1922, the cotton industry was more or less satisfied with existing conciliation machinery, while in the heavier sections of the iron and engineering industries the radical movement among the shop stewards for the control of the industry by workers was also unfavorable to the adoption of the Whitley scheme.

The Ministry of Labor also considerably slackened its efforts to form Joint Industrial Councils when the urgent need for reconstruction immediately following the war had somehow been met. This was admitted by Miss Bonfield when she stated in Parliament that, although it was the policy of the Government to give assistance in the formation of Joint Industrial Councils, it was necessary to allow employers' and workers' organizations in each industry to adopt the form of joint machinery that seemed to them to be best fitted to their own circumstances. She thought that mistakes had been made in attempting to apply Joint Industrial Councils to certain unorganized industries in which trade boards would have operated with more effectiveness.[13]

The greatest cause of decline of the Whitley scheme is to be found in the fact that the war-time idealism, in which it had been conceived, receded with the return of industry to normal conditions of production with a resulting general lack of interest in the scheme among employers and workmen. This is well demonstrated by the fact that only a single new council has been created since 1921.

The unprecedented and universal depression, on the other hand, caused many councils to break up. The majority of these lacked experience in corporate government under strong trade unionism. Effective organization was the keynote of the Whitley scheme and it was not to be created overnight. Both time and training are required, but the post-war hailstorm of industrial changes did not afford much time for the less organized employers and workmen to acquire the skill and patience necessary for handling either the difficult questions of wage adjustment or the diverse sectional and district interests which often proved fatal to the existence of National Joint Industrial Councils.

By 1934 eight councils out of the 45 existing national councils covered the public administration, 4 the public utility services, while the remaining 33 councils governed industries which, except for a small number of trades such as printing, wool, hosiery, boot and shoe, pottery, chemical, and the flour milling industry, were of minor importance. The Councils govern altogether about three million workers and their activities, which spread in many directions, are attended with varying success.

[13] Parl. Deb. Commons (246), 511, Dec. 11, 1930; also *ibid.* (174), 811, May 30, 1924; *cf. Toward Industrial Peace*, pp. 162-3, per Captain L. H. Green. Under the Trade Boards Acts, 1909-1918, the Ministry of Labor is authorized to establish Trade Boards in unorganized industries with powers to determine minimum wage rates, which are enforceable by law.

2. THE JOINT INDUSTRIAL COUNCILS SYSTEM AT WORK

A. The Works Committees and District Councils

Decentralization by means of District Councils and Works Committees was an integral part of the Whitley scheme. By the end of 1918 it was reported that Works Committees had been established in practically all the industries where a National Joint Industrial Council was formed. The number which by the end of 1921 had reached more than a thousand, has since decreased considerably. The idea seems to have failed to take deep root, except in a small number of industries such as the match manufacturing, pottery, electricity supply, cement making, flour milling, printing, and the Government industrial establishments. There is no apparent need of formally instituted works committees in certain industries with their relatively small individual workshops; and in others, indifference on the part of both employers and trade unionists seems to be the principal reason against the establishment of such committees.[14] The functions of the Works Committees are generally of a consultative or advisory character, the final power of decision resting with the management. The ordinary agenda of the Committees comprises the application of trade agreements to individual works, the promotion of safety, ventilation, sanitation, and other welfare work, the arrangement of working time, time keeping, investigation into the waste of materials and other unnecessary production costs, and suggestions for improvement to promote the efficient working of the establishment concerned. The handling of grievances is a common item in the agenda. In certain cases managerial matters also come before the Works Committee in the form of comments on the proposed appointment of a foreman or the

[14] J. B. Seymour, *The Whitley Councils Scheme*, ch. ix, Appendix VII; *cf.* B. Selekman, *British Industry To-day*, chs. 5-6.

dismissal of a workman. The organization of the Committees also varies according to circumstances, but the common feature is the joint representation of workers and management.

The general scheme obtaining in the Government industrial establishments may be cited as an illustration. This plan provides for separate joint committees for shop, department, and works, and also for trade committees in order to deal with trade questions separately from questions of a more general character, such as matters of discipline and welfare. The workers' side of the shop committee includes at least one representative of the trade unions having membership in the shop. The workers also elect representatives to the Department Committees, which in turn send representatives to the Works Committee. The management is represented on the committees by responsible officials in charge of the shop, department, or works as the case may be. The broad objects of the Committees are (1) to provide a recognized means of consultation between the management and workers, (2) to give the workers a wider interest in and greater responsibility for the conditions under which their work is performed, (3) to insure that the regulations made in collective agreements shall be duly carried into effect in the workshops, and (4) to prevent friction and misunderstandings. If a question of a general nature arises at a workshop, it is to be discussed, in the first instance, between the workmen concerned and their foreman; if not settled in this manner the matter may be taken up successively by the shop, department, and works committees, the final reference being to the Department Joint Council. Questions concerning wages and other trade matters may be taken up by the trade committees and by them referred to the Joint Trade Council for final settlement.

For the purpose of comparison an account of the successful operation of the Works Committee at the Park Works of Mather and Platt, Ltd., Manchester, one of "the show places" of the country, is given below.

The Committee was first organized in 1917 and reorganized in 1920 according to the York Agreement in the engineering industry.[15] The workers elect, in the first place, a representative committee of shop stewards, roughly one steward for each department under the auspices of the trade unions having membership in the establishment. The shop stewards committee then elects seven of its members to the Works Committee on which the management is represented by another seven members. The Committee covers a wide area of activities, dealing with questions of overtime, piecework, apprentices, time keeping, shop discipline, settlement of grievances, elimination of waste, accidents, administration of dining rooms and the disbursement of various funds established for the benefit of the workers. As routine work the committee, with a view to removing unsatisfactory working conditions, conducts a scrutiny of the reasons given by workers for their leaving the firm's employment. Following the meeting of the Works Committee, meetings are held by a committee of the foremen and by the stewards to take any necessary action on the points raised at the previous Works Committee meeting. The Works Committee thus gives more than a mere hint as to the course or policy to be followed by the company.

Another interesting feature is the Suggestions Scheme which gives opportunity for any workman to bring forward his ideas for the prevention of accidents, for better organization of work, for improvement in the machinery operation, etc. If the idea is of any value the designer is remunerated

[15] *The Engineering Industry is not governed by Joint Industrial Council*, see p. 259.

suitably, and after due experiments a patent may be taken out without any cost or risk to the workman. The procedure is for the designer to write out his suggestion, preferably on a specially printed form, which may be obtained from the secretary of the firm or from a box in the canteen; it is then sent to the Suggestions Committee consisting of the director of research, the works manager, a department head, and one representative each of the works office and of the Works Committee.

To provide facilities for the annual summer holiday the firm has established a fund called "the Ernest Mather Work-people's Fund," the proceeds of which are distributed among the workers in amounts ranging from 30s. to 50s. under the recommendation of the Works Committee. Another fund is the Mutual Help Fund to which all workers contribute voluntarily and from which they receive assistance when in a straitened financial situation owing to illness. The disbursement of the fund is under the control of the Works Committee, as is also the Manchester and Salford Hospital Saturday and Convalescent Homes Fund. The company also maintains an Employees' Benefit Fund which applies to all workmen in need of financial help, and a pensions scheme for the officials, foremen, technical and clerical members of the staff. The firm maintains also a Day Continuation School which is attended by all apprentices between 14 and 17 years of age. Evening classes are held in the school during the winter months to help the junior girls to improve their knowledge of business methods and the young men on the clerical staff to learn bookkeeping. Good physique of the workers, a special concern of the Works Committee, is fostered by various means of sport and drill. In the dining room, which is under the charge of the Works Committee, over 1,400 workmen may sit down to a hot dinner at a reasonable price, provisions also being made for those who bring their own brew of tea or coffee. Washing conveniences are provided at the lavatory where soap and clean towels are furnished every day free of charge. A separate dining room is provided for women and girls and also for the staff members of the works. The whole policy of the firm is well expressed in its motto: "It's toil's reward that sweetens industry," and "Freemen freely work." [16]

As for the effect of the Works Committees it is generally agreed that they provide an effective means of nipping grievances in the bud and give to the workers a greater share in the determination of their working conditions. These Committees also promote the technical efficiency of the workshops concerned.[17] It has sometimes been charged that the employers are not fully aware of the opportunities offered by the committee system and do not take the trouble to acquaint the employees with their commercial difficulties, such, for instance, as problems of credit, production, raw materials, merchandising, and competition. Such information, if imparted with open-mindedness and frankness, would ensure more confidence and good will between employers and their workmen. With a view partially to overcoming this indifference and securing a more rapid spread of the works committees, the Liberal Party in 1930 and 1932 presented to Parliament Works Council Bills providing for the establishment of consultative works councils in factories and workshops, for the abolition of arbitrary dismissal of workmen, and for submission by the management of commercial and financial statements to the councils. The Bills have not been acted upon mainly because they do not provide for joint

[16] The author wishes to express his gratitude to Mr. Mather, Secretary-Director of the company, who kindly gave the author permission to visit the works in 1931.

[17] Committee on Industry and Trade, *Survey of Industrial Relations*, p. 306.

bodies and proceed on a compulsory basis of workshops organization, a form of legislation that is basically opposed to the traditional method of voluntary co-operation between British employers and workmen.[18]

Among the District Joint Industrial Councils practices again vary according to the different circumstances of the trades concerned. In those industries that are substantially localized, such as, the pottery, hosiery, tin plate, and heavy chemical trades, District Councils have not been established, while in a number of trades such as the woolen textile, electrical contracting, flour milling, and public utility services District Councils have been of great value especially in the settlement of wage questions. The National Industrial Councils have generally the right to deal with questions affecting the industry as a whole and the District Councils, to varying extents, enjoy local autonomy. In the wool and electricity supply industries, for instance, wage variations are negotiated by the District Councils, while in the flour milling industry the National Council prescribes standard rates of wages on a double basis of classification by areas and the roller capacity of the mills in each area, the actual grading of the individual mills in the areas being determined by the respective District Councils. The District Councils in the municipal and public utility services are similarly authorized to grade undertakings in their respective areas and fix schedules of wages for each grade within the scope of their respective national agreements. In the quarrying industry sectional councils have been established for the five branches of the industry with more or less complete autonomy in wage matters and on other questions, the National Council concerning itself mainly with safety regulations in the industry. The district councils thus vary widely as to their powers and

[18] Parl. Deb. Commons (244), 665; Nov. 4, 1930; (262), 393; Feb. 24, 1932.

status, but their general functions are (1) to consider matters referred to them by the National Council, (2) to take action on matters decided by the central authority, (3) to make recommendations to the national agency, (4) to consider matters of interest to their districts, including subjects referred to them by the Works Committees, (5) to co-operate with other district councils in matters of common interest, and (6) to settle disputes.

B. The National Joint Industrial Councils

The size of the Councils varies with the scope of the industries and the variety of organizations represented on the councils in question. The membership of the councils ranges from 72 in the printing trade to 14 in the cement industry. The average membership is about 24. In the majority of cases the Council has a chairman and a vice-chairman, one from each side, and separate secretaries who are usually officials of the employers' and workers' organizations affiliated with the Council. It is the secretaries who, with the help of the chairman, prepare the agenda of the council. Preliminary meetings are held by each side before a meeting of the Council in order to ascertain their respective attitudes on the questions at issue. In most cases the Councils meet regularly, vote by sides, and work either through standing committees or committees appointed for specific purposes, the necessary expenses being borne by the organizations affiliated with the councils. The different methods of Council organization may be best illustrated by the citation of a few actual examples.

In the Government industrial establishments [19] there are two types of councils, namely, the five Departmental Joint Councils for the Admiralty, Office of Works, Stationery

[19] For the Civil Service see L. D. White, *Whitley Councils in the British Civil Service.*

Office, War Office, and the Air Ministry, and the four Trade Joint Councils for the engineering, building, shipbuilding and miscellaneous trades with a Co-ordination Committee for the Government industrial establishments. Each Departmental Council is headed by responsible officials appointed by the Department concerned, together with a representative of the Ministry of Labor. The employees' interests are handled by representatives of the trade unions having membership in the various establishments under the control of the Department. Since, however, it is a common practice of the trade unions to settle wages and certain other matters on a trade rather than on an industrial basis, and since there is need of securing uniformity of action in all Government Departments, Trade Joint Councils have been established for the purpose of dealing with wages and other matters customarily settled on a trade basis. Each Council is headed by representatives of all the Government Departments employing its particular class of labor, while the employees are represented by members of the unions in the trade concerned. Thus, for instance, questions regarding building wages in Government establishments would be negotiated by a joint body composed of official representatives and trade unionists; official representatives, appointed by the Office of Works, the War Office, the Admiralty, and other Departments having building trade operatives, together with Treasury and Ministry of Labor representatives; the trade unionists representing building trade operatives employed by the various Departments. It had been feared that difficulty might be experienced in separating the functions of the two types of Council, but in practice no serious difficulties have been found because of the fact that many persons are members of the two types of Council.

The National Maritime Board for the shipping industry consists of five Panels, each panel being made up of twelve members of each side, and dealing respectively with (1) masters, (2) navigating officers, (3) engineers, (4) sailors and firemen, and (5) the catering department. The employers' representatives on the panels are elected by the Shipping Federation with which most of the ship owners of the country are federated, and one seat is allocated to the Railway Staff Conference as representing the railway companies owning steamers, and one to the Admiralty as representing the naval auxiliary vessels, such as colliers and oilers. The seamen concerned are represented on their respective panels by the nominees of their respective unions; the masters and navigating officers by the Imperial Merchant Service Guild and the Mercantile Marine Service Association; the engineer officers by the Marine Engineers' Union and the Amalgamated Engineering Union; and the sailors, firemen and stewards by the National Sailors' and Firemens' Union and the Amalgamated Marine Workers' Union. The panels sit separately and independently to negotiate wages and other conditions of employment on a national basis for the grade or grades which they represent. Two chairmen, one elected by and from each side, take the chair at alternate meetings. Questions on which the panel do not agree may be referred by either side to the Full Board composed of the five panels sitting together. Each panel has power to appoint District Committees known as District Panels. These panels may then be subdivided into three sections to deal with particular classes of vessels. The District Panels appoint one or two representatives of each side of each panel as Port Consultants whose duty it is to settle any local difference arising between masters and crews.

In the quarrying industry five sectional councils have been established for the lime and limestone, granite and roadstone, freestone, slate, and chalk branches of the industry. The Councils, which possess virtual autonomy in regard to wages and other matters affecting their respective branches, have established district or area councils covering various localities. In each section of the industry the employers' local associations are federated in a national organization which is further linked with the Federated Quarry Owners of Great Britain. The majority of the workers are organized in the National Union of General and Municipal Workers, the Transport and General Workers' Union, and the Amalgamated Union of Building Trade Operatives. The National Joint Industrial Council, on which the sectional councils are represented as distinct sections, does not deal with questions of wages and other ordinary conditions of employment except when the Sectional Councils appeal to it on a disputed matter, as to an arbitration court.

In the electricity supply industry we find another method of organization. There are two Joint Industrial Councils, namely, the National Joint Industrial Council, which covers the manual workers, and the National Joint Board, which governs the technical staffs. The employers' side of the National Joint Council consists of representatives of the municipal employers' section of each of the 13 District Councils and an equal number of representatives of the company associations, while the workers' representatives are elected by the Amalgamated Engineering Union, the Electrical Trades Union, the National Union of Enginemen, Firemen, Mechanics, Motormen, and Electrical Workers, and a number of general labor unions. The National Joint Board consists of representatives appointed from the employers' side, as in the case of the Joint Industrial Council, and representatives of the staff side appointed by the Electrical Power Engineers' Association. The Board has also established 12 District Boards.

A slightly different principle of representation applies to the Joint Industrial Council for the pottery industry, the members of which are appointed, 30 each, by the employers' association and various trade unions. Representation of the workers, originally confined to the craft unions, was later extended to the unions of general labor, clerks, commercial travellers, and managerial staffs. The representatives of the managerial staffs, with reserved freedom in voting, sit on the employers' side. The Council has three honorary members and works through various committees on organization, statistics, research, invention, design, wages and conditions of employment. The chief duties of the last mentioned committee are " the regular consideration of wages and conditions with a view to establishing and maintaining equitable conditions throughout the industry, to assist the respective associations in the maintenance of such selling prices as will afford a reasonable remuneration to both employers and employed, the regulation of production and employment as a means of insuring to the workpeople the greatest possible security of earning, and to consider and settle all disputes between the different parties in the industry."

In the printing industry the employers are organized in local associations grouped together in a number of geographical Alliances. The Alliances are then federated in the Federation of Master Printers and Allied Trades of the United Kingdom, with a membership employing probably 90 per cent of the printers in the entire country. The workers are organized in some 14 trade unions which are brought together in the Printing and Kindred Trades Federation of the United Kingdom. These two federations are represented on the Joint Industrial Council by 36 members each. Representation of the newspaper offices caused some difficulty in the early stage of the formation of the Council, but now two seats on the Council are allocated to both the National Union of Journalists on the workers' side and the Newspaper Society on the employers' side. The open or closed shop question, which also caused considerable discussion and delay, has finally resulted in the definition of the employers' side of the Council as "an association of employers who employ members of a Federated Trade Union." This provision is not, however, interpreted as a limiting clause, but as a ground upon which representation might be granted. The Council works through various committees such as the general purpose, finance, organization, health, unemployment, betterment, and conciliation committees. The Council has also established a number of district committees to deal with purely local matters.

As the organization varies so does the work of the various Joint Industrial Councils. The pottery Council, for instance, has defined its general purpose as "the advancement of the pottery industry and all connected with it by the association of its government with all engaged in the industry," while the printing Council has specified as its general objects: to secure complete organization of employers and employees, to promote good relationship between employers and workmen, to devise ways of settling difference, to do everything for the improvement of the trade and its conditions, to establish uniform working hours and conditions, to assist in maintaining reasonably remunerative prices, to minimize unemployment, to secure recognition, by all persons engaged in the trade, of agreements as to wages and working conditions, to take in hand the question of apprenticeship conditions, to insist on clean healthy workshops, to encourage friendly intercourse, sports, and social clubs in the industry, to encourage welfare committees, and to consider any proposed legislation affecting the trade. Several councils, such as those for the boot and shoe and the printing trades, have excluded from their purview the consideration of wages, while others in the pottery and the heating and domestic engineering industries, though empowered to deal with wage questions, have in practice excluded them from their activities. In these cases it is generally felt that the elimination of such controversial questions would more effectively help cooperation initiated by the Councils.

The majority of the Councils have, however, made the regular consideration of wages and allied questions one of their most important activities and have made notable achievements in the form of wage standardization and national agreements on working weeks, shifts, overtime, and holidays with pay. Unemployment has received close attention by various councils whose practices in dealing with it varies from short time operation, transference of workers from one locality to another, to the provision of unemployment benefits. In the match making industry a scheme of supplementary voluntary unemployment benefit has been in operation for many years, for the purpose of which a fund, one per cent of their wages bill, is maintained by contributions from the employers. To receive benefits from the fund a workman must have been in service with a given firm for at least six months prior to his " lay off ", and must be receiving benefits from the Government unemployment insurance scheme. He must also have contributed at least 2d. per week to his union unemployment fund for the previous six months. Fulfilling these conditions the unemployed workman is entitled to receive the amount of money necessary to make up his unemployment benefits from the other sources—50 per cent of his average earnings, plus 10 per cent for each dependent child. In the flour milling industry there has been established an Assistance and Resettlement Fund for the purpose of providing weekly relief and the necessary means of resettlement in new careers for those workmen who have been displaced in the process of rationalization of the industry. In 1930 approval was also given by the Council to a group pension scheme requiring employers and workmen to contribute 1s. per week for the purpose of pensioning workers who have reached the age of 65. A similar scheme has been in operation in the wallpaper making industry.

Broader problems such as the improvement of trade and consequent alleviation of unemployment, have also been considered by certain councils. The three Councils operating in the electrical industry, for instance, have considered measures of electrification and have urged the Government to speed up their electrical scheme as much as possible. In the printing industry the Betterment Committee of the Council has been urging affiliated employers to modernize their workshops by installing time-saving machinery with safeguards against the possible displacement of workmen. In those industries where craft skill has not yet completely given way to advancing mechanization the question of apprenticeship and technical education has received close attention, especially by the Councils for the heating and domestic engineering, printing, pottery, and the electrical contracting trades. In the pottery industry there is an open technical scholarship, with a value of £50 per annum, offered by the Council for three years. Candidates for funds must satisfy the Council that they have an intimate knowledge of the industry as well as a satisfactory general education. When elected the candidate is required to attend the Central School of Pottery at Stoke-on-Trent. Close contact has also been kept by various Councils with the Government and other educational authorities. In certain cases training in a junior technical school for a certain specified number of years is counted as part of the period of indenture, while in others advisory committees have been established to cooperate with the City and Guilds of London Institute in their examination schemes. In some cases a thorough survey of the question of juvenile employment in various industries has been made and various means, such as continuation classes and lectures, have been adopted for technical education in behalf of the industries concerned as a whole.

The question of health and safety is one of the principal concerns of various Councils. Some of them have cooperated with the Government through the Industrial Fatigue Research Board and the Home Office for the purpose of reducing accidents and fatigue, and promoting the improvement of sanitation, ventilation, lighting, and other welfare measures. Certain Councils have also established regular machinery of their own to give continuous attention to this subject. The Pottery Council has, for instance, carried out joint research in such matters as atmospheric conditions in the potters' shops, the efficiency of various types of drying stoves, and provisions for welfare, and has made certain recommendations which have been accepted by the Home Office. The Wool Council, which has carried on investigations of the relationship between accidents and the lifting of heavy bales, has also studied certain defects in factory buildings. In the flour milling industry the question of skin diseases has engaged the special attention of the Council. Fact finding is also one of the principal functions of certain Joint Industrial Councils. In the pottery industry the Statistical and Enquiries Committee, which took a census of production in 1922, has since been issuing returns on the average percentage of profit on turnovers. The printing industry has adopted a standard system of costing and has appointed a special committee " to study its details and application to all sections of the industry." In the tramway industry it has become an established practice in connection with wage negotiations to appoint a joint committee to investigate the cost of living, the wage levels prevailing in comparable industries, and the general financial condition of the industry. The constitution of the Wool Council provides that upon the introduction of new machinery wage rates must be revised according to the findings of a joint investigation committee.

A considerable amount of time has also been spent by various Councils on the commercial problems of their respective industries. The building and pottery councils have concerned themselves at one time or another with the questions of supply and the rationing of raw materials and fuel, while the china clay and quarrying councils made representations to the Ministry of Transport on the subject of railway facilities in behalf of their industries. Numerous councils have also appointed a joint deputation to the Government to secure protective measures under the Safeguarding of Industries Act or under the Merchandise Marks Act.

Among the functions assigned by the Whitley Committee to a Joint Industrial Council was "the establishment of regular methods of negotiation for issues arising between employers and workpeople, with a view both to the prevention of differences and to their better adjustment when they arise." The model constitution issued by the Ministry of Labor included a similar clause, which has been adopted either literally or in principle by practically all the Councils established. Nearly every Council has constitutional provisions for the convening of special meetings at short notice in case of dispute, and a large number of them further provide that no stoppage of work shall take place until the matter in dispute has been considered by the Council. Even where no formal procedure has been established, matters of difference in appropriate cases may be brought before the National Council in the usual manner, through the local works committees and district councils. In certain cases machinery for negotiation has been retained from existing agreements made previous to the establishment of the Council. The conciliation machinery operating in the boot and shoe manufacturing industry, for instance, has been in existence in substantially its present form since 1895, when a national agreement was reached between the Federated Associations of Boot and Shoe Manufacturers and the National Union of Boot and Shoe Operatives. The agreement provided, inter alia, for the reconstruction of the existing various local Boards of Arbitration and Conciliation with full power to settle all questions submitted to them concerning wages, hours of labor, and other conditions of employment. In case of disagreement by the Board the matter in dispute is to be referred to two arbitrators, to be mutually agreed upon, or to an umpire to be appointed by the Board of Trade. No strike or lockout may be entered into by either party represented on the Boards, provision also being made for monetary penalties in the event of either party's not complying with the agreement or awards by the Boards. At a national conference held in 1914 a Standing Committee consisting of three representatives of each of the parties was created to deal with all disputes that might arise out of the national agreements. On account of this well established machinery the National Joint Industrial Council does not concern itself with questions of wages and other allied conditions of employment.

In some cases the conciliation and arbitration machinery adopted by Joint Industrial Councils presents interesting features. In the Civil Service differences arising over remuneration, hours of work, and leaves of civil servants as a class may be referred to the Industrial Court. The Court for this purpose consists of a chairman, who may be the president, or the chairman of a division of the Industrial Court, and one member drawn from the panel appointed by the Minister of Labor as representing the Chancellor of the Exchequer, and another from the panel appointed by the staff side of the National Joint Council for the Civil Service.[20] In the tramway industry questions of national importance, if not settled by the Council, are referred to a Tribunal consisting of 14 persons, 5 elected by each side of the Council from among their members and 2 from non-members, with an independent chairman mutually agreed upon, usually the President of the Industrial Court. In the electricity supply industry differences affecting the technical staffs are referred to arbitration under the Industrial Courts Act, while those affecting the manual workers are reported to a Tribunal for examination of the facts and recommendations as to the course to be followed by the National Joint Industrial Council. An elaborate procedure of arbitration has also been adopted by the National Joint Industrial Council for the quarrying industry. If a dispute is not settled through local machinery written notice may be given by either party to the Secretary of the Council stating that a dispute is imminent. Within three days of the receipt of such notice the secretary is required to submit to the parties concerned a panel of arbitrators consisting of all members of the Council, from which the parties are each to select from the respective sides two persons not directly involved in the dispute. The court of arbitration then consists of the four persons thus selected together with an independent chairman who may be mutually agreed upon or may be nominated by the Ministry of Labor. The Court is to meet within 14 days and to issue an award within seven days of its hearing. Before the hearing the parties are required to sign an agreement to abide by the decision of the Court. The Council may also arrange a Conciliation Committee which may proceed to the actual locality of the dispute and endeavor to effect a settlement by

[20] For a fuller account see L. D. White, *Whitley Councils in the British Civil Service*, ch. 5.

conciliation. A similar scheme has been adopted by the silk Council.[21]

In the wool and allied textile industry an arbitration court is selected by the parties to a dispute from two standing panels of chairmen and members of the arbitration court annually nominated by and from among the members of the National Council. The court, within seven days of its hearing, is required to issue an award which is binding on both parties to the dispute, at least for 42 days. Should the court fail to agree upon an award the matter in dispute may be referred for final settlement to an umpire to be nominated from another standing panel of four independent umpires yearly elected by the National Council. Special Committees to deal with cases of dispute have also been established by various Councils. In the printing and allied trades although the National Council does not deal with questions of wages, its constitution provides that no strike, lockout, or other aggressive action shall take place until the matter in question has been considered by the District Committee, and, failing a settlement there, by the National Council, which is required to meet within seven days to consider the question. Before a full meeting of the Council the question in dispute is usually referred to and settled by the Conciliation Committee composed of the chairman and the vice-chairman of the Council and of six members nominated by the contend-

[21] The scheme provides for the constitution of an Emergency Committee consisting of the chairman, the vice-chairman and the secretaries of the Council. This Committee has power to decide, within seven days of receipt of notice, as to whether the dispute should be referred to local machinery or should be dealt with under the scheme of the Council. If the decision favors the latter method the Emergency Committee selects from a rota of the entire membership of the Council suitable persons to act as mediators. Should the parties apply for arbitration by an umpire the Committee is to ask the Ministry of Labor to appoint from outside the Council an umpire who may sit with trade assessors appointed by the Emergency Committee.

ing parties. The Committee "do not observe any legal formalities of any kind, we interrupt each other as much as we want, and no decision has ever been come to by the Committee—they merely express an opinion. They express what is the opinion of the Committee, and I think that in only one case has that opinion been turned down by both sides. . . . They are not even asked, when they come, whether they are prepared to accept the findings or not. We simply take our chance and hope we shall find some way out, and usually we do, and I hold the opinion that if we can find the way out by argument before strike notices are tendered and before the men come out, it is so much better than trying to do it afterwards." [22] In the pottery industry disputes may be referred to a small committee consisting of an equal number of manufacturers and operatives with one of the honorary members of the Council as chairman. The chairman has a casting vote in case of disagreement by the two sides of the Committee.

3. A REVIEW OF JOINT INDUSTRIAL COUNCILS

The Joint Industrial Councils were initiated with high hope. It was believed that they would give workers an effective voice in industry and lay a basis for better understanding and cooperation between employers and workmen. The basic conflicting forces of capital and labor were still there, but it was thought that bringing them together at a council table would throw into relief matters of common interest and would foster a general desire for the welfare of the industry as a whole, as distinct from individual private interests. The brief review of the actual working of the Councils, however, gives us another instance of the disillusionment of high hopes by the cold facts of reality. The

[22] Parl. Deb. Commons (174), 775-76; May 30, 1924, per Mr. G. A. Isaacs.

Works Committees and District Councils, an essential part of the Whitley scheme for self-government in industry, have admittedly been a failure. With the exception of a small number of active Councils whose notable achievements in the form of the standardization of wages and hours, relief of unemployment, promotion of health, joint fact-finding, and technical education have been mentioned, the majority of the National Councils are merely wage negotiation machineries. It will be noticed, furthermore, that the achievements mentioned are by no means a contribution that can be made only by the Councils since similar achievements are recorded by industries that are governed by the ordinary type of negotiation machinery.

It is a matter of further disappointment that the Councils have often failed even in their capacity as the official standing consulting committees to the Government on matters affecting their respective industries. In this connection Sir Henry Betterton, Minister of Labor, stated in the House of Commons in 1934:—" I will tell the House what my experience has been when I have asked Joint Industrial Councils for their opinion and advice on matters of great importance. From time to time recently the question of a forty-hour week has been raised in the House. . . . I asked the Joint Industrial Councils what they thought about it. . . . In practically every case—there were only two or three exceptions—the answer I got from the employers was, 'Please apply to the Employers' Confederation,' and the workers said, 'please apply to the Trade Union Congress, because that is a matter they have in hand.' In both cases I was referred to the separate organizations of the two sides. The Royal Commission on Unemployment Insurance asked the 45 or 50 Joint Industrial Councils what they thought of certain specific proposals which the Commission was then considering. The experience of the Commission was precisely the same as mine. Excepting in a very few cases, seven or eight, the Joint Industrial Councils said, 'if you want our views, you must ask, on the one hand, the organization of the employers and, on the other hand, for the views of the Trade Union Congress."[23] This shows incidentally the relative position and strength of the Association of Joint Industrial Councils and Interim Industrial Reconstruction Committees, on the one hand, and of the national organizations of capital and labor, on the other, in respect of the discussion of national policies concerning the industry as a whole.

In 1928 the Turner-Mond Conference proposed the establishment of a National Industrial Council. The Council was to be composed of representatives nominated, on the workers' side, by the General Council of the Trade Union Congress, and, on the employers side, by the Federation of British Industries and the National Confederation of Employers' Organizations. The three main functions prescribed for the proposed Council were (1) to hold regular quarterly meetings in order to consult on the widest possible range of questions concerning industry and industrial progress, (2) to provide through a standing joint committee for the appointment of conciliation boards, and (3) to establish a direct machinery for continuous investigation of industrial problems.[24] The proposal was not accepted by the two national organizations of the employers because of their "limited capacities," but toward the end of 1929 it was agreed that the Trade Union Congress, the Confederation, and the Federation of British Industries might enter into discussion of any matter within their respective provinces that was of common interest to British industry. The following list of subjects was drawn up as an indication of the type of questions suitable for such discussion: (1) unem-

[23] Parl. Deb. Commons (286), 723-4, Feb. 23, 1934.

[24] Selekman, *British Industry Today*, p. 241.

ployment, (2) industry and finance, (3) taxation, (4) education and industry, (5) inter-Empire trade, (6) international trade, (7) trade facilities, (8) international labor questions, (9) industrial and commercial statistics, (10) social service, (11) delegated powers of Government Departments. Although nothing much has been done as a result of the joint discussions, the arrangement shows at least the trend of thought in the country toward joint action for industrial reconstruction, not through the Joint Industrial Councils, but through the direct cooperation between the Trades Union Congress, on the one hand, and the Federation of British Industries and the National Confederation of Employers' Organizations, on the other.

As a wage negotiation machinery the Joint Industrial Councils still face the old problem of "the ebb and flow of trade", a condition that tempts the Councils on one side or the other, to try to use what is called "the whip hand."[25] As in the case of the old method of collective bargaining, complaint is made that the employers fail to show their full hand. "The Conference table has an attraction for us all," says a critic, "but invariably, when we meet, the procedure is on these lines. The representatives of the workmen state their case, ethical and economic. The employers thank them courteously, leave the room, and then come back and say, 'We have considered your case, but we are sorry we cannot concede anything.' The workers' representatives then ask for evidence that will enable them to go back to the workers and explain the reasons why the demand has been refused. The employers shrug their shoulders and say, 'we are not in a position to supply the evidence that you require; we have given your case sympathetic consideration, and we regret that circumstances do not permit us to go any further.'

[25] Parl. Deb. Commons (174), 802; May 30, 1924, per Mr. C. Dukes.

In such circumstances the workers' representatives have to go back to thousands of workpeople and say there can be no change, and when some inquisitive person asks why, they can only say, 'The employers have told us so.' That is the extent of Whitleyism." [26]

Another difficulty confronting many of the Councils is the question of non-federated firms whose unfair competition outside the scope of agreements made by the Joint Industrial Council renders the position of the federated concerns difficult and often untenable. To remedy this difficulty several Bills have been introduced in Parliament. An Industrial Councils Bill, introduced in the House of Commons in January, 1924, by Mr. Frank Murrel, a member of the printing Council, enjoined the Minister of Labor to encourage the formation of Joint Industrial Councils and authorized him to issue an Order making the decisions of a Joint Industrial Council to be legally binding upon all employers engaged in the industry concerned. The Bill also proposed the establishment of a Central Industrial Board whose duty it would be to consider appeals that might be made against the Order of the Minister, to give general advice and assistance to the various Joint Industrial Councils, and, when requested by both sides, to act as a Board of Arbitration. The Independent Labor Party objected to the Bill on the ground that the Whitley scheme was the antithesis of socialism and split industry permanently into two sections of employers and workmen, a condition to which the Labor Movement was fundamentally opposed. A warning was issued, on the other hand, by Mr. Vivian who stated that the organization of employers and workmen might be "crystalized" to such an extent as to make the entry of newcomers, with initiative and genius, difficult in any private

[26] *Towards Industrial Peace*, p. 177.

industry. The Bill was read a second time on May 30, but because of the fall of the first Labor Ministry [27] the proposal was abandoned.

In 1931 Mr. Hayday, then President of the Trades Union Congress, presented a Rates of Wages Bill that differed from the previous Joint Industrial Councils Bill in two respects. In the first place it proposed to give legal sanction to only those rates of wages that might be agreed upon by a collective negotiation machinery representing a majority of both the employers and workmen concerned. This Bill also was shelved for lack of time.[28] In 1934 the Liberal Party again brought in the Industrial Councils Bill in its revised form which proposed to give legal effect to any wage agreements that might be entered into by a Joint Industrial Council. Mr. George Hicks representing the Labor Party objected to the Bill on the ground that it unduly favored the Joint Industrial Councils, which were not the only type of collective negotiation machinery, and that if the Bill passed the legal position of the trade unions might be seriously disturbed. Questions might arise as to whether the unions were contracting parties liable to suit for any alleged breach of agreements. Mr. L. Jones pointed out that fixing of wage rates was an intricate and delicate job, with 200 or 300 different rates running in some cases to three decimals, and that it was impossible under such circumstances to expect Order after Order to come before the House for its approval and sanction. Sir G. Hurst on behalf of the Conservative Party took up the cause of independent employers and moved the rejection of the Bill on the ground that it was " inconsistent with the grit, initiative, independence, and self-reli-

[27] Parl. Deb. Commons (169), 392 (174), 759, 780, 811, 823, 842.

[28] Parl. Deb. Commons (254), 630, June 25, 1931; (256), 841, Sept. 16, 1931.

ance," that had been the main factors in giving British industry its present position of supremacy. Sir Herbert Samuel supported the Bill on the ground that trade unionism had been weakened under the strain of the depression and that the Bill was essential to uphold the necessary machinery of collective bargaining. The Bill was defeated by a vote of 87-44.[29]

The outlook of the Joint Industrial Councils is further dimmed[30] by the fact that, while the less organized trades are looking forward to the establishment of Trade Boards, the union leaders in the well organized industries are advocating socialization of their industries by means of nationalization and public control, whether under direct government management or through independent statutory corporations. But it is typical of the British people to employ piecemeal measures and to amend according to experience and the merits of each particular case. Many industries may become socialized and more trades may come under the Trade Boards system. Even so, there is hope that the Joint Industrial Councils may improve their position in the private industries which will continue for a long time. Their position will indeed become stronger with the growing need for what is called the professionalization of industry,[31] and as the necessity that each industry have a corporate body of government becomes more fully and generally realized. Their position will also be strengthened by the grant, in due time, of necessary legislative powers, a development foreshadowed by the passage of the Cotton Manufacturing Industry (Temporary Provisions) Act of 1934 to which we

[29] Parl. Deb. Commons (286), 647, Feb. 23, 1934.

[30] *Cf.* Seymour, *op. cit.*, chapter xvii.

[31] See Sir Arthur Salter, *The Framework of an Ordered Society*, *passim*.

have briefly referred in Chapter 4. However, for their success, whether as a piece of negotiation machinery or as a council for the attainment of broader objects, much depends on the actual capacity for leadership and the strength of the practical idealism existing in each industry,—these qualities really count more than any particular piece of machinery and they cannot be exacted by legal decree.[82]

[82] *Cf.* White, *op. cit.*, p. 350.

CHAPTER VI

The Negotiation Machinery in the Five Major Industries

I. INTRODUCTION

Direct negotiation between the parties immediately concerned is of predominant importance in the British system of industrial peace.[1] In the present chapter it is proposed to give a general description of the negotiation machinery obtaining in some of the staple industries, namely, the coal mining, railways, iron and steel manufacturing, engineering, shipbuilding, and the cotton industries. The choice of these industries is made for two principal reasons. In the first place their importance in the national economic life is paramount, and secondly they are the best organized industries and exhibit the features most characteristic of the British system of industrial peace.

According to the population census of 1931 there were in Great Britain about 34,662,000 persons of working age, that is, 14 or over. The number of those actually following definite occupations was about 21,055,000, of which about 9,100,000 were concerned with agriculture, commerce and finance, public administration, professions, entertainments, domestic service, and office work, and about 11,955,000 were engaged in the extractive and manufacturing industries. Of the total industrial employment the five staple industries under consideration accounted for nearly one third, as is shown on the following page:[2]

[1] See the conclusion of ch. 4, p. 173.

[2] *The 21st Abstract of Labor Statistics*, pp. 4-14.

Coal and shale mining	1,012,000
Metal working (exclusive of electrical and precious metal)	1,640,000
Textile trades	986,000
Railway service	305,000
Total	3,943,000

In the same year the exports of British produce amounted to about £391,000,000, of which coal, iron and steel, machinery, and cotton manufactured goods accounted for about £170,000,000, or more than one-third.[3] In other words these great industries provide employment for a vast number of workers whose products form the basic foundation of British industrial power and national well-being.

It was the rise and expansion of these industries during the last century that made Great Britain the workshop of the world and the leading nation in international trade; it is their recent decline, comparatively speaking, that creates the most acute of the present-day problems of unemployment and industrial reconstruction that the country has to solve. They had grown up as a result of the Industrial Revolution and at the expense of agriculture.[4] In the past their products commanded a world market in exchange, on good terms, for food and raw materials from other nations. Their prosperity, which provided work for the growing population concentrated in the industrial cities around the coalfields and in the leading ports,[5] gave wide scope to the shipping, commercial, and financial activities of the nation. It was these industries that in the main constituted the backbone of national prosperity and it was the interests of these industries that largely determined the economic policy of the

[3] *Statistical Abstracts for the United Kingdom for 1913-1932*, pp. 382-93.

[4] Committee on Industry and Trade, *Survey of Industrial Relations*, p. 62.

[5] Committee on Industry and Trade, *Further Factors in Industrial and Commercial Efficiency*, p. 199.

nation along the lines of free trade. Since the Great War the many causes that have combined in threatening the supremacy of these industries both in international trade and in the domestic industrial structure,[6] have raised many questions of great importance, such as unemployment, the transference of surplus labor forces, reorganization of industry on a more efficient basis, the revival of agriculture in order to ensure to the nation a sufficient food supply, and the protection of the home market. The two latter considerations have already led to the adoption of a tariff, a complete reversal of the free trade principle that had been the fixed fiscal policy of the country for nearly a hundred years. These broad questions of social and industrial reconstruction are not within the scope of the present study, but there is a consensus of opinion that whatever methods may be applied for industrial reconstruction the improvement must be accompanied by fuller cooperation between employers and workmen.[7] The methods and possibilities of such cooperation we propose to examine in this chapter.

There are certain features of the five staple industries which may explain, on the one hand, their common characteristics, and, on the other, the rich variety of arrangements made by the industries for the adjustment of disputes. In the first place the industries under review employ a higher proportion of male labor than do the other industries in the country. The coal mining, railway, iron and steel, engineering, and shipbuilding industries are staffed almost exclusively by men and boys. Only in the cotton textile are women in a majority. Secondly, particular branches of the industries, with the exception of the railway service, have become concentrated in particular districts, specializing in

[6] G. C. Allen, *British Industries and Their Organization*, ch. x, p. 277.

[7] *Cf. The Report of the Royal Commission on the Coal Industry*, 1926 (CMD. 2600), p. 237.

certain processes of production suited to the districts concerned. The nature of the labor forces thus employed, the specialized character of the work pursued, and the geographical concentration of these industries have been responsible for the creation of strong trade unionism and a highly developed form of collective bargaining. Thirdly, these industries are highly unstable, partly because they are, with the notable exception of the railways, dependent on foreign markets and partly because many of them are concerned with producers' goods. Consequently wages and employment in these industries, as well as prices and profits, are subject to violent fluctuations. These in turn form the chief source of frequent disputes between employers and workmen. Since the industries are well organized on both sides these conflicts, in many instances protracted, assume great magnitude. In the fourth place these are basic industries, on the smooth operation of which the entire industrial system of the country depends for its success. Coal is the foundation of iron and steel manufacture which in its turn provides the basis for mechanical engineering. Engineering trades supply machinery to all trades and industries which in the main are still dependent on coal for motive power and on the railway service for transportation. The interdependent nature of these industries is complete. Furthermore they are, for the most part, engaged in bulk production of homogeneous commodities suited to standardization and national control, a condition that to some extent justifies the claims of labor for nationalization of the industries, especially coal mining, railways, and the iron trades.[8]

Apart from these common features, however, the individual industries present bewildering diversity,[9] not only in

[8] The Trades Union Congress, *Annual Reports*, 1932, p. 206; 1933, p. 210; 1934, pp. 189, 376; 1935. pp. 202, 208.

[9] John Hilton and others, *Are Trade Unions Obstructive?*, pp. 40, 57, 137, 204, 253, 272.

their material equipment and organization for production and distribution, but also in the leadership of those engaged therein. The coal miners are noted, for instance, for their strong corporate spirit, stronger perhaps than among any other class of working people. This is due partly to the conditions of their work which involves a large degree of mutual dependence and helpfulness often in circumstances of danger, and partly to the fact that coal mining, as a rule, leads to the growth of separate villages for the workers in the locality where their work is to be carried on. They thus form a homogeneous community with the fullest opportunities for common action, which is not the case with ordinary factory workers. On the other hand, however, the coal mining industry is scattered in widely separated districts which differ from one another, not only in their geological character and geographical situation, but in the history of their development. The mining industry is not really a collection of more or less uniform undertakings, employing so many men under conditions fairly similar, producing a single article, with the costs of production and the price obtained varying little among the mines at any time. The Samuel Commission on the coal industry reported in 1926 that at that time there were in Great Britain 1,400 colliery undertakings which owned 2,500 mines, some of them producing coal at a cost of 12s. per ton, others at a cost of 30s.[10] Under the circumstances it is therefore impossible to treat the mining industry as a single unit for the purpose of wage regulation. That is the precise reason why the mine owners are determined to maintain the principle of local negotiation by districts, while the miners are equally insistent on the need for nationalization of the coal mining industry.

[10] *The Report of the Samuel Commission*, pp. 45, 293.

The iron and steel manufacturing industry is also a collection of many different trades located in separate counties.[11] There is, however, a redeeming feature in the fact that a small number, about 12, of the large groups of iron and steel making concerns possess about 47 per cent of the pig iron capacity of the country and about 60 per cent of the steel capacity.[12] The engineering industry is another example of a vast aggregation of different trades which, though linked together by their common operation on metal materials, vary in their finished products. These products differ in the extent to which their prices are influenced by the state of industry in general. The manufacturing of textile, agricultural, or ship machinery, for instance, is dependent on the prosperity of the industries concerned, whether at home or abroad, while the production of motor cars and cycles is dependent on the general purchasing power of the public. In consequence these different sections may exhibit very different degrees of prosperity at a given time. The diverse nature of the industry has also been responsible for the rival claims of different craft unions, claims from which arise questions such as demarcation, piecework, or what is generally called "the managerial functions," the prominent cause of disputes in this industry.

The railway industry, on the other hand, is a "sheltered" industry and, since it is in its nature more or less monopolistic, it accepts more discipline by the State. Its operation was co-ordinated to some extent under the Railways Act, 1921. This co-ordination is responsible for the highly centralized form of the negotiation machinery and the great extent of standardization of working conditions in the industry. It is not a single, but a composite industry, includ-

[11] Committee on Industry and Trade, *Survey of Metal Industries*, pp. 2, 117-19.

[12] *Ibid.*, p. 33, Appendix III, p. 125.

ing a large number of trades whose joint action in negotiation with the employers has been a matter of considerable difficulty, owing to the different methods of trade-union organization employed. The cotton industry is practically concentrated in one locality, Lancashire, within which, however, specialization has been carried out to the extreme. This localization of the industry explains the strong growth of trade unionism in spite of the predominant element of female labor, while the extreme specialization is responsible for the sectionalism prevailing among the cotton trade unions. The complicated process of production in the industry has also produced a distinct method of wage regulation, namely, the minute regulation of piece prices, or price lists, a form of regulation that had a considerable influence on the method of adjusting disputes.

In short the negotiation machinery existing in each of the five industries is unique both in its history and in its principal features because the industries are built differently, with different requirements to meet and with varying degrees of leadership. Taken as a whole the peace agencies in these industries are characterized by great flexibility and many-sidedness, on the one hand, with the inevitable lack of uniformity and coordination, on the other. A detailed study of the peace agencies now follows.

2. THE COAL MINING INDUSTRY

A. Historical Note

It will be recalled that in the 'sixties the spread of industrial conciliation and arbitration had led to the passage of Mr. Mundella's Arbitration Act in 1872.[13] It was in this general setting that in 1872 the system of conciliation and arbitration was first introduced in the coal-mining industry in the form of a standing joint committee for the Durham

[13] See Chapter 2, p. 42.

coal trade. For the first time in coal-mining history the Durham colliery owners had agreed that year to meet representatives of the miners' unions as such and had effected wage agreements in an amicable fashion. It was soon found to be in their common interest that questions arising out of the agreement thus made should be withdrawn from incessant wranglings and should be settled by peaceful means. There was accordingly constituted a standing committee of an equal number of delegates from the miners' and mine owners' associations with the purpose of settling, by arbitration or otherwise, all questions that might arise at any particular colliery, with the exception of general wage questions that affected the county as a whole. The Committee worked so well that similar committees were soon formed in other districts, including Northumberland, Cleveland, Staffordshire, and South Wales,[14] which in turn, by producing a friendly spirit and mutual understanding between mine owners and miners, prepared the way for the establishment of joint conciliation boards for the further purpose of dealing with general county wage questions. The first board of this kind, formed for the coal mining trade of Northumberland in 1894, was followed by the formation of similar boards in Durham, Cumberland, the Midlands, the Forest of Dean in 1894-5, in Scotland in 1900, and in South Wales and Monmouthshire in 1903. Before the Great War the entire coal fields of the country were thus covered by eight separate conciliation boards established for Scotland, Northumberland, Durham, Cumberland, the Federated Area, Forest of Dean, Somerset, South Wales and Monmouthshire.[15]

[14] *Summaries of Evidence taken before the Royal Commission on Labor, 1894* (C. 7421), pp. 66-83.

[15] *Cf.* G. D. H. Cole, *Labor in the Coal Mining Industry*, pp. 9-10.

The development of these conciliation boards was closely connected with the growth of trade unionism in the various coal fields which, as we have seen, are widely distributed in separate counties and form the basic factor that gives a distinct colour to the negotiation machinery in the industry. Trade unionism in the coal-mining industry has a chequered history of at least a century, but the real beginning was not made until 1860 when the miners' right to appoint their own checkweighmen was recognized by the Mines Regulation Act, 1860. During the 'sixties the miners' unions were not recognized by the colliery owners and scarcely a single important change in wages or the methods of work was effected without a strike or lockout. By 1872, however, trade unions had grown so strong among the miners of Northumberland and Durham [16] that, when the unionists employed at various mines in the districts presented their demands for a rise in wages to the individual owners in accordance with their usual practice, the mine owners declined to deal with the proposals separately, but agreed to receive a deputation from the trade unions and confer jointly upon the applications. This conference, which led to the first successful collective bargaining between the colliery owners and miners in Durham, resulted in the establishment of the first standing joint committee, to which we have referred above.

Toward the end of the 'Seventies severe depression in the industry swept out of existence most of the district unions except those of Northumberland and Durham, but in the 'Eighties a revival took place with the formation of the Yorkshire Miners' Association in 1881, the Lancashire and Cheshire Miners' Federation, 1882, the Lanarkshire Federation, 1883, and the Midland Federation, 1885. In 1888 the Yorkshire and the Midlands unions combined in the

[16] Welbourne, *The Miners' Unions of Northumberland and Durham*, p. 151.

Miners' Federation of Great Britain. The immediate purposes of the new organization were to abolish the selling price sliding-scale system of wage regulation, which had been prevalent since 1877,[17] and to bring about an eight hour day for the mine workers. The unions of Northumberland and Durham, which had opposed these policies, stood aloof. The militant new Federation, however, had a rapid growth, rising in membership from 36,000 in 1888 to more than 200,000 in 1893 when it organized the first great mining strike against wage reductions, a strike in which more than 300,000 miners took part in Yorkshire, Lancashire, and the Midlands. As a result of this strike the Conciliation Board of the Federated Districts was formed in 1894. The Scottish Miners' Federation had joined the Federation immediately before the strike and four years later the South Wales Miners' Federation also came in. The passage of the Coal Mines Eight Hour Act in 1908, and the Coal Mines Minimum Wage Act in 1912, had secured the two primary objects of the Miners' Federation which, by the acceptance of its constitution by the two northern district associations of Northumberland and Durham, became a truly national representative body of all mine workers in the country.[18]

The miners began to think of their industry as a whole and directed their efforts to securing a uniform standard of wages throughout the country. For this purpose the Miners' Federation had included in its pre-war program the demand for a national wages board and direct negotiation between itself and the Mining Association of Great Britain. The plan was rejected by the Mining Association on the ground that the Association had no authority to deal with

[17] Welbourne, *op. cit.*, pp. 180 *et seq.*

[18] *Cf.* Herbert Tracey, "Makers of the Labor Movement: The Miners and Their Union," an article published in the *Labor Magazine*, July, 1923, p. 99.

wage questions, which were under the jurisdiction of the separate conciliation boards of the different mining districts.

This situation was radically changed in February, 1917, when the coal-mining industry was taken over by the Government under the Defence of the Realm Act and its administration was placed in charge of the newly created Coal Controller.[19] With the imposition of Government control wage issues automatically passed from consideration by local conciliation boards to negotiation between the Government, on the one hand, and the Miners' Federation on the other. The coal owners had previously maintained that national wage negotiations were impracticable because of the varying financial circumstances of the different mining districts, but the difficulties were removed by Government control which carried with it a national pool of profits under a unified financial policy. The advantage of this unified national policy was so clear that the miners pressed for nationalization of the coal mining industry and its joint control by the miners and the State.

This demand caused serious strikes in 1919 and led to the appointment of the Sankey Commission. In his final report the Chairman, Mr. (now Lord) Justice Sankey, recommended that both the coal measures and colliery undertakings should be purchased by the Government, that a series of joint councils, local, district, and national, should be created for administrative purposes, and that under such a reorganization of the industry no stoppage of work should take place until the matter in dispute had been referred to the local and district mining councils[20] and had failed of a settlement. The plea for nationalization was rejected by the Lloyd George Administration, but the value of joint committees was recognized in the Mining Industry Act of 1920,

[19] Cole, *Labor in the Coal Mining Industry*, pp. 49-55, 60-63.

[20] CMD. 360, 1919, Report by the Honorable Mr. Justice Sankey.

which provided for the establishment of a pit committee for each colliery, a number of district committees, area boards, and a national board. It was the area board that was authorized to formulate actual schemes of wage adjustments for the area concerned. For this purpose the mine owners were asked to furnish necessary particulars as to the output, cost of production, proceeds, and profits. For their actual operation these provisions were dependent upon the voluntary cooperation of the Miners' Federation and the Mining Association. The miners decided to boycott the Act, seeing in it an attempt on the part of the Government to defeat their claim for a true national wages board and to force them back to the pre-war system of local negotiations. When they changed this attitude in 1921 the Mining Association refused to take part in the operation of the provisions which therefore became inoperative in March, 1922.[21]

In the meantime the coal strike [22] of 1920 had been settled by an agreement reached between the Miners' Federation and the Mining Association. This agreement called for the establishment of a national board and a number of district committees for the purpose of dealing with wage questions. The subsequent actual negotiations on wage issues were disrupted, however, by the Government decision to relinquish control of the mining industry at the end of March, 1921. With the abolition of Government control the mine owners were determined to go back to the old system of local negotiations, considering it impossible to effect any wage settlement on a national basis in view of the great variations in the local conditions of the different coal fields; the miners,

[21] *The Ministry of Labor Gazette*, July, 1920, p. 357; Jan., July, Dec., 1921, pp. 7, 337, 625; Feb., March, 1922, pp. 56, 110; *cf.* the *Report of the Royal Commission on the Coal Industry*, 1926, pp. 213-214.

[22] See International Labor Office, *The British Government and the Miners' Federation of Great Britain*, Studies and Reports, Series A, No. 5, No. 10, Oct., 1920.

on the other hand, were no less strongly determined to continue national negotiations, demanding not only a national wages board, but also a national pool of profits so that the poorer mining undertakings might be enabled by subsidy to meet the necessary wage bills. The Government refused to adopt a policy of a national pool of profits, and the great national stoppage of work that took place in the coal fields lasted from April 1 to July 1, 1921.

The strike was terminated by an agreement entered into between the Miners' Federation and the Mining Association. Under its terms there were set up a National Board and 13 District Boards consisting of an equal number of representatives of employers and of workmen, chosen by the Mining Association and the Miners' Federation in the case of the National Board, and by the district associations in the case of the District Boards, with an independent chairman for each Board. The 13 districts, with the exception of the Federated districts which were divided into four separate districts, corresponded closely to the pre-war conciliation board areas. Each of the 13 District Boards were periodically to fix wages in the form of a percentage addition to the base rates prevailing in the district concerned, in accordance with the ascertained proceeds of the industry. The main function of the National Board was to interpret certain terms used in the Agreement such as "the proceeds of the industry," "standard wages," and "the cost of production other than wages." [23]

The National Wage Agreement of 1921 continued in force until January, 1924, and, with certain important modifications, until the end of June, 1925, when the Mining Association gave a month's notice of its termination. A Court of Inquiry was appointed under the Industrial Courts Act,

[23] *The Ministry of Labor Gazette*, March-July, 1921, pp. 122, 174, 228, 280, 336.

1919. As a result of the report of this Court the Government decided to appoint a Royal Commission, and, in the meantime, to grant a subvention for a period of nine months from August, 1925, in order to make up the deficit between the level of wages as provided in the National Wage Agreement of 1924 and the level of wages that would result from the colliery owners' proposals for a new agreement. The Royal Commission, under the chairmanship of Sir Herbert Samuel in March, 1926, issued its report recommending a continuance of the national wage agreements with a downward revision in the minimum percentage additions to the standard rates of wages.[24] The principle of national agreements as to the ratio between profit and wages, the method of ascertainment and the definition of the proceeds of the industry was accepted by the mine owners, who however insisted that the actual amount of the minimum percentages to the base rates as well as the amount of subsistence wages should be referred to the district associations for determination subject to approval by the national conference. The Miners' Federation, however, declined to accept any reduction in wages and refused consent to the abolition of the national minimum percentage. The deadlock was so complete that it could not be solved except by a national stoppage of work. This took place on May 1 and lasted until the latter part of November, 1926.

The Trades Union Congress General Council came to the aid of the miners by ordering a General Strike effective on May 4. It was called off, however, on May 12, leaving the miners to wage alone their own fight of exhaustion. After a four months' bitter struggle the miners were forced to accept a reduction in wages, and early in September they

[24] The Royal Commission also recommended changes in the organization of the industry with a view to securing more economical production, utilization, and marketing of coal and coal products. CMD. 2600, 1926.

asked the Government to arrange a joint meeting between the Mining Association and the Federation, but the Mining Association declined to enter into any discussion of wage questions with the Miners' Federation. After a considerable discussion between the Government and the Association the question was referred to the constituent members of the Association, but the 24 principal district associations refused to authorize the Association to negotiate in their behalf. None of the district associations had raised any objection to the principle of regulating wages by reference to ascertained results, fixing a minimum percentage below which wages should not fall, and insisting on subsistence wages. They maintained, however, that the quantitative determination of these points and others should be settled only by the local associations. Under these circumstances the Miners' Delegates Conference, held on November 19, passed a resolution recommending that all the district unions open negotiations with the colliery owners in their respective districts in order to arrive at a settlement of the dispute. District agreements were accordingly made in the 18 principal coal-mining districts, in the main on the terms proposed by the mine owners.[25]

B. The Negotiation Machinery

1. The Joint District Minimum Wages Boards

After a long and bitter struggle, which called two royal commissions into being and several times forced Government intervention, the miners were finally thrown back to their old system of local negotiations. The negotiation machinery differs from district to district and varies according to the nature of their subject matter. Questions arising under the Coal Mines (Minimum Wages) Act, 1912, are dealt with

[25] *The Ministry of Labor Gazette*, August-December, 1926, pp. 280, 320, 358, 394, 434.

by the Joint District Wages Boards established under the Act. For this purpose the country is divided into twenty-two districts, each of which has a Joint Board consisting of an equal number of representatives of employers and employees in the district, with an independent chairman who is appointed by the Board or, in case of disagreement, by the Board of Trade. The Board is authorized to fix minimum rates of wages for the underground workers employed in the district and to form general district rules as to the procedure and conditions under which such minimum rates shall be applied. The district rules may also provide for the settlement of disputes arising under the arrangement. As a matter of fact the Coal Mines Minimum Wages Act, 1912, recognized the competence of the existing conciliation boards to act as Joint District Boards, and in practically all the coal fields the conciliation boards have become Joint District Boards for the purpose of carrying out the provisions of the 1912 Act.[26]

2. The Standing Joint Committees

Questions affecting an individual colliery are generally dealt with, in the first instance, by the men concerned or by their representatives and the colliery management. If no settlement results in this manner the miners' agent for the district is called in, and, if no agreement is reached, the question may be referred to the district Conciliation Board, which generally appoints a special small committee to investigate and report on the matter so referred. In some districts the conciliation board does not deal with local disputes at all, such disputes falling within the jurisdiction of a separate Standing Joint Committee. In Northumberland, for instance, such a committee, consisting of an equal number of representatives of the mine owners' and miners' associa-

[26] The Ministry of Labor, *Report on Collective Agreements*, vol. i (1934), pp. 16–18.

tions has been in operation since 1873. The Committee has full power to deal with all questions relating to wages, working practices, or any other subject which may arise in any particular colliery. For the general guidance of the Committee it is expressly provided in the rules that "before any change in hewing prices be entertained it must be shown that the average wage on which the claim is made is at least 5 per cent above or below the county average," and that "all applications for advances or reductions in any portion of a pit shall open up the question of the prices paid to the same class of workmen throughout the whole of the pit", except in the case of a bona fide change in the working method or of the opening up of a new seam of coal.[27]

3. The District Wages or Conciliation Board

The district agreements made in the various coal fields since 1926 provide for the establishment of district wages or conciliation boards. Generally speaking, the boards, which are formed for the purpose of regulating the general rates of wages affecting the district as a whole, consist of an equal number of representatives of the mine owners' and miners' district organizations. The boards vote by sides and, in order to avoid a deadlock, they usually provide for the appointment of a permanent or ad hoc independent chairman. The agreement of 1926 made between the Durham Coal Owners' Association and the Durham County Mining Federation may be cited as an example. The agreement merely stipulates that a District Board shall be established, consisting of such number of members as may be determined by the parties, and that the rules of procedure shall include a provision for the appointment of an independent chairman and for voting by sides. According to a well established

[27] The Board of Trade, *Report on Rules of Voluntary Conciliation and Arbitration Boards and Joint Committees*, 1910 (CD. 5346), pp. 87-90; *cf.* the Ministry of Labor, *Report on Collective Agreements*, 1934, vol. i, pp. 32-81.

custom in the district an umpire, a chairman, and a vice chairman are annually appointed, together with a secretary for each side of the Board. This Board meets ordinarily in quarterly sessions to consider and decide upon all claims for a change in the county rates of wages and upon any other questions that may be referred to it by either party, except those falling within the jurisdiction of the separate joint standing committee. Questions submitted to the Board are stated in writing and may be supported by verbal, documentary, or such other evidence as the parties may desire to submit and as the Board may deem relevant. If the Board fail to agree on any question the independent chairman is called in at an adjourned meeting, and after further discussion he gives a final decision which is binding for a certain specified period of time.[28]

4. Coal Mines National Industrial Board

Above the district conciliation boards is the Coal Mines National Industrial Board, which was established in November, 1930, under Part IV of the Coal Mines Act, 1930, with power to investigate and report on any dispute arising over a proposed agreement on wages or on any other working conditions after such dispute has failed of settlement through the ordinary conciliation arrangement existing in the mining district concerned. The Board consists of 17 members appointed by the Board of Trade, with Sir Harold Morris, President of the Industrial Court, as chairman. The other members were appointed after consultations with the Mining Association and the Miners' Federation each as to six members,[29] the Federation of British Industries and

[28] The Ministry of Labor, *Report on Collective Agreements*, 1934, vol. i, pp. 75-81; the Board of Trade, *Report on Rules of Voluntary Conciliation and Arbitration Boards and Joint Committees*, 1910, pp. 91-3.

[29] The Miners' Federation is represented on the Board, but the Mining Association declined such representation; the *Ministry of Labor Gazette*, December, 1930, p. 441, Jan., Feb., 1931, pp. 7, 50.

the Association of British Chambers of Commerce as to one member, and the General Council of the Trades Union Congress, the Cooperative Union, and the National Confederation of Employers' Organizations each as to one. The Board, which sits in private, has so far issued nine reports covering disputes in South Wales, Scotland, Lancashire and other districts. In one case the South Wales Mine Owners' Association declined to accept the report issued by the Board in August, 1934.[80]

C. The Principle of Wage Determination

The long practice of collective bargaining in the coal-mining industry developed a well defined principle of wage determination. In the early 'Seventies the Northumberland and Durham coal trades had agreed to effect changes in wages according to the selling prices of coal either through the conciliation boards themselves or by arbitration. This method spread into other districts until by 1879 it had become a common practice in all the principal coal fields of the country. Early in the 'Eighties a reaction set in, especially in Yorkshire, Lancashire, and the Midlands where the militant trade unionists who believed that wages should be the first charge on industry, were dissatisfied with the " bottomless " reductions in wages according to the market price of coal. By 1910 the sliding scale system had practically come to an end, the general changes in wages being effected by means of percentage addition to, or reductions from, certain basic rates prevailing at a particular date in the district concerned, with provisions, in some districts, for minimum and maximum percentages upon such basic rates. This method prevailed until 1917, when the coal-mining industry was taken over by the Government and wage increases were granted on a uniform national basis in order to meet the

[80] The *Ministry of Labor Gazette*, Aug., Nov., 1934, pp. 270, 395.

increased cost of living. Under the National Wage Agreement of 1921 there was adopted a new principle which has since been adhered to throughout the country.

Under the terms of the National Wage Agreement of 1921 wages were to be regulated by district conciliation boards. This regulation was in the form of a percentage of the basic rates prevailing in each district in accordance with the proceeds of the industry as ascertained by returns to be made by the owners and checked by joint test audits of the owners' books by independent accountants appointed by each side of the conciliation board. A standard wage was payable to each grade of workers and a corresponding standard profit to the owner, the standard profit to be 17 per cent of the total cost of the standard wages. In no district should wages fall below 20 per cent above the standard wage, and if any rates determined according to the terms of the agreement did not provide a subsistence wage to the low-paid day workers such additional allowances should be made per shift worked as the Board or the independent chairman might deem necessary. Any surplus remaining after the payment of the standard wages, standard profits, and other costs of production was to be divided between the men and the owners in the proportion of 83-17. If, during any accounting period, the proceeds of the industry after the costs of production and the standard wages were paid, should not be large enough to yield the owners their standard profits, the deficiency was to be carried forward to the next accounting period as a first charge on the then available surplus.[81]

[81] The National Board for the Coal Industry, established under the National Wage Agreement of 1921, ruled that the coal mining industry comprised all the operation of the coal mines including the incidental raising of other products, but excluding such activities as coke ovens, by-product plants, selling agencies, farms, and cottages. The proceeds of the industry included all sales and transfers, not only of coal, but also of such other products as mineral waters. The standard wages were

Under the terms of the national agreement of June, 1924, the standard profit was reduced from 17 to 15 per cent, while the minimum percentage of basic rates was increased from 20 to 33 per cent, and the surplus proceeds were to be allocated to wages at 88, instead of 83 per cent. In the ascertainment of any surplus proceeds the items of reduction to make up for a previously deficient standard profit were to include (1) the costs of production other than wages, as before, (2) standard wages plus the minimum percentages, instead of the standard wages alone, (3) standard profits and a minimum profit corresponding to the minimum percentage of wages, instead of the standard profits alone. In no case was more than one-third of any surplus proceeds in any single accounting period to be used to make up the loss resulting from previously deficient standard profit. In the latter part of 1924, although coal prices dropped, the coal owners were obliged to pay the minimum rates of wages irrespective of the agreed proportions in which the proceeds of the industry were to be divided. It was this deficiency that caused the termination of the agreement of 1924 and finally led to the General Strike of 1926. The minimum percentages on the basic rates as fixed in the district agreements after the General Strike were, in some districts, the same as, and in others, higher than, those under the 1921 Agreement, but were in all cases lower than those under the Agreement of 1924. The general principles of wage regulation laid down in the 1921 Agreement were, however, adhered to throughout the country.

those paid to all colliery workers at the basic rates and percentages, but did not include the remuneration of the clerical and administrative staffs. The costs of production other than wages included such items as timber, stores, depreciation, renewal, damage, royalties, and the various obligations imposed by Acts of Parliament, but did not include interest, the income tax, or the corporation profit tax. *Cf. National Board for the Coal Industry*, the Chichester Press, London, 1921; *The Ministry of Labor*, "Report on Collective Agreements," 1934, vol. i, pp. 75-81.

3. THE RAILWAY INDUSTRY

A. The Traffic Grades

1. Historical Note

The railway industry has two different sets of negotiation machinery for its two main functions, namely, traffic service and maintenance work. In both cases they are highly organized in respect of the national issue of standard wages and other standard conditions of service with due devolution of powers for the settlement of local disputes. The high centralization is, however, a comparatively recent development growing out of the particular nature of the industry. As we have seen the railways accept more discipline by the State than does any other industry, and the idea that collective bargaining is inimical to that discipline has been a serious obstacle in the development of railway trade unionism.[32] Secondly the railway industry is governed by a long series of official hierarchies receiving instructions from, and reporting back to headquarters. This procedure is not followed by other industries, where responsible managers are more or less on the spot to deal with labor questions as they arise. Under such circumstances it has been almost impossible to secure local action by union branches, and when effective trade unionism was introduced into the railway industry it was on a practically national scale and compelled the railway companies to recognize its power by virtue of its immediate concern with the State and the community at large. Thirdly, the railway industry is not a single but a composite industry including as it does a large number of different trades, which have taken a long time to devise a joint machinery owing to their divergent interests.

[32] As late as 1892 a railway manager considered trade unionism "totally incompatible" with the railway service. "You might as well expect to have trade unionism in Her Majesty's Army." Summaries of evidence taken before the Royal Commission on Labor, 1894, p. 228.

It was not until 1871 that the Amalgamated Society of Railway Servants was formed with a small number of members, not more than 20,000 among a quarter of a million railway workers.[33] It did not adopt a strike policy until 1880. The first sign of active trade unionism did not appear until after 1889, when the General Railway Workers' Union was formed to organize unskilled workers not eligible for the Amalgamated Society. The first "All Grades" movement was started in 1896, and the second in 1906, when the railway unions made a demand for an eight-hour day with increased pay for overtime and for Sunday work and a demand for recognition of the trade unions by the railway companies. The companies' refusal to meet the union officials led to the threat of a national strike in October, 1907. The strike was averted by the intervention of the Government. A settlement was reached by some 11 railway companies and the three principal railway unions, namely, the Amalgamated Society of Railway Servants, the Associated Society of Locomotive Engineers and Firemen, and the General Railway Workers' Union, covering in all about 420,000 workers.[34] Under the terms of the settlement each of the companies was to have its own separate system of sectional and central conciliation boards for the purpose of dealing with questions of wages and hours of labor. The trade unions as such, however, were not recognized, their officials being definitely prevented from taking part in the operation of the conciliation scheme under the provision that the workers' representatives on the boards should be those actually employed by the companies concerned.

[33] *The Railway Review*, Aug. 5, 1921; *cf.* Herbert Tracey, "The Railwaymen in Action," *The Labor Magazine*, June, 1924, p. 51; *cf.* G. W. Alcock, *Fifty Years of Railway Trade Unionism*, chs. 2-3.

[34] *The 7th Report of Proceedings under the Conciliation Act, 1896, for 1909*, p. 3; *cf.* the 1st Report of the same, p. 22.

As the unions grew in strength the question of recognition became a burning issue. The pot boiled over in August, 1911, when a national strike actually took place in the railway service. The Government again intervened, a Royal Commission was appointed to report on the actual operation of the 1907 conciliation scheme,[35] and the House of Commons finally intervened by passing a resolution expressing the opinion that a joint meeting should take place between the railway companies and the unions for a discussion of the recommendations made by the Royal Commission. The railway companies finally agreed to a joint conference and an amended conciliation scheme was adopted. Under the new scheme the old central conciliation board was abolished, while the local conciliation procedure was considerably speeded up. The companies were required to give a written reply within a specified time to any request made by the workers for a change in the conditions of service. The sectional conciliation board was asked, in case of disagreement on any matter referred to it, to request the independent chairman appointed by the Board of Trade to give a final decision. This decision was to have a binding power for at least two years. While the trade unions still remained unrecognized, it was made possible for their officials to be elected to the secretaryship of the workers' side of the conciliation boards.[36]

Toward the end of 1913 the railway unions gave a year's notice of the termination of the conciliation scheme of 1911. The railway companies were ready to recognize the unions by agreeing to meet their representatives, not through the Board of Trade, but directly. The two railway unions [37]

[35] CD. 5922, 1911.

[36] *The 9th Report of Proceedings under the Conciliation Act, 1896*, pp. 5-7.

[37] In 1913 the Amalgamated Society of Railway Servants, the General Railway Workers' Union, and the United Pointsmen and Signalmen's

were not, however, able to settle upon a common policy. They agreed that the conciliation boards to be proposed should be competent to deal with questions of discipline and management, a power not granted to the existing conciliation boards, and that the system of deputation and petition should be abolished. But they were not able to come to an agreement on the question as to whether the boards should be composite or sectional in their constitution. The A. S. L. E. & F. made a categorical demand for a separate board on each railway for locomotive men, while the N. U. R. stood as firmly for the principle of a single all-grades board for each railway system.[88] The situation was radically changed immediately after the declaration of war in 1914, when the railways were taken over by the Government under the Regulation of Forces Act of 1871. With Government control of the railway industry, wage questions passed automatically from consideration by local conciliation boards to negotiation between the railway unions and the General Managers' Committee representing the Government. War bonuses were granted on a uniform national basis in order to meet the increased cost of living.[89]

The policy of industrial truce, to which the railway trade unions had agreed in October, 1914, was terminated early in 1919, and a national strike of the railwaymen took place in September over a national program of the N. U. R. for improved conditions of service. As a result of the settle-

Society united in a new organization, the National Union of Railwaymen, but the Associated Society of Locomotive Engineers and Firemen remained outside pursuing a policy of craft unionism as against the industrial unionism which the new organization had adopted; G. D. H. Cole and R. P. Arnot, *Trade Unionism in the Railways*, chs. 3-4.

[88] *The Railway Review*, April 3, 10, June 19, 1914.

[89] *Ibid.*, Aug. 7, 14, Sept. 18, Oct. 9, 1914; Charles W. Baker, *Government Control and Operation of Industry in Great Britain and the United States during the World War*, ch. 4.

ment of the strike it was agreed that during the period of Government control standard wages and other conditions of service affecting the conciliation grades should be dealt with by a Central Wages Board, and, on appeal, by a National Wages Board, and that local disputes should be settled by local committees. In 1920 the N. U. R. and the A. S. L. & F. came to an agreement as to the constitution of the local committees. It was proposed that these committees should have power to deal with questions of discipline and management, but to this the railway companies raised a strong objection.[40] In the meantime the Ministry of Transport had issued a statement outlining the Government policy on the future organization of the railways. It was proposed that the railways should be amalgamated into a limited number of groups, each group to be governed by a Board of Management to be composed of representatives of the shareholders and the railway employees, including both administrative and manual workers.[41] The Board as proposed by the Government was strongly opposed by the railway companies, while the railwaymen, who had stood strongly for the nationalization of the railway industry and for its joint control by the State and the workers,[42] were also reluctant to sit upon a capitalist board of directors. The proposed Board of Management was therefore made use of as an instrument for securing improvement in the proposed negotiation machinery. An agreement reached on May 3, 1921, between representatives of the railway companies, on the one hand, and of the N. U. R., the A. S. L.

[40] *The Ministry of Labor Gazette*, April, October, December, 1919, pp. 125, 416-8, 516; February, June, July, 1920, pp. 59, 290, 356; *The Railway Review*, January 23, 1920, February 11, 1921.

[41] *The Ministry of Transport, the Outlines of Proposals*, 1920 (CMD. 787).

[42] Cole and Arnot, *Trade Unionism in the Railways*, ch. 20, p. 105.

E. & F., and the Railway Clerks' Association, on the other, was subsequently given legal effect by the Railways Act, 1921 (11 & 12 Geo. 5, c. 55, Pt. 4).[43] The agreement continued in force until February, 1935, when it was replaced by another agreement now in force.

2. NEGOTIATION MACHINERY

A. The Local Departmental Committees

The Agreement of 1921,[44] as revised in 1935, regulates wages, hours, and other conditions of service of the traffic grades, including station masters and clerical staffs. Generally speaking, local questions or matters affecting individual railways are dealt with, in the first instance, by the workmen and the railway company concerned, while questions affecting the industry as a whole are taken up directly by the headquarters of the trade unions and the Railway Staff Conference, a committee of the general managers of the four principal railway companies.

For the purpose of local negotiation a Local Departmental Committee is established at each station or depot, where more than 75 regular workers are employed in a de-department. This Committee consists usually of four representatives of the workers and of the management. In case the employees number less than 75 they may appoint representatives to discuss matters with the local officials of the railway. The workers' representatives on the Departmental Committee, who are eleced by and from the adult staff having at least a year's continuous service with the company, hold office for a year. Each side of the Committee elects a secretary from among its own members, the

[43] Parl. Deb. Commons (142), 345, May 26, 1921, per Sir Eric Geddes; J. H. Thomas, "Railwaymen's Wages," *The Labor Magazine*, July, 1922, p. 99.

[44] *The Railway Review*, May 13, 27, June 10, August 26, 1921.

Committee meeting as often as circumstances may require. The primary objects of the Committee are to provide a recognized means of communication between the workers and the local management and to give the workers a wider interest in the determination of the conditions under which their work is performed. Thus the Committee may make suggestions for a more satisfactory arrangement of working hours, breaks, time recording, holidays, publicity, improvement in the method and organization of work, and general welfare work among the workers. Any proposal for a change in the conditions of service must be taken up, in the first instance, by the workmen and the company concerned. In the absence of a satisfactory answer within two weeks the question may be reported to the Local Committee, and, upon its failure to reach an agreement, to the Sectional Railway Council which ranks above the Departmental Committee.

B. The Sectional Railway Councils

Each railway has ordinarily five sectional railway councils, each council consisting of an equal number, usually 12, of representatives of the company and the workers concerned. Each side of the council elects its chairman from among its own members and appoints a secretary from any source that it pleases. The council meets as occasion may require, with at least two regular meetings in each year. The primary functions of the council are to deal with any of the following subjects affecting the workers represented on the council: (1) the application of national agreements in so far as the individual railway is concerned; (2) suggestions for improvement in the method or organization of work; (3) other matters in which the company and the workmen are mutually interested, such, for instance, as cooperation for increased business, greater efficiency and economy, the well-being of the staff, general principles governing recruits, promotion, discipline, and tenure of service; (4) appeals from the Departmental Committees. For the electoral purpose of the councils the various grades of workers employed on each railway are grouped in five sections, in each section they are further sub-divided into two or more groups having a common interest. Each of the groups then elects representatives to the sectional council for a term of three years on a proportional basis, but not more than 12 representatives in any case.[45] Should any of the councils fail to settle a ques-

[45] Five Sectional Railway Councils

Group of Grades	No. of Employees	No. of allotted representatives
No. 1		
A. Stationmasters, Agents, Yardmasters, and Traffic Controllers	950	2
B. Clerical Staff	7,200	7
C. Traffic and Good Department Inspectors and Foremen, etc.	1,250	2
D. Engineering and Signal Department Inspecors and Foremen, Locomotive, Carriage and Wagon Department Inspectors and Foremen	480	1
Total	9,880	12
No. 2		
A. Engine Drivers, Firemen, and Cleaners	12,000	10
B. Electric Train Motormen	.....	..
C. Shedmen and Hydraulicmen	2,100	2
Total	14,100	12
No. 3		
A. Signalmen, etc.	4,300	3
B. Guards and Shunter, etc	6,700	4
C. General Porters, Parcel Staff, etc.	5,400	3
D. Carriage and Wagon Examiners, Carriage Cleaners, Electric Lightmen, etc.	2,000	2
Total	18,400	12

tion referred to it, the case may be taken up by the trade union and the company concerned. If no agreement is reached by this group the question may be referred to a joint meeting of the Railway Staff Conference and the leaders of the trade unions. Ordinarily, however, questions coming before the sectional councils should not be carried beyond this stage unless the issues involve national agreements.

C. The Railway Staff National Council and the Railway Staff National Tribunal

As originally provided in the agreement of 1921 questions failing of settlement at a Sectional Council could be referred to a Railway Council and from there to the Central and National Wages Boards for final settlement. The Central Wages Board consisted of 16 members representing the four principal railway companies and the three railway unions, while the National Wages Board was composed of 17 members, 6 representing the railway companies, 6 the railway unions, 4 the railway users as represented by the Trades Union Congress General Council, the Cooperative Union, the Associated Chambers of Commerce, and the Federation of British Industries, and an independent chairman representing the Government. The National Wages Board sat in public for the hearing of cases but deliberated in private to arrive at its final decisions. Up to February, 1935, the Board had issued more than 160 awards, dealing mostly with

No. 4		
A. Goodsshed and Yard Staff	5,300	8
B. Cartage Staff	2,100	4
Total	7,400	12
No. 5		
A. Gangers, Sub-Gangers, and Undermen	8,100	9
B. Signal and Telegraph Linemen	1,700	3
Total	9,800	12

appeals from local decisions. There had been only two occasions on which the workers refused to accept the award of the Board.[46] It was complained, however, that the long process of negotiation caused delay in the settlement of disputes,[47] that it was open to the influence of organized propaganda, and that the National Wages Board was too large to act as a judicial body. The truth of the last charge was demonstrated early in 1933 when the railway companies demanded a reduction in wages, but the representative members of the Board were not able to agree on an award. The railway unions declined to accept the independent chairman's ruling.[48] It was in the light of these difficulties that the railway companies gave notice, on March 3, 1933, that they were about to terminate the reference of cases to the Central Wages Board, or, on appeal, to the National Wages Board. A new agreement was reached in February, 1935.[49]

Under the new agreement the Railway Council and the Central and National Wages Boards were abolished and their places were taken by a Railway Staff National Council and a Railway Staff National Tribunal. The National Council consists of 8 representatives of the four principal railway companies and 8 representatives of the three railway unions. It deals only with questions relating to standard salaries, wages, hours, and other conditions of service covered by national agreements, and may not deal with minor issues which fall under the jurisdiction of local negotiation machinery and which in no event should be carried beyond the stage of joint meetings between the Rail

[46] *The Annual Register for 1924*, p. 21; *The Amalgamated Engineering Union Monthly Journal*, Feb., 1924; the *Ministry of Labor Gazette*, Feb., 1933, pp. 46-7.

[47] *The Railway Review*, June 6, 1930.

[48] *The Ministry of Labor Gazette*, Feb., 1933, pp. 46-7.

[49] *Ibid.*, March, 1935, p. 89.

Staff Conference and the railway unions concerned. Questions coming before the National Council may not ordinarily be carried beyond the Council itself, though some classes of questions may, by the consent of the parties concerned, be referred for decision either to the chairman of the Railway Staff National Tribunal or to the Tribunal itself. The Tribunal consists of three members, one selected for each particular case by the railway companies, another by the trade unions from standing panels of persons previously nominated by them, with a chairman appointed by agreement between the companies and the unions, or, failing agreement, by the Minister of Labor. He may be appointed for a specified period of time or for each particular case. No official of the companies or of the trade unions is eligible for membership in the Tribunal, but the Tribunal may have the assistance of representatives of the parties sitting as assessors. Issues involving the interpretation of a national agreement as well as cases involving other than minor issues may, by agreement of the parties concerned, be referred to the chairman of the National Tribunal, while the Tribunal itself may hear and decide cases that have been adjudged by the National Council or by the chairman of the National Tribunal to be issues of major importance to the railway company or companies or to the railway trade union or unions concerned. The decisions of the Tribunal are to be printed and published, but its hearings are private, unless otherwise decided by the Tribunal or by the parties.

The broad lessons of the new agreement are that local disputes should be settled locally as far as possible, and that in dealing with national issues the highest court of appeal should be strictly judicial in its composition and its hearings.

It is significant that when the railway companies gave notice of the termination of the agreement of 1921 they did not desire to interfere with the work of the existing local negotiation machinery, the mutual advantages of which have been fully recognized by them. A recent examination of the minutes of proceedings of the Local Departmental Committees shows that the subject matter of their discussions has changed from purely personal grievances to matters of more general interest, such, for instance, as the best method of dealing with traffic or the possibilities of increased business. In some cases the provision of cheap excursion fares was discussed as a means of increasing business, and in others the extension of areas for the collection and delivery of goods. In one case the chairman of the employer's side expressed his appreciation of the business increase that had "undoubtedly" been brought about by the efforts of the workers. In other words the actual experiences of the workers and the responsibility of the local management were pooled by means of the Local Departmental Committees. The sectional railway councils have also been generally recognized as of great value, especially as a medium for the satisfactory application of national agreements.[50]

D. The Shopmen and the Power House Staff

The railway shopmen are employed on the manufacturing and repairing sides of the industry, such as the carriage, wagon, shed, engineering, signal, telegraph, dock, and marine departments of the various railway companies. They are organized in a number of trade unions, whose policies of organization are not identical. The question of setting up joint negotiation machinery for them was taken up as early as September, 1914, between representatives of the National Union of Railwaymen and a large number of craft unions, but they did not agree upon a common policy until June 1926. Early in 1925 the Railway Staff Conference had submitted

[50] *The Railway Review*, June 29, 1923; December 4, 1928, October 11, 1929, January 18, 1930.

an outline of negotiation machinery to the various trade unions having members in the railway shops. The general object of the scheme, it was explained, was to provide full facilities for discussion and for the settlement of all questions of wages, hours, and other conditions of labor in the shops, except matters of management and discipline. Questions of national application were to be discussed by the Railway Staff Conference, on the one hand, and the trade unions jointly, on the other, while local disputes were to be settled by local committees to be established at each shop, works, and department. These Committees were to consist of an equal number of nominees of the company and elected representatives of employees in the particular grades. In the case of arbitration the reference was to be to the Industrial Court. The craft unions were desirous of limiting the scheme to their members only, but this was refused by the railway companies. Thereupon representatives of the craft unions and the N. U. R. met in conference, and finally came to a common understanding on the questions of membership and negotiation machinery in June, 1926. According to the agreement all questions affecting the railway shopmen as a whole were to be negotiated jointly by the unions concerned, but purely craft questions were to be handled by individual unions separately.[51] This agreement, although criticised by members of the N. U. R. as being contrary to their "All Grades" movement, was eventually accepted by the annual general meeting of the union held at Carlisle in July, 1927.[52] The draft proposal of the Railway Staff Conference was accordingly signed on August 15, 1927, by representatives of the railway companies and of the various trade unions.

[51] *The Amalgamated Engineering Union Journal*, Aug., Sept., 1924, April, July, Sept., Nov., 1925, July, Aug., 1926, Jan., June, 1927, May, 1928; *The Ministry of Labor Gazette*, Sept., 1927, p. 329.

[52] *The Railway Review*, July 1, 15, 22, 1927.

A week later a similar agreement was made, covering the power house staffs.[53]

The agreement covering the shopmen provides for the establishment, at each shop where more than 75 and less than 150 workers are employed, of a Shop Committee consisting of an equal number of representatives of the railway company and the employees. The workers' representatives are elected for a term of three years by those who have had at least a year's continuous service with the company. In case the workers number less than 75 they may appoint a representative to take up matters with the local management. Where there are two or more shop committees in a department at any plant or depot, there may be appointed a works committee consisting of not more than ten elected representatives of the various shop committees and of an equal number of nominees of the company. As for those workers who are employed in small detachments at various centers of a railway line a Departmental Line Committee may be established on the basis of the whole line. Each side of the various committees elects its chairman and secretary from among its own members, the committees meeting as circumstances may require. Questions falling within the scheme must, in the first instance, be dealt with by the foreman of the shop and the workers immediately concerned. If they

[53] The parties to the agreement are: on the employers' side, the Great Western Railway, London and North-Eastern Railway, London, Midland, and Scottish Railway, Southern Railway, and the Metropolitan Railway; on the employees' side, the National Union of Railwaymen, Amalgamated Engineering Union, National Society of Coppersmiths, Braziers, and Metal Workers, Electrical Trades Union, United Pattern Makers' Association, National Union of Foundry Workers, United Operative Plumbers and Domestic Engineers' Association, Workers Union, Amalgamated Machine, Engine, and Glaziers' Society, Amalgamated Union of Building Trade Workers, Shipconstructors and Shipwrights' Association, and the Federation of Engineering and Shipbuilding Trades comprising about 25 trade unions.

fail to settle the question it may be successively referred to the shop, works, or the departmental line committees, and finally to the National Railway Shopmen's Council, whose primary purpose is to deal with questions of national application. The Council consists of the Railway Staff Conference and of 10 delegates appointed by the trade unions, 3 by the N. U. R., 2 each by the Amalgamated Engineering Union and the Engineering and Shipbuilding Federation, and 1 each by the Foundry Workers' Union, the Electrical Trades Union, and the Pattern Makers' Union. The Council meets regularly in January, April, July, and October, in addition to occasional special meetings. Pending consideration of disputes by these organizations or arbitration by the Industrial Court no stoppage of work is to take place.[54]

Similar arrangements are made for those workers employed at the electricity generation stations and sub-stations.[55]

The negotiation machineries for the shopmen and the power-house staffs were put into full operation in July, 1928.[56] As a medium of discussion between management and staff they have proved on the whole to be of great value both to the employers and workers, although in some cases it is complained that the scope of discussion by the com-

[54] *The Amalgamated Engineering Union Monthly*, Nov., Dec., 1927, Jan.-March, 1928, Oct., 1930.

[55] *The Railway Review*, July 29, 1927, Aug. 23, 1929.

[56] The number of committees established on the various railways in June, 1928, was reported to be as follows:

Railways	No. of Shop & Works Committees	Committees	No. of Com- Power Houses
L. N. E. R.	188	13	3
L. M. S. R.	206	9	5
G. W. R.	122	6	2
Southern R.	55	5	3
Metro. R.	1	—	1

The Railway Review, July 29, 1928.

mittees is too limited, since such important matters, for instance, as piece prices are not included.[57]

4. THE IRON AND STEEL MANUFACTURING INDUSTRY

A. Pig Iron Manufacture

The iron and steel manufacturing industry is highly organized on both sides by employers and workmen. On the employers' side the principal organization dealing with labor questions is the Iron and Steel Employers' Association, which was formed early in 1922 by an amalgamation of leading associations of iron masters in the country.[58] On the workers' side the main organizations are the Iron and Steel Trades Confederation and the National Union of Blastfurnacemen, Ore Miners, Coke Workers, and Kindred Trades. The maintenance craftsmen are for the most part organized in the various craft unions, while the semi-skilled workers are enrolled partly in the Confederation and partly in the general unions, such as the National Union of General and Municipal Workers and the Transport and General Workers' Union. The Iron and Steel Trades Confederation, which claims to represent about two-thirds of the organized workers in the industry, was formed in 1917 by the amalgamation of some leading unions, the principal of which was the British Steel Smelters' Union originally founded in Lanarkshire in 1886.[59]

[57] *Ibid.*, Aug. 16, 1929.

[58] The Steel Ingot Makers' Association, the North of England Iron and Steel Manufacturers' Association, the Midland Steel Rolling Mill Employers' Association, the Scottish Steel Makers' Wages Association, and the employer members of the Conciliation Boards in the West of Scotland and the North East district of England.

[59] S. Webb, *The History of Trade Unionism*, 1920, ed. p. 491; Herbert Tracey, "Arthur Pugh, A Statesman of Industry," *Labor Magazine*, Nov., 1925, p. 291; the Balfour Committee, *Survey of Industrial Relations*, pp. 267-9.

Although the industry is well organized in capital and labor it is not really a single industry, but an aggregation of a large number of different trade groups widely distributed in separate counties. The negotiation machinery obtaining in the industry varies from one section to another and from district to district. It may be broadly classified under three headings: (1) joint conferences between organized employers and workmen, (2) conciliation and arbitration boards, and (3) joint industrial council.

In most of the important districts of pig iron production general questions of wages and other conditions of employment are directly taken up at joint conferences between employers' associations in the districts concerned and the National Union of Blastfurnacemen, Ore Miners, Coke Workers, and Kindred Trades. In Cleveland and Durham, the most important pig iron district, such collective bargaining has been in operation since 1872, and wages have been regulated by a sliding scale based on the selling price of certain standard products.[60] Should any dispute arise over the operation of the sliding scale system or as to the rates of wages applying at any particular plant it may be decided either by a joint committee consisting of an equal number of representatives of the employers and the blastfurnacemen, or, failing an agreement, by an umpire mutually agreed upon. A similar arrangement in principle prevails in Cumberland, North Lancashire, North Lincolnshire, North and South Staffordshire, and the Northampton districts.

In the West of Scotland a conciliation board, which has been in operation since 1900 and in the Nottingham district since 1906, also regulates wages by selling-price sliding scale. General questions may be submitted to and decided by the

[60] Von Schulze-Gaevernitz, *Social Peace*, pp. 207-12, 221; see *infra*, p. 257.

boards. In case of disagreement, they are then referred to a neutral chairman whose decision is final and binding.[61]

B. Iron and Steel Production

The conditions of employment in this section of the industry, namely, iron puddling, iron and steel rolling, steel melting, and steel sheet rolling, are covered by agreements made in most cases directly between employers' associations and trade unions, in some cases by conciliation boards, and still another by a joint industrial Council. The Iron and Steel Trades Employers' Association covers the heavy steel industry in England and the West of Scotland, and the wrought iron trade on the North East Coast. The heavy steel industry in the Sheffield district and iron and steel manufacture in South Wales and Monmouthshire are covered by separate employers' associations, while iron puddling and iron and steel rolling in the Midlands and the West of Scotland, and steel sheet rolling in South Wales and other districts are covered by conciliation boards. A joint industrial council governs the tin plate and sheet industry in South Wales. The trade union most generally party to these arrangements is the Iron and Steel Trades Confederation.

Joint Conferences. The workers employed at various steel melting shops and steel rolling mills on the North East Coast,[62] in Cumberland, Lancashire, South and West Yorkshire, Lincolnshire, the Midlands, and the West of Scotland are governed by long established practices, which have never been formally incorporated in written agreements, with the exception of the agreement that was entered into on March 3, 1925, between the Iron and Steel Trades Employers' Association and the National Union of General and Municipal

[61] *Report on Rules of Voluntary Conciliation and Arbitration Boards and Joint Committees*, 1910, pp. 134, 146, 148, 151.

[62] Including the wrought iron trade on the North East Coast which was regulated by a Conciliation Board from 1869 to 1922.

Workers.[63] The negotiation machinery as provided in this agreement is briefly as follows. Questions arising at individual works are dealt with, in the first instance, by the works management and the workers concerned, and, failing a settlement, by the employers' and the workers' organizations. If the question is not one of general principle and affects only the works in question the matter is generally referred to a neutral committee composed of two neutral representatives of the organized employers and workmen. After careful consideration of the cases presented by each side the committee issues a memorandum of settlement, which is subject to confirmation by the respective trade associations. Failing an agreement the committee may refer the case back to the associations or submit it to arbitration. When questions of a general character arise they may be dealt with by joint conferences between the employers' and the workers' associations, and, failing a settlement, by arbitration. Pending these negotiations no stoppage of work is to take place either by a strike or a lockout.[64]

Conciliation Boards. The iron puddlers and millmen in the Midlands are governed by the Midland Iron and Steel Wages Board. The Board, originally formed in 1872, following the good example of the Conciliation Board for the North of England,[65] was reconstituted in 1886 under the

[63] There is another agreement establishing similar practices for the blastfurnacemen and iron and steel workers in South Wales. The agreement was made in December, 1919, superseding the South Wales Iron and Steel Wages Board which had been in existence since 1890, between the South Wales and Monmouthshire Iron and Steel Manufacturers' Association, on the one hand, and the Iron and Steel Trades Confederation, the South Wales Blastfurnacemen, and a number of general labor unions, on the other. *Report on Collective Agreements*, 1934, vol. i, pp. 168-175.

[64] *Ibid.*, pp. 142-159.

[65] *Report on Rules of Conciliation and Arbitration Boards and Joint Committees*, 1910, pp. 156, 161, 166, 168, 169, 175; von Schulze-Gaevernitz, *Social Peace*, pp. 213-16.

present title, covering the Midlands, south Yorkshire, and part of Lancashire. Its objects are " to discuss, and, if necessary, to arbitrate on wages or any other matter affecting the respective interests of the employers and operatives, and by conciliatory means to interpose its influence to prevent disputes and put an end to any that may arise." The Board, consisting of one employer and one workman representing each plant joining the Board, annually elects a chairman from the employers' section, a vice chairman from the workers' side, an independent President, and a Standing Joint Committee. Any question arising at a particular plant is discussed, in the first instance, by those immediately concerned, and, failing a settlement, by the standing joint committee, and finally by the independent President. If the question is of a general character it may be referred by the committee to the full Board, and if the Board fails to settle, it may be decided by the independent President. Pending these negotiations no withdrawal of labor is to take place.[66]

Similar conciliation boards have been in operation for the malleable iron works and steel sheet rolling mills in the West of Scotland since 1897, the steel sheet rolling industry in South Wales and Monmouthshire since 1926, and the galvanizing of iron and steel sheet industry in South Wales, the Midlands, and the North East Coast since 1921.

Joint Industrial Council. In the tin plate and sheet making industry, which is confined almost entirely to South Wales, collective bargaining has been in operation since 1872 and has reached a high degree of development. The industry was governed by a conciliation board from 1899 to 1919, when the board was reorganized as a Joint Industrial Council.[67] The Council carries on its work largely through

[66] *Report on Collective Agreements*, 1910, pp. 73-85; *Report on Collective Agreements*, 1934, vol. i, pp. 159-165.

[67] The trade unions represented on the Council are the Iron and Steel Trades Confederation, the Transport and General Workers' Union, the

a standing joint committee, which meets bi-monthly to deal with all questions coming within the jurisdiction of the Council. The joint committee acts in many cases through special sub-committees appointed for various sections of the industry, and reports to the annual meeting of the full Council which is held in May.

C. The Selling-Price Sliding-Scale System

The iron and steel manufacturing industry has a long record of peace and has often been referred to as the brightest spot in the country's industrial relations.[68] This is primarily due to " the complete recognition of trade unionism, unequivocal observance of agreements, and the mutual acceptance of the principle of arbitration as a final resort in the settlement of disputes." [69]

Another contributing factor is the long established practice of regulating wages by a sliding scale based on the selling prices of certain standard products. This system of wage regulation was described by Professor Munro as " the greatest discovery in the distribution of wealth since Ricardo's enunciation of the law of rent." [70] It is a natural product of the practice of collective bargaining in an industry that is most sensitive to the influence of the trade

National Union of General and Municipal Workers, the Welsh Artizans' Association, and the Amalgamated Engineering Union, while the employers are represented by the Welsh Plate and Sheet Manufacturers' Association.

[68] *British Wages*, Trade Promotion Series, no. 42, Washington, D. C., 1926, p. 10.

[69] A summary of the evidence given before the Balfour Committee on Industry and Trade by Mr. (now Sir) Arthur Pugh, then General Secretary of the Iron and Steel Trades Confederation, in the issue of *Man and Steel*, a monthly publication by the Confederation, for March, 1925.

[70] " Sliding Scales in the Iron Industry," a paper read by Prof. Munro before the Manchester Statistical Society, *Transactions*, 1885, p. 26.

cycle. In such an industry wage demands naturally follow fluctuations in the market price, both employers and workmen pointing to the selling price as an index of the state of their trade. When this is repeated time and again, whether at a conference table or before a court of arbitration, it is only common sense to suggest, in order to save time and trouble, the establishment of a scale of automatic changes in wages in accordance with fluctuations in the market prices. This was what actually occurred in the North of England where the first selling-price sliding scale was adopted by the Conciliation Board in 1872. It now applies in one form or another to the whole of the pig iron, wrought iron, steel, and tin plate trades, except the Sheffield steel industry.

According to the broad principle of the system a standard selling price for a certain defined standard product is fixed for a corresponding standard rate of wages, each rise or fall of a certain agreed amount in the selling price automatically causing a corresponding fluctuation of a certain percentage above the standard rate of wages. For this purpose the sliding-scale agreements between organized employers and workmen usually provide that joint accountants shall, every two or three months, ascertain from the books of certain specified firms in the district concerned the net average prices of the defined standard products during the preceding period. After the War a system of output bonuses and a special allowance to low paid workers was adopted in addition to the sliding scales.[71]

The selling-price sliding scale system has been adversely criticised on various grounds. It is based on the theory, it is said, that supply and demand should determine wages, while, according to the general trade union view, an adequate wage should be the first charge on the industry, irrespective

[71] For details see *Report on Collective Agreements*, 1934, vol. i, pp. 124-159; *Report on Collective Agreements*, 1910, pp. 62-85.

of market conditions. Secondly, the wage fluctuations resulting from the operation of the scheme bear no close relationship to the cost of living, which is determined by a different set of circumstances. Thirdly, the march of civilization should in normal times result in the lowering of prices together with a higher standard of living. Fourthly, although the system puts the workers in the position of a partnership with the employers and gives the former a share in the prosperity of the industry, it denies them a voice in the management of the industry. Furthermore the partnership of employers and workmen may tend to keep prices up to a level that is detrimental to the general interest of the community.[72] On the other hand, the system has been defended by the argument that it has at any rate secured for the industry a long period of peace and supplied it with the most effective means of meeting foreign competition. Furthermore wages in the industry are not entirely dependent upon market conditions, because the sliding scales do not apply to the basic rates, which are stable and really the first charge on the industrial proceeds.[73] Perhaps there is truth on both sides; but the most convincing fact is that the overwhelming majority of the iron workers are not prepared to part with the system.

5. THE ENGINEERING AND SHIPBUILDING INDUSTRY

A. The Negotiation Machinery on National Issues of Wages and Other Conditions of Service

As in the railway industry the negotiation machinery in the engineering and shipbuilding industry has reached a high degree of logical development. Generally speaking,

[72] The coal miners had tried sliding scales, but abandoned them mainly on the grounds mentioned here; see The Trade Union Congress, *Industrial Negotiations and Agreements*, pp. 46-50.

[73] W. A. Stevens, "A Defence of Price Sliding Scales," an article published in *Man and Steel*, Oct., 1923.

local disputes are dealt with locally, subject to national review, while national questions on wages and other conditions of employment are dealt with directly at joint conferences between the national authorities of the organized employers and workmen. Another similar feature in the two industries is the widely recognized institution of works committees, which play an important role for peace in both industries. A third point of similarity is the fact that the national negotiation machinery in the engineering and shipbuilding industry is also a recent development owing to the particular nature of the industry.

As we have seen the engineering industry covers a wide range of trades which, although linked together by their common operation on metal materials, are nevertheless widely different in their finished products. This diverse nature of the industry was a great obstacle to the development of trade unionism. As early as 1822 there were numerous trade societies among the engineers, smiths, patternmakers, and other skilled mechanics at various engineering centers, such as London, Manchester, New Castle, Bradford. All of them were in keen competition. The movement for "one concentrated union" achieved a great result in 1851 when a large number of engineering trade unions were merged in the Amalgamated Society of Engineers, Machinists, Smiths, Millwrights, and Patternmakers, with a definite policy of restricting systematic overtime and piecework. Various independent societies, such as the Boilermakers, the Steam Engine Makers, and the Cooperative Smiths, declined, however, to join the new organization, with the result that as late as 1897 there were altogether 268 engineering unions with a total membership of only about 288,000. Similar conditions of disorganization prevailed among the employers who, by the end of the 'Eighties, had in most of the districts, associations mainly of a technical character. Wage negotiations under these conditions were carried on between individual employers and the local branches of the various trade unions.

This situation was fundamentally changed in 1897 by the great engineering strike which took place nominally over the London engineers' demand for an eight-hour day but really over the issues of systematic overtime and piecework. The strike was settled by an agreement signed, on January 28, 1898, between representatives of the Engineering Employers' Federation, formed in 1896,[74] on the one hand, and representatives of the Amalgamated Society of Engineers, the Steam-Engine Makers' Society, and the United Machine Makers' Association, on the other. The agreement recognized the principle of local collective negotiation on wage questions and placed certain general principles of employment on a national basis. It was agreed that the federated employers should not interfere with the proper functions of the trade union, and the trade unions were prohibited from interfering with the employers in their management of business. The employers and workmen were entitled to work piecework on the understanding that the piece prices should be agreed upon between the employer and employed concerned, with each man's day rate guaranteed, irrespective of his piece earnings. Overtime could be worked with extra pay, but systematic overtime was to be deprecated as an ordinary method of production. On the question of wage negotiations it was agreed that, while the trade unions disclaimed any right to interfere with the wages of workers other than their own members, they should have the right to fix the rate of wages at which their members might accept work. General alterations in the district rates were therefore to be determined by negotiation between the employers'

[74] Labor Research Department, *Labor and Capital in the Engineering Trade*, p. 10.

and the workers' local associations. Provisions for avoiding disputes both by local measures and by national review were then made. Should any dispute arise at a particular plant a deputation of the workers concerned were to be received by their employer for a mutual discussion of the matter at issue. Failing an agreement the question might be referred either to the secretary of the trade union for discussion with the local secretary of the employers' association, or to a local conference between the employers' and workmen's associations concerned. All questions, including wage issues, failing of settlement at a local conference, might then be referred to a Central Conference at York between the Executive Board of the Engineering Employers' Federation and the national authorities of the trade unions. No stoppage of work was to take place pending this procedure.[75]

The agreement of 1898, although subsequently revised, continued in force until February, 1917, when wage negotiations in the engineering industry were placed on a national basis under the National Wages Agreement.[76]

The National Wages Agreement was terminated in November, 1920, but general wage negotiations affecting the engineering industry as a whole have since continued to be conducted on a national basis between the Engineering and Allied Employers' National Federation, on the one hand, and the national organizations of the workers jointly, on the other. The Employers' National Federation was reported in 1923 to represent about 2,600 engineering firms with an employment capacity of about 750,000 workers. On the workers' side the principal organizations are the Amal-

[75] *The 10th Report on Strikes and Lockouts*, 1897, pp. 151-5; *The Report on Collective Agreements*, 1910, pp. 85-91; *cf. Second Report on Rules of Voluntary Conciliation and Arbitration Boards and Joint Committees*, 1910, pp. xii-xiii.

[76] *Ante*, p. 87.

gamated Engineering Union, the National Union of Foundry Workers, the United Society of Boilermakers and Iron and Steel Shipbuilders, and the Electrical Trades Union. There is in addition a large number of unions which act jointly with the principal organizations in national negotiation with the employers.[77]

The national negotiation machinery in the shipbuilding industry, naturally concentrated on or very near the coasts, the North East Coast, the Clyde Side, and Belfast in Northern Ireland[78] is also of comparatively recent development. It was not until 1909 that a joint machinery covering the industry as a whole was agreed upon between the representatives of the Shipbuilding Employers' Federation and some 17 leading trade unions. The agreement provided for cen-

[77] The Amalgamated Engineering Union was formed in July, 1920, by a combination of ten engineering unions, namely, the Amalgamated Society of Engineers, Steam-Engine Makers' Society, United Machine Makers' Association, Amalgamated Instrument Makers' Society, Amalgamated Tool Makers, Engineers, and Machinists, Associated Brassfounders, Turners, Fitters, Finishers, and Coppersmiths' Society, East of Scotland Brassfounders' Society, London United Metal Turners, Fitters and Finishers' Society, North of England Brass Turners, Fitters and Finishers' Society, and the United Kingdom Society of Amalgamated Smiths and Strikers. The National Union of Foundry Workers was also formed in 1920 by the amalgamation of the Friendly Society of Ironfounders, the Associated Ironfounders, and the Amalgamated Society of Coremakers. The other craft unions are the United Pattermakers' Association, the National Brass and Metal Mechanics, the National Society of Coppersmiths, Braziers, and Metal Workers, the National Union of Vehicle Builders, the Amalgamated Society of Woodcutting Machinists, and the National Union of Sheet Metal Workers and Braziers. The unskilled and female workers are mostly organized in the National Union of General and Municipal Workers and the Workers' Union section of the Transport and General Workers' Union. The Federation of Engineering and Shipbuilding Trades also sometimes associates itself in the engineering joint trades movement. *Cf.* Committee on Industry and Trade, *Survey of Industrial Relations*, pp. 269-70.

[78] Committee on Industry and Trade, *Survey of Metal Industries*, ch. 4, *Further Factors in Industrial and Commercial Efficiency*, p. 205.

tral conference between the parties to the agreement for the settlement of national issues of wages and for an elaborate machinery for the avoidance of local disputes. The scheme was in broad outline similar to that prevailing in the engineering industry.[79] This agreement, with subsequent revisions, continued in force until November, 1926, when the Shipbuilding Employers' Federation entered into a new agreement with the Federation of Engineering and Shipbuilding Trades.[80]

There is no specific provision in the new agreement as to the procedure governing general wage fluctuations in the shipbuilding industry, but according to a well established practice such questions are dealt with directly by a Central Wages Conference between the national representatives of the Employers' Federation and the national organizations of the workers engaged in the industry. The Employers' Federation represents practically all of the important firms in the country, including the ship repairing industry on the Thames, Mersey, Bristol Channel, and at Manchester. On the workers' side some 24 trade unions, representing shipwrights, blacksmiths, woodcutting machinists, cabinet makers, french polishers, and unskilled workers, are associated in the Federation of Engineering and Shipbuilding Trades, established in 1889. There is a large number of organizations outside the Federation,[81] but they act jointly with the Federation in national negotiation on wages and other conditions of service.

[79] *Report on Collective Agreements*, 1910, pp. 92-96.

[80] *Report on Collective Agreements*, 1934, vol. i, pp. 263-80.

[81] Including the Amalgamated Engineering Union, the United Society of Boilermakers and Iron and Steel Shipbuilders, the Electrical Trades Union, the Amalgamated Society of Woodworkers, the National Amalgamated Society of Operative House and Ship Painters, the Plumbers, Glaziers and Domestic Engineers' Union.

The Central Wages Conference has been successful in many cases in bringing about important changes in the wages scheme without a strike or lockout, its procedure of negotiation being marked by "harmonious relationships" between the two sides.[82]

B. The Provisions for Avoiding Local Disputes

The provisions in the 1898 agreement for avoiding local disputes were amplified in June, 1922, by the agreements that settled the great engineering strike over the question of what is called the "Managerial Functions."[83] The new agreements recognized the shop stewards and works committees as an established institution in the engineering industry[84] by authorizing the workers at each of the federated engineering establishments to elect their representatives, or shop stewards, subject to the control of the trade unions that were parties to the agreements. For each department there may be set up a works committee consisting of not more than seven members each from the management and the shop stewards. If any question arises at a plant it is to be dealt with, in the first instance, by the worker and his foreman. Failing a settlement, the question may be taken up successively by the shop manager and the appropriate shop steward, the works committee, and the local and central conferences. The local conference is required to meet within a week to discuss any matter thus referred to it. The central conference meets regularly on the second Friday of each month to settle cases brought before it.

[82] The author is greatly obliged to the Secretary of the Shipbuilding Employers' Federation for his supply of information on this important subject.

[83] Report by a Court of Inquiry concerning the Engineering Dispute, 1922, CMD. 1653.

[84] As for the welfare work of the works committees see ch. 5, pp. 191-93.

It is expressly provided in the agreements that, whenever any alteration in the recognized working conditions in a particular workshop is contemplated, the management shall give the workers directly concerned, or their representatives in the shop, at least ten days' notice and shall afford an opportunity for mutual discussion of the matter in question. Should the discussion fail to bring about a settlement, work is to be continued under a temporary decision to be made by the management, pending settlement by the ordinary procedure under the provisions for avoiding disputes.[85]

Similar arrangements in broad outline prevail in the shipbuilding industry. If questions other than general wage fluctuations or piecework arise at a shipyard a deputation of the workers concerned is received by the employer within two days after the receipt of the application for an interview. Failing an agreement, a further meeting may be arranged between the employer, with or without the attendance of a representative of his association, and the official delegates of the workers' union concerned. Still failing a settlement the question may then be dealt with successively by a local conference between the employers' and the workers' organizations, a central conference between the national representatives of the employers' National Federation and the trade unions concerned, and finally, either by arbitration or by a General Conference between the representatives of the employers' National Federation and those of all the trade unions parties to the agreements. The General Conference, under an independent chairmanship appointed by mutual agreement or alternatively by the Minister of Labor, meets within two weeks to discuss the matter so referred.

Questions on piecework are required to be settled as far as possible by those immediately concerned. Failing a settle-

[85] *The Amalgamated Society of Engineers Monthly Journal,* July, 1919; *The Amalgamated Engineering Union Monthly,* July, 1922.

ment in this manner the matter may be dealt with by a neutral committee, and then successively by the local, central, and general conferences, excepting cases where the issues involve only the yard in question or a matter of interpretation of the district piece prices. In such cases the dispute may be referred to arbitration by mutual agreement after the local conference has failed to settle it. The arbitrator may be drawn from a panel of disinterested persons locally elected and he may be assisted by assessors. Demarcation questions are also settled primarily by the management and the workers concerned. Failing a settlement in this manner the management may give a temporary decision pending the final and binding decision of the matter by a joint committee. The joint committee consists of three representatives of the local employers' association and three representatives of each of the local trade unions concerned. Its decision is applicable only to the plant in question and is binding for a period of twelve months.

C. The Operation of the Negotiation Machinery in the Engineering Industry

A few examples illustrating the actual operation of the negotiation machinery in the engineering industry may show the impossibility of enforcing collective agreements without strict discipline imposed by efficient organization. They may also reveal the long process of negotiation between well organized employers and workmen, negotiation which, by bringing up the questions at issue for parliamentary discussion, enlightens the workers, on the one hand, as to the economic and financial conditions of the industry as a whole, and informs the financial interests, on the other, as to the human needs and common aspirations of labor.

The Hoe Strike Case. Toward the end of November, 1925, the shop stewards employed at the workshop of Messrs.

R. Hoe & Co. in London requested the management to cease working overtime. This step had been recommended by the London District Engineering Committee in response to the national application for an increase of 20s. a week, an increase then under negotiation between the national authorities of the engineering employers and workers. The company refused on the ground that the question was a matter for negotiation between the Employers' National Federation and the national authorities of the trade unions. The workers went out on strike without authorization from the central offices of their unions.[86] On February 25, 1926, a joint meeting was held by representatives of the Employers' National Federation and the unions concerned in the strike. Sir Allan Smith, Chairman of the Federation, reviewed the history of the strike and requested the unions to instruct their members to return to work immediately and observe the Provisions for Avoiding Disputes. After a short speech by Mr. Brownlie, President of the Amalgamated Engineering Union, the union leaders retired for consultation and reported back to the conference that they could not comply with the employers' request in view of the previous action of the firm in question and the circumstances surrounding the strike. Sir Allan then replied by saying: "We requested you to honor your agreement, and you say you are not in a position to honor your agreement. It is a strange thing for you to say . . . If any individual firm contravenes the provisions and you let us know, we see that the firm is kept in order. We only ask you to do the same and see that your men regularize their position." Then he informed the conference that he had obtained from the feder-

[86] The Amalgamated Engineering Union, the Electrical Trades Union, the National Brass and Metal Mechanics, the United Patternmakers' Association, the National Union of General and Municipal Workers, the Transport and General Workers' Union, and the Workers' Union.

ated firms a mandate that authorized the Management Board of the Federation to take the steps necessary to enforce the provisions for avoiding disputes, even to the extent of a national lockout. On the following day the unions were informed that instructions had been sent out to the federated concerns to post lockout notices effective as of March 13.

The executive representatives of the trade unions met in several conferences, together with representatives of the strikers, and decided to order an immediate return to work. A mass meeting of the strikers was held on March 10. At this meeting Mr. Brownlie and other union leaders stressed the irregularity of the strike and urged an immediate resumption of work. But the workers were hostile and refused to comply with the executives' instructions. After having obtained a week's suspension of the lockout notices the executive council of the A. E. U. called at Manchester on March 13 and 14 a special meeting of the National Committee of the Union. Mr. Brownlie again stressed the irregular nature of the strike and appealed to the Committee to endorse the action of the executive council. After a long discussion the motion was carried by 44-7 votes.

At another mass meeting of the strikers, held on March 17, the union leaders, including the London District Committee, recommended an immediate resumption of work; but the workers declined to do so. Thereupon Mr. Brownlie declared that the executive council of his union would give effect to the decision of the National Committee by enforcing a strict discipline upon the members. In the afternoon the various trade unions issued instructions ordering an immediate return to work, and on the following day the situation was reported to the chairman of the Employers' National Federation. In the meantime the workers on strike had another meeting and decided to resume work on March 22. This decision was made in secret, but the executives of the trade unions got information of it, and conveyed the news to Sir Allan, who agreed to cancel the lockout notices. A national lockout was thus averted at the eleventh hour.[87]

The National Agreements on Wages and Conditions of work of 1927 and 1931. National application for an increase of 20s.[88] a week was made in April, 1924. After protracted negotiations which bore no results the representatives of the trade unions concerned with the movement met in conference, on March 16, 1926, and decided to apply for the same increase in the various engineering districts. Sir Allan Smith, chairman of the Employers' Federation, suggested that "the mere transference from national to district discussion" would not afford any means of arriving at a satisfactory settlement of the questions, which were "more fitting for discussion with the General Negotiation Committee of the Federation than in a Central Conference." This suggestion was accepted by the unions and a memorandum was signed at a Central Conference. The Memorandum stated that in view of the large number of applications the negotiation committee of the employers' federation and the national authorities of the unions should meet together and endeavor to arrive at an amicable solution of the problem. A solution was reached in August, 1927, by granting to the plain time workers a special bonus of 2s. a week as against the original claim for 20s. The negotiation had lasted for more than three years.[89]

Toward the end of January, 1931, a conference was held between representatives of the Employers' National Federa-

[87] *The Amalgamated Engineering Union Monthly*, March, April, 1926.

[88] Wage reductions had been effected in the engineering industry in 1921 and 1922. These amounted in the aggregate to 6s. per week off the basic time rates, 16s. 6d. off the war bonuses, and the complete withdrawal of the 12½ per cent and 7½ per cent bonuses granted by the Ministry of Munitions.

[89] The *A. E. U. Monthly*, April, May, 1926, April, 1930.

tion and a large number of unions representing about 600,000 workers. The employers submitted a comprehensive proposal dealing with general conditions of work, including hours of labor, overtime, night work, the shifts system, payment by results, and other allied matters. After having heard a long and detailed statement by the employers the union representatives retired for consultation among themselves and reported back that they had agreed to submit the proposals to their respective executive committees. Another joint conference was held about the middle of March and a joint committee was appointed to examine the employers' proposals. The proposals were eventually rejected by a meeting of the union executives held on May 7. This decision was conveyed to the employers, and the negotiations were broken off until June 4, when the negotiation committee of the employers' Federation informed the negotiation committee of the trade unions that the position had been reported to the federated firms and instructions had been secured to put the proposals into effect as of July 6. This situation was immediately reported to the conference of the union executives. The Conference expressed "regret at the employers' decision to impose the conditions," but nevertheless authorized the negotiation committee to reopen negotiations with the employers. A joint meeting was accordingly held on June 18, and the employers made some modifications in their proposals. The modified scheme was accepted by the union executives on June 23 by 61-38 votes. These negotiations had lasted for five months.[90]

Although such a long process of negotiation means delay and indecision it has the merit of affording an opportunity to consider a situation from all possible aspects of the interests involved through the active participation of those leaders who are well acquainted with the industry. The confer-

[90] The *A. E. U. Monthly*, January–July, 1931.

ence scenes are thus often a battleground of closely knit arguments based on well observed facts as well as on broad visions and ideals. The chairman of the employers reviews the industrial situation both at home and abroad and the difficulties that beset the industry, while the representatives of the workers plead for a better system of costing and distribution so that the stability of the industry may be secured on a firm basis of contentment and justice.[91]

That the negotiation machinery in the engineering industry works satisfactorily on the whole was proved at the 12th meeting of the National Committee of the Amalgamated Engineering Union, held at Manchester in May, 1930. A resolution was moved proposing to terminate the York Memorandum which contains the Provisions for Avoiding Disputes. The resolution was defeated by a large majority. This was the third time within four years that the Committee had been asked to consider the question of withdrawing from the York Agreement, and on each occasion the proposal received only six votes.[92]

6. THE COTTON INDUSTRY

A. The Negotiation Machinery

The cotton industry, which has a long history of oppression and misery behind it, supplies an example of how a strong organization among the workers and the compulsory regulation of working conditions by the State can produce an efficient and comparatively contented industry. In the early stage of the Industrial Revolution the cotton operatives were unorganized and oppressed under the relentless operation of the Iron Man. Driven by want and despair, the operatives turned either to revolutionary movement or to sporadic riots in the "aimless strikes of the belly." With

[91] The *A. E. U. Monthly*, June, 1924, December, 1925.

[92] *Ibid.*, June, 1930.

the introduction of factory legislation working conditions began to improve and the growth of organizations changed the old revolutionary ideas and unlawful activities of the workers while the employers came around to meet their employees on an equal footing in trade disputes.

The growth of organization was materially assisted by the fact that the cotton industry is practically concentrated in a locality, namely, Lancashire and the adjoining fringes of Cheshire and Derbyshire. Within Lancashire itself, however, there are further sub-divisions and specializations. The spinning section of the industry is concentrated in the south-eastern part of the county. This district consists of two continuous areas, the smaller area around Bolton and the larger Oldham, connected by a number of small spinning towns. The weaving area, lying immediately to the north of the spinning section, while separated from it is linked to it by a number of towns doing both spinning and weaving. The weaving area is also subdivided into two groups, one in the neighborhood of Burnley and the other at Blackburn.

The majority of the employers in the spinning section are organized in a number of local associations, combined in the Federation of Master Cotton Spinners' Associations, while the weaving employers are federated in the Cotton Spinners and Manufacturers' Association. On the workers' side a majority of the spinners are organized in the Amalgamated Association of Operative Cotton Spinners and Twiners and the Amalgamated Association of Card and Blowing Room Operatives, organizations which were established in 1853 and 1886 respectively. The operative weavers are organized in a number of local associations, federated in the Northern Counties' Textile Trades Federation, which originated in 1884. These trade unions are all combined in the United Textile Workers' Association, which deals with the more general interests of the operatives, particularly with factory legislation.

Wages in the cotton industry are regulated by a complicated system of price lists. The essential principle of this system is that it does not fix the actual amounts of wages, but determines certain percentage increases or decreases in certain standard rates in accordance with the state of the market. The principal lists governing the spinning section are the Bolton and Oldham Lists, which were first negotiated between the employers' and the operatives' organizations in 1853 and 1876 respectively. In the weaving section the Uniform List, adopted in 1892 for plain goods, serves as a standard for the smaller lists governing fancy and colored goods.

It is not an easy matter to compute accurately the operatives' earnings under the operation of the complicated lists system. This difficulty caused both employers' and workers' organizations to appoint more or less expert officials in the adjustment of local disputes arising out of existing agreements on piece prices. This practice had been firmly established long before it was formally incorporated in the Brooklands Agreement, signed in 1893 after a great strike in the spinning section.[93] The agreement which was subsequently revised and strengthened is still in force so far as the provisions for settling disputes are concerned.

Under the terms of the agreement questions arising at a particular factory are dealt with, in the first instance, by the management and a deputation of the workers concerned and, failing a settlement, by the secretaries of the local employers' and workers' organizations. It is their duty jointly to investigate the actual facts and give their decision, which is final in the majority of cases.[94] If the secretaries fail to

[93] *Report on Collective Agreements*, 1910, pp. 136-169; the Committee on Industry and Trade, *Survey of Textile Industries*, pp. 28-9.

[94] In 1923 Mr. John Smethurst, then Secretary of the Master Cotton Spinners' Federation was reported to have said that out of a total number

agree the question may then be dealt with by a local joint committee, and finally by a national joint committee representing the employers' federation and the operatives' amalgamations. Until this procedure has been tried no stoppage of work is to take place on account of any local dispute.

General questions affecting the spinning section as a whole are dealt with directly by a joint conference between the Wages Committee of the Federation of Master Cotton Spinners' Associations and the Executive Committees of the operatives' Amalgamations.

This is the normal negotiation procedure in the spinning section. As a result of another great strike in 1932 a new Conciliation Committee was added to the normal procedure. The Conciliation Committee consists of not less than four or more than six representatives each from the employers' and workers' national associations, with an independent chairman appointed by agreement or alternatively by the Minister of Labor. The chairman, a standing chairman holding office for a specified period of time, may be assisted by two standing independent members nominated by the parties. Any matter that has gone through the normal procedure of negotiation and failed of a settlement may be referred to the Conciliation Committee. This Committee is required in the first instance to try to settle the case by agreement between the parties. Failing a settlement by conciliation the standing chairman may, after consultation with the independent members, make a recommendation, or issue an award if invited to do so by the parties to the dispute.[95]

In the weaving section arrangements similar to those existing in the spinning section were in force until 1932. These

of disputes affecting the Federation, between 600 and 700 in a year, not more than 20 had ever reached the central joint committee. *The Manchester Guardian*, April 27, 1923.

[95] *The Ministry of Labor Gazette*, Nov., 1932, pp. 412-3.

regulations, known as "Joint Rules for the Settlement of Trade Disputes," had originally been negotiated in 1909 between the North and North-East Lancashire Cotton Spinners' and Manufacturers' Association and the Northern Counties' Textile Trades' Federation.[96] After a long dispute over the question of "more looms to a weaver" an agreement, signed on September 27, 1932 between representatives of the Cotton Spinners and Manufacturers' Association and the Northern Counties' Textile Trades Federation, amended the old joint rules in three ways, namely, by the institution of a Conciliation Committee, a Prices Committee, and a Standing Joint Committee.

The Conciliation Committee, in its constitution and powers, is similar to that in the spinning section. The Prices Committee is composed of four representatives from each of the parties with full power to settle any question arising over the interpretation of existing price lists. If the committee fails to agree the question at issue may be brought under the normal procedure of the joint rules. The Standing Joint Committee does not deal with labor questions, but meets regularly for examination of general economic and legislative matters affecting the section as a whole.

The new agreement of 1932 reaffirmed the old principle of collective bargaining as an essential requirement "for the preservation of equitable arrangements as between employers and employers and as between employers and operatives." The reaffirmation is important as a recognition of the value of collective agreement for the maintenance of fair standards of competition and also as an indication of the growing difficulties that have been experienced in keeping such agreements by voluntary efforts under the unsettled conditions in the cotton manufacturing industry. In fact the organized employers and workmen in the trade in April, 1934, came

[96] *Report on Collective Agreements*, 1910, pp. 170-187.

to the conclusion that collective agreements could not be maintained by private efforts and that, therefore, agreed wage rates should be made legally binding on all employers by legislation. The Government accepted this position and passed the Cotton Manufacturing Industry (Temporary Provisions) Act, 1934 (24 & 25 Geo. 5, c. 30). The Act authorized the Minister of Labor, upon a joint application from a majority of the organized employers and workers engaged in the cotton weaving trade and upon unanimous recommendation by an independent investigation board to be appointed by him, to make orders directing wage rates agreed upon by representative organizations in the trade to be binding on all employers, under monetary penalties.[97] This legislation is a purely temporary and experimental measure, but its importance cannot be exaggerated. It is the first recognition of the power of organized employers and workmen to legislate for their industry, subject to Government supervision and control. Secondly, it signifies the delegation of power by Parliament to the Executive Department, a measure of control that is becoming increasingly necessary for the efficient functioning of modern representative government.

B. The Joint Committee of Cotton Trade Organizations

Another important feature of the recent movement in the cotton industry is the Joint Committee of Cotton Trade Organizations, which was established in 1925 with a view to "adopting cooperative actions which would facilitate the removal of the difficulties facing the industry in general." As reconstituted in 1928 the Committee consists of representatives annually appointed by each of the main cotton

[97] *The Ministry of Labor Gazette*, March, 1931, p. 89, Oct., 1932, p. 360, April, May, July, 1934, pp. 118, 157, 231; Parl. Deb. Commons (289), 1961, 1969, 1973, 1977; May 17, 1934.

trade organizations, including the United Textile Workers' Association.[98] It acts through an executive committee of 18 members, and makes no attempt to deal with wage questions and other allied conditions of employment. It is not organized in two sections, one for the employers and the other for the workers, as in the case of a Joint Industrial Council, but the whole Committee acts as a single body with the same officials and the same working staff.

The Committee has been actively engaged in the task of reorganizing the cotton industry. It is generally recognized that if Lancashire wishes to check the progressive decline in her trade she must endeavor by large scale amalgamations to secure economies in specialization, standardization, bulk-buying, and bulk-selling. Since the Committee endorsed this policy in December, 1928, a number of combinations have been created, the most important of which is the Lancashire Cotton Corporation registered in January, 1929.

7. SUMMARY

The basic principle underlying these peace machineries is voluntary approach to the settlement of disputes. This has the merit of enabling the different industries to adopt methods appropriate to their own changing needs and varying conditions of production, according to their ability and

[98] The trade organizations affiliated to the Joint Committee are as follows: The Federation of Master Cotton Spinners' Assns., the Cotton Spinners' and Manufacturers' Assn., the Bleaching Trade Advisory Board, the Federation of Calico Printers, the Piece Dyers' Assn., the Employers' Federation of Dyers and Finishers, the Master Packers' Assn., the Employers' Federation of Cotton Yarn, Bleachers, Dyers, and Sizers, the Shipping Merchants' Committee of the Manchester Chamber of Commerce, the Manchester Cotton Assn., the United Textile Factory Workers' Assn., the Joint Dyers' Societies, and the Joint Board of Inside Warehouse Workers. The author is greatly obliged to Mr. P. W. Lacey, secretary to the Joint Committee for his kindly supply of information on this very important subject.

actual experience. Naturally the methods adopted are not uniform but diverse. A comparison of the differences and a recognition of the common characteristics may make clear the position of the individual industries and indicate the possibilities of a further development.

In line with its specialization the cotton industry has created two sets of negotiation machinery for its two principal sections, one for the spinning section and the other for weaving, with respect to wages and other conditions of employment. It has the most elaborate system of piece prices with expert officials of trade unions and employers' associations to adjust difficulties arising over the interpretation or actual application of the system. On the broader questions affecting the industry as a whole there is a Joint Committee, representing the various cotton trade organizations collectively, and actively engaged in the task of rationalization of the cotton industry. The railway industry has also two parallel sets of negotiation machinery, one dealing with the traffic grades and the other dealing with the shopmen. The divergent nature of the work of the two groups, however, has so far prevented the creation of an "all grades" peace machinery competent to treat the railway service as a single unit. Within each separate sphere the negotiation machinery is well balanced and highly developed. For the traffic grades, for instance, there are, on each railway, department committees and sectional railway councils, on which, together with representatives of the management, the various grades of workers organized in different trade unions are represented on a proportional basis. For the railways as a whole there is the Railway Staff National Council composed of representatives of the railway companies and the railway trade unions, and above all comes the Railway Staff National Tribunal, an arbitration authority to which questions of national importance may be referred for final settlement.

In the engineering industry there is no arbitration element, the principal feature of its machinery being joint conferences, both local and national. The industry is noted for the presence of shop stewards and works committees. The shop stewards are representatives of the workers and are subject to the control of the unions concerned, while the works committees are in most cases joint representative bodies. The committee is valuable as a means for the peaceful settlement of disputes, local application of national trade agreements, and the administration of welfare work. It also serves as a channel through which the financial and economic conditions of the particular concern may be conveyed to the workers. Through the operation of the committees, indeed, the workers who might otherwise become mere cogs in the machinery under existing industrial organization may freely express their personality. The arrangements existing in the shipbuilding industry are similar in broad outline to those obtaining in the engineering industry. But the interesting feature is that different sets of questions are dealt with in a different manner. The question of piece work is settled primarily by a neutral committee in the yard concerned, and that of demarcation by a joint committee representative of the employers and of all the trade unions in the district concerned. Other questions may be dealt with by local, central, and general conferences.

The iron and steel manufacturing industry has developed an elastic system of peace agencies. The heavy steel sections are governed by joint conference, the Midlands iron trade by a conciliation board, while the tinplate and sheet industry in South Wales is under a Joint Industrial Council. The industry as a whole, however, has a uniform method of wage regulation in the selling price sliding scale system, which the industry has been able to maintain for more than a half century. Although the coal-mining industry also tried this method it found it wanting and replaced it with the principle of minimum wage and profit sharing which is administered invariably by local conciliation boards. For the ascertainment of industrial proceeds, upon which both the sliding scale and profit sharing schemes are dependent for their operation, the coal mining and the iron and steel industries have adopted a joint auditing system, a method that is not found in other industries.

The different industries have also adopted various methods for the final review of disputes. The Coal Mines National Industrial Board is a permanent statutory body consisting of 17 members appointed by the Board of Trade and representative of the miners, mine owners, and the public. It has jurisdiction in disputes over the terms in a new proposal for district agreement on wages and other conditions of employment. In the railway service a National Wages Board similarly constituted and governing the traffic grades was in operation until 1935 when it was replaced by a railway staff National Tribunal. The chief complaints against the old Wages Board were delay in settlement of disputes and lack of impartiality. The new Tribunal consists of three members, nominated for each particular case by the railway companies and trade unions, and an independent chairman appointed by the Minister of Labor. The Tribunal may deal only with questions involving national agreements. The final appeal court for the shopmen is the Industrial Court.

Arbitration by single arbitrators is the usual practice in the iron and steel industry as well as in the shipbuilding industry. There is no set rule in the engineering industry for the final review of general issues of national importance, but for the settlement of local disputes the central conference at York is the final authority. The conciliation committee in the cotton industry consists of an independent chairman and a small number of independent members. Its duty is to conciliate in the first instance, and, failing conciliation, to issue an arbitration award if required to do so by the parties concerned.

As a general rule in all of the five major industries local disputes, usually arising out of existing agreements, are dealt with primarily by those immediately concerned. Failing agreement, such disputes are subject to local and national review by representatives of the organized employers and workmen concerned. Proposals for new agreements on wages and other conditions of service affecting the industry as a whole are taken up directly by the national authorities of the trade unions and employers' associations, except in the coal mining industry. The national treatment of these wider industrial issues has both merits and demerits. It may mean delay in settlement, and the agreement reached may be too rigid and restrictive for a rapidly changing industry. Should the national authorities fail to reach an agreement industrial disturbances and dislocation may take place on a national scale. This method has, on the other hand, the merit of establishing on the widest possible basis a uniform common rule that may serve well as a fair standard of competition in the industry concerned. The differentiation between cases concerning existing agreements and those resulting from fresh demands is a great forward step in the clarification of the two essentially different issues. The dispute belonging to the first category is a matter of interpretation of existing rights and therefore a proper subject for judicial settlement, while questions coming under the second heading are matters of rights, not already agreed upon, but to be conceded in the process of negotiation. There is another well established common practice. In case of a deadlock nearly all the industries under review call in a third party, either an arbitrator or a conciliator. This practice is significant not only as an expedient for the solution of a deadlock, but also as an indication of a growing conscience on the part of the industrial disputants and a realization that labor troubles should be considered as judicially as possible in a calm atmosphere, and that account should be taken both of the interests of those immediately concerned and the interests of the community at large.

The basic operative force behind these negotiation machineries is trade unionism. The extent to which trade unionism is recognized and the ability of leadership to apply it to the changing needs of a particular industry are, therefore, the chief determinant of the adequacy or inadequacy of the resulting peace agencies. The coal mining industry, for instance, is well organized on both sides, but the Mining Association has failed to recognize the value of the Miners' Federation as a national negotiation authority on wages and other issues of great importance, while the leaders of the miners missed a good chance by refusing to accept the Mining Industry Act, 1920.[99] The result has been unfortunate for the industry as a whole, creating, generally speaking, a lack of confidence between the miners and the mine owners. In contrast the iron and steel industry is noted for its long record of peace, a record due partly to the complete recognition of trade unionism and partly to the able leadership of the employers and workmen engaged in the industry. In the railway industry there is friction between the craft and the industrial unions. This is also the case in the cotton and the engineering industries where the rival claims for membership and employment by numerous different unions often cause serious difficulties. Taken as a whole trade unionism even in these well organized industries is still in the crucible. It requires more consolidation and cordination, both against the organized force of capital and within

[99] Hilton, *Are Trade Unions Obstructive?*, p. 55.

its own inner councils. As Mr. Conley pointed out at the Annual Trades Union Congress in 1934, it is certainly high time that the "sporadic and uncoordinated movements (by separate unions) should be linked together in a disciplined and ordered effort to carry forward the unions as a united body."[100] Until this objective has been attained the defects of the existing peace machinery will probably remain, defects that consist mainly in a lack both of uniformity and of full power to deal with industrial problems as comprehensively as is desired by the unions.

The primary value of the negotiation machinery thus far described lies more in the prevention than in the cure of industrial disputes. Unfortunately, however, there are no published statistical materials showing the actual number of cases settled peaceably by means that have not involved a stoppage of work. Such cases must reach an enormous figure each year.[101] The only available material is in the form of figures covering cases of strikes and lockouts. These figures may be taken as an indirect measurement of the adequacy or inadequacy of the peace agencies in the industries under discussion. The following table shows the number of stoppages of work for the 15-year period from 1919 to 1933.

The total number of strikes and lockouts, it will be noticed, was 9,191, of which 62.03 per cent took place in the five staple industries, coal-mining accounting for 26.21 per cent, the metal trades, 19.38, textile, 8.32, and transport, 8.12. The total number of workers affected was 13,146,000 with a total loss of about 386,331,000 working days. The industries under review accounted for 81.03 per cent of the total number of workers involved, and for 92.08 per cent of the working days lost. From these figures it may be argued

[100] *The Annual Report of the Trade Union Congress for 1934*, p. 73.

[101] See the remarks of Mr. Smethurst referred to on p. 274.

NUMBER OF STRIKES AND LOCKOUTS FOR THE 15 YEAR PERIOD, 1919-1933 *

No. of Disputes	Industries under Study: Mining	Metal, Engineering Shipbuilding	Textile	Transport	Total	Other Trades	Total
Total Nos. ..	2,409	1,781	765	746	5,701	3,490	9,191
Yearly Average ..	161	119	50	50	380	232	612
Percentage to all disputes ..	% 26.21	% 19.38	% 8.32	% 8.12	% 62.03	% 37.97	% 100.00
Number of Workers Involved (in thousands)							
Total Nos. ..	6,053	1,292	2,217	1,090	10,652	2,494	13,146
Yearly Average ..	404	86	148	73	711	166	877
Percentage to all disputes ..	% 46.04	% 9.83	% 16.87	% 8.29	% 81.03	% 18.97	% 100.00
Working Days Lost (in thousands)							
Total Nos. ..	258,705	46,628	41,887	8,501	355,721	30,610	386,331
Yearly Average ..	17,247	3,109	2,792	567	23,715	2,041	25,756
Percentage to all disputes ..	% 66.97	% 12.07	% 10.84	% 2.20	% 92.08	% 7.92	% 100.00

* The 21st Abstract of Labor Statistics, p. 126.

that the negotiation machinery in the most important industries of the country is less effective than is generally believed. A further detailed study of the strike figures, however, indicates that this conclusion is more apparent than real. The following table shows that the cases in which less than 100 workers were involved constituted 49.16 per cent of all disputes and accounted for only 0.69 per cent of the working days lost, while the large scale stoppages of work, in which more than 5,000 workers were involved, constituted less than 2 per cent of the disputes, but accounted for more than 91 per cent of the working days lost. In other words, although the well organized industries have occasional outbursts of disputes causing great damage to the

NUMBER OF DISPUTES AS CLASSIFIED BY NUMBER OF WORKERS *

Workers Involved	1919-1926	Percentage to all Disputes	1927-1933	Percentage to all Disputes	Total	Total Percentage
		%		%		%
Under 100	3,235	35.20	1,283	13.96	4,518	49.16
100-250	1,251	13.61	565	6.15	1,816	19.76
250-500	756	8.23	337	3.67	1,093	11.90
500-1,000	641	6.97	241	2.62	882	9.59
1,000-5,000 ...	545	5.93	173	1.88	718	7.81
5,000-10,000 ..	66	.72	13	.14	79	0.86
Over 10,000 ..	68	.74	17	.18	85	0.92
Total	6,562	71.40	2,629	28.60	9,191	100.00
Working Days Lost in Above Disputes (in thousands)						
		%		%		%
Under 100	2,127	.55	517	.14	2,644	0.69
100-250	2,850	.74	709	.18	3,559	0.92
250-500	3,234	.84	876	.23	4,110	1.07
500-1,000	4,480	1.17	979	.25	5,459	1.42
1,000-5,000 ...	12,702	3.29	3,938	1.02	16,640	4.31
5,000-10,000 ..	6,885	1.77	821	.21	7,706	1.98
Over 10,000 ..	324,346	84.01	21,629	5.60	345,975	89.61
Total	356,624	92.37	29,469	7.63	386,093	100.00

* *The 21st Abstrict of Labor Statistics,* p. 129.

country, ordinarily the negotiation machinery operating therein secures more or less lasting and stable peace.

This does not, of course, mean that the well organized workers are satisfied with the present machinery. On the contrary from their broad point of view of socialization and public control of industrial production and distribution it is entirely too narrow in its scope. In this respect it is worth noting that 71.40 per cent of the disputes shown in the table above occurred in the years between 1919 and 1926 when the temper of labor ran exceptionally high. It will be readily recalled that the outstanding strikes in this period were those on the railways in 1919 and those in the coal fields culminating in the General Strike of 1926.

According to the coal mining and the railway trade unionists industrial peace is impossible so long as industry is organized on the private profit seeking motive, without regard either for the human needs of the workers or for the value of their past work.[102] This view is shared by cotton and iron trade workers who advocate a thorough reorganization of their industry on a scientific basis. For this purpose they propose that the individual industry should be governed by a public utility corporation which would serve the public interest by having a Government-appointed central planning board and several sectional or regional administrative boards, with or without representation of the workers. For the settlement of disputes they propose a tripartite organization consisting of the works councils representative of the workers employed at the individual workshops, regional councils, and above all a national council consisting of representatives of the corporation and the trade unions concerned. For the industry of the country as a whole there would be a National Joint Council which in its turn might be linked up with an economic committee of the Cabinet or an industrial board on a separate footing. When this is done and the conception of the industry as a national service is properly understood, trade unionism will become, they believe, a complementary rather than conflicting force in the process of production.[103] This contention is fully admitted; yet there still remains the question whether mere social machinery or arrangement, no matter how perfect and well advised, will be able to secure a complete harmony of the conflicting human interests which are, in the final analysis, the real cause of disputes, and which can only be harmonized by a broader and deeper interpretation of man's inner life itself.

[102] *The Railway Review*, Nov. 26, 1926.

[103] Trades Union Congress, *Annual Report*, 1931, pp. 439, 441; 1932, p. 206; 1934, pp. 189, 419; 1935, pp. 202, 208.

CHAPTER VII

Past Experiences and Future Prospects

The question of peace, as we observed in the introductory note, is not one of mere avoidance of strife. It is a quest for the cooperation of all for the harmonious growth of each, just as in the springtide a thousand and one elements combine in the production of the glory of the floral kingdom. It is the mission of democracy to view each individual personality as in itself of ethical value, and to seek to insure to every man the opportunity to live a full and free life. The practical difficulty besetting this great principle is proverbial. No man can hope to realize his best self without social cooperation, but social cooperation is all too liable to be secured by methods involving exploitation and oppression. For it is an age-old truism that it is not the wise but the strong who rule the actual social situation.

Industrial peace is the harmonious cooperation of all the agencies participating in the production of goods through which the community obtains its livelihood. No one denies the need for such cooperation, but strife is rampant on all sides, differences naturally arising between capital and labor, not only over the division of industrial proceeds and the arrangement of working conditions, but also over the existing industrial order itself. Peace is desirable; but without justice it is a mere cloak for tyranny. To render each his due is to do justice; but, unless tempered by good will, this formal principle of justice may become merely a source of division instead of cooperation. Good will is of no avail, however, in a society where Brother Sambo is sold for three kegs of rum and an ell of cloth; where the human soul is so "seared with the brute idolatry of sense" that to him "going to Hell is equivalent to not making money," where "all promises and moral duties, that cannot be pleaded for in the Courts of Requests, address themselves in vain." [1] Industrial peace is clearly then not a mere question of improvement in the cash payment arrangement which obviously is not the sole relationship of human beings. It is an essential part of the broader question of what will bind man's allegiance to peace and what will form the best order of society; a society in which the development of each becomes a condition of the development of all, a question that is indeed the central theme of political science.

Democracy rejects as precarious and unstable a social order that is imposed by force, whether of mere numbers, wealth, or armed power, because force can not create the inner order of human personality which is the core of all social cohesion and cooperation. Human personality develops to the extent to which a person directs his action according to his own sense of right or wrong. To coerce anybody by telling him what to do or what not to do is to deprive him of his free exercise of will and reason and thereby pauperize his moral nature. Self-determination is just as essential to the growth of moral character as it is to the effective functioning of modern democracy. Democracy therefore seeks social order, not by coercion or suppression of the individual personality, but by seeking its fuller attainment and free expression; not that individual freedom always means harmony, but that, in the final analysis, peace and order must rest upon the bedrock of man's capacity to control his own nature.

Needless to say, man's spiritual power requires for its full growth certain social conditions of fulfillment, just as the

[1] Thomas Carlyle, *Past and Present*, Everyman's Library, pp. 141, 179-80.

appearance of the violet requires sunshine and the spring soil. Man is free and at peace with himself when his basic requirements for existence are satisfied and when he finds full cooperation not only in the state, but also in the daily exercise of industry,[2] art, science, and religion;[3] when, in other words, his better self is realized in full measure. It is obviously, however, beyond the power of the State to guarantee to every individual citizen a maximum attainment of life. At the best it can secure only a certain minimum standard of decency by prescribing certain systems of rights that civilization may create and determine as necessary conditions of social life.

British democracy has created two primary rights, the right to social security and the right of free association. These are the basic foundation of the British system of industrial peace.

Behind the system of social security lies a long history of social struggle. In the old days labor was regarded as a duty to the State, and as such it was strictly regulated in respect both of wages and freedom of movement. This was an inevitable result of the then widely held social theory that individual citizens should be governed in their action, not by private interest, but by the interest of the community at large. The community was not a free community, and the State was frankly a class State. As civilization marched on, with the ever-growing complication of the national life, this policy became untenable, and a reaction set in under the philosophy of laissez-faire. Each man was now regarded as being free to rise to the top, but the Industrial Revolution brought the factory workers to a state of practical slavery. A reaction again set in, taking the form of State interference based on the plea that liberty did not

[2] L. A. Hartley, *Human Engineering and Industrial Economy*, p. 320.

[3] Stanley Baldwin, *This Torch of Freedom*, pp. 80-81.

mean the power of the rich to destroy the poor in the course of trade, but the guarantee to every man of a decent standard of living through regulated social cooperation. This tenet won a great victory in the passage of factory and social legislation which collectively constitute the comprehensive British system of social security. It is this broad background of security that, because of the spirit of fair play thus exhibited on the part of the community and the atmosphere of good will prevailing among the workers, has made it possible for the agencies for industrial peace to work smoothly and effectively.

In the meantime it was found unjust to fetter the freedom of the workers to combine, because only by numbers and concerted action could they hope to get a square deal from their employers. This right of combination or free association has been fully recognized, and trade unionism is now an established institution of the country. As soon as labor began to combine effectively the employers were forced to enter into counter combinations. Through the bitter experience of strikes and lockouts the employers and workmen learned the broad lesson that their interests, though conflicting seriously, were inevitably bound up in a common cause of production and prosperity; that the basic elements in conflict were not entirely immutable economic forces, but human beings, who, though selfish and slow in learning, were nevertheless open to reason. With this knowledge in their possession they began to sit around a table and talk things over. At the council table of industry which before had been reserved exclusively for the employing classes, now sat representatives of the employed. A foundation was laid upon which British industry has since built a form of self-government. Trade unionism has become the basic operative force by which the negotiation machinery in the various industries has been organized and through which self-discipline, education, and organization have been achieved among the workers, thus preparing them for a further democratic control of industry in the future.

As trade unionism gained wide influence with the growth of voluntary conciliation boards and arbitration courts the obsolete measures of compulsory industrial regulation were abolished. Government intervention in trade disputes was placed on an entirely new basis under the Conciliation Act of 1896. Compulsory arbitration, an outgrowth of the old practice of direct regulation by State authorities of wages and condition of employment, had been found wanting. Not only was there no definite principle upon which industrial differences could be equitably arbitrated, but it was also difficult to find an effective arbitration agency whose impartiality and intimate knowledge of trade would command the full confidence of the parties immediately concerned. Industrial disputes could not, however, be allowed to drift along. They were destructive to industrial production, inimical to social peace, and oppressive to the poor working class families. Democracy by this time had reached a higher stage and public opinion veered from the individualistic to a corporate view of society. The Government could not properly evade its responsibility for industrial peace, upon which the security of livelihood of the entire nation was dependent. It therefore assumed the duty of intervention in trade disputes and arrangements were made for the peaceful settlement of such disputes on a voluntary basis.

Although resting on the slender basis of voluntary agreement these arrangements were taken advantage of extensively and with significant results. Encouraged by Government propaganda and assistance the voluntary conciliation and arbitration boards grew both in number and in influence, while Government intervention itself soon began to throw light on different aspects of the difficult problem of adjusting industrial disputes. The function of intervention was to be discharged by an independent Government Department, far removed from any political influence. This Department was expected to exercise its power as conservatively as possible so that employers and workmen might come together and compose their differences among themselves. It was, after all, their responsibility to work together for their mutual benefit in industrial production. In case of intervention, however, it was shown that different situations required different methods of treatment to be administered by different agencies. Conciliation required speed in action, patience in heated controversy, and deep human understanding of the difficulties of the parties concerned, a function properly to be discharged by the conciliation officers of the Government. Arbitration on the other hand required a calm atmosphere and a judicial mind with an intimate knowledge and actual experience of trade as a broad background. Because of these requirements courts of arbitration constituted on the basis of tripartite representation were preferable to single arbitrators, while a permanent court representing the industry of the country as a whole was more suited than such ad-hoc courts of arbitration to meeting the growing need of securing unity in the awards that the essentially interdependent nature of modern industry demanded of the arbitration authorities. For this purpose the Industrial Council was created, but it was premature. Furthermore it failed to make a clear distinction between the parliamentary government of industrial relations in general and the judicial settlement of industrial disputes in particular. It died a quiet death.

The Government assumption of responsibility for industrial peace and the growing practice of voluntary conciliation and arbitration had quickened the conscience of the industrial disputants and thus to a great extent prepared the nation to accept the compulsory arbitration that served it well during the Great War. Under the strain of war the ordinary method of voluntary settlement of industrial disputes was slow and cumbersome. In munitions production, the basic need of the country at the time, this method was therefore discarded, and compulsory arbitration was resorted to as a necessary part of the trio-code of labor regulation, essential to the Government policy of industrial mobilization for war purposes. This was purely a war measure; as soon as hostilities ceased it was dropped as a part of national policy; and the old method of voluntary settlement was brought back with some important improvements, chief among which was the establishment of a permanent court of arbitration and of the Joint Industrial Councils. The brief episode of the war experiment, however, demonstrated with more convincing force the well known fact that free British workers would not countenance blind allegiance to the State. Their active cooperation could be won only through persuasion and understanding and by measures that satisfied their sense of fair play and justice. This lesson prompted the Whitley Committee to recommend a fuller measure of self-government in the industry, as it had motivated the post-war governments when they passed legislation for unemployment insurance and other measures to insure social security, an essential requirement of peace in modern democracy.

As they exist at the present time the British methods of industrial peace may be classified under two headings. For the immediate purpose of settlement of disputes there are the methods of inquiry, conciliation, and arbitration, which may be set in motion either through governmental or nongovernmental agencies. For the purpose of preventing disputes through closer cooperation and better understanding between employers and workmen there are the methods of discussion and consultation on matters of broad common interest through joint committees and councils between organized employers and workmen.

Of the Governmental agencies the Ministry of Labor is the chief office of conciliation; the Industrial Court the principal of the arbitration authorities, affording, as a standing court, a speedy, inexpensive, and regular means for the peaceful settlement of disputes; while single arbitrators and ad-hoc courts of arbitration meet the special requirement that arises from time to time, such as the local hearing of cases of comparatively small importance or specially desired arbitration personnel in whom the parties may have more confidence. The court of inquiry has in many cases, through its operation, enabled the Government to enlist intelligent public opinion and sympathy for a peaceful settlement of grave disputes affecting the vital interests of the community.

The methods of Government intervention are so varied and flexible as to meet any set of industrial situations; but intervention itself can take place only on the voluntary submission of the parties concerned, the Government having no power either to enforce its decision, if any, or to prohibit strikes and lockouts. This policy of voluntary intervention is a direct result of the old policy of laissez-faire, and has the merit of enabling industries to adopt methods appropriate to their own changing needs and varying conditions of production and according to their own actual experience. This policy is becoming hard to maintain in its existing form as industry becomes more consolidated both in composition and operation and as the State assumes more responsibility for social security and industrial peace. We have seen that the courts of inquiry have expressed opinions on certain fundamental issues of industrial peace. These issues are really a part of the larger claim of democracy for the opportunity of every member of the community to attain a full life; no democratic Government, therefore, can fail to settle them and expect to survive. We have also seen that the Industrial Court, though it has rendered valuable service, is not the place for the determination of these fundamental issues of industrial policy. The Government itself must sooner or later make a definite decision unless it is prepared to fail in its high mission.

Of the non-Governmental agencies there are two types, namely, the Joint Industrial Councils and the ordinary negotiation machinery. The Joint Industrial Councils lay more stress on the cooperative side of industrial production than do the ordinary negotiation machineries whose function is mainly concerned with the settlement of wage questions and other conditions of employment, questions concerned mainly with the distributive side of industrial production. This difference of stress is of vital importance from the point of view of industrial peace, because it is only by the unity of a higher aim and common interests that the divisions arising inevitably in any form of cooperative production can be harmonized. Theoretically speaking, therefore, the Joint Industrial Councils system, with its broader purview and more logical form of tripartite organization, is a considerable improvement on the ordinary type of negotiation machinery. Industrial peace does not in fact, however, depend so much on any set form of machinery or constructive theory as on the actual spirit of leadership of those engaged in the trades. The Whitley scheme has failed of its main object in many cases because of the lack of interest or the absence of broad vision among the employers and workmen engaged in the industries covered by it. Certainly it has failed to catch the imagination of the well organized industries, such as coal mining, iron and steel, engineering, and the cotton trades. In these industries the organized workers believe that neither peace nor prosperity is possible so long as industry is organized on the basis of profit-seeking, a motive that of necessity implies conflict of interests not only between employers and workmen, but also among employers themselves. They propose therefore industrial reconstruction and socialization on the broader basis of public ownership and control through the means of a statutory corporation to be established for the several individual industries, with or without representation of the workers on the governing board.

Apart from this ultimate goal of industrial organization, in the case of both the Joint Industrial Council and the ordinary negotiation machinery, it is a well established practice that discussion and negotiation are carried on jointly between organized employers and organized workmen, with provisions for settling local disputes primarily at local conferences and for dealing with matters of national importance on a national basis. National negotiation has both dangers and advantages. It has the merit of enabling industries to be governed with regard to the conditions of competition on a broad basis of common rule, and through the coordination of different local trade policies, coordination that it is impossible to secure when negotiations are conducted on a local basis. Differences may also be brought to the notice of those national peace agencies whose broader view and higher prestige may afford a better assurance of settlement than is offered by those immediately concerned, because the judgment of the latter might have been prejudiced by limited knowledge and personal grievances. Furthermore, with the growth of national negotiation there is also developed on both sides a larger sense of responsibility and a greater willingness to examine the facts at issue from every possible angle. This attitude often has the result of narrowing down the marginal differences between the two sides. National negotiation may mean, on the other hand, delay in the settlement of disputes, and, should settlement not be arrived at, a national stoppage of work throughout the entire industry. National agreement may also have the handicap of rigidity and uniformity, features that make it difficult for industry to meet the requirements of a rapidly changing industrial world with its varied sectional interests.

The remedy does not lie, however, in a return to the old method of individual bargaining between separate employers and workmen. It lies, on the contrary, in a closer contact between them through representative government of industry in its entirety. For it is close contact such as this that enables both employers and workmen to understand each other and truly to appreciate the economic situations that they have to face with knowledge and wisdom. The chief defect of the existing negotiation machinery is, indeed, its lack of power to deal with industrial problems comprehensively and with a close coordination of policies, not only as between the component part of an individual industry, but also as between different industries.

The basic operative force behind these negotiation machineries is, as we have seen, trade unionism, the evolution of which from the Industrial Revolution is a distinct feature of modern society. Its functions so far have been confined mainly to negotiating with regard to wages, hours, and other working conditions. As democracy broadens its base and shifts emphasis from the political to the industrial government of the country the conception of trade unionism is also becoming wider and deeper; a new order of industry is being sought, an order in which labor, not a commodity to be bought and sold at the market price but a personality inherent in democratic citizenship, may find a freer scope of expression.[4] The adequacy or inadequacy of negotiation

[4] Warburton, *History of Trade Union Organization in the Potteries*, Introduction by R. H. Tawney, pp. 15-16; *cf.* R. M. MacIver, *Labor in the Changing World*, pp. 174-76.

machinery is therefore to be determined by the extent to which this broad claim of labor is met by the employers whose attitude is in turn determined by the effective organization of the workers in particular industries. Taken as a whole British trade unionism is still "patchy," with a large territory of industrial fields still unorganized.[5] Even in the small number of well organized industries the extreme diversity of trade-union organization, a surprising curiosity to an American observer in 1919,[6] is still a great handicap to the development of a well planned and coordinated national policy on wages and other issues of great importance to the working class as a united force.

Considered as a whole the British system of industrial peace works fairly well. During the 41-year period from 1893 to 1933, for which statistics are available,[7] there occurred 26,892 strikes and lockouts involving approximately 23,832,000 workers and costing the country about 596,-591,000 working days. A yearly average would amount to less than 656 disputes and would involve less than 582,000

[5] According to the census of 1931 the number of persons gainfully occupied in Great Britain was about 21 millions, of whom about 4,500,000, or more than one-fifth, were organized in trade unions. The principal unions were in coal mining, metal works, textiles, railways, and other transport and general labor, which accounted for 554,000; 508,000; 525,000; 406,000, and 720,000, respectively, making a total of about 2,713,000 out of the total 4,500,000 trade unionists in the country. The high degree of centralization among this small group of well organized trade unions is indicated by the percentage of figures showing the proportion between total membership and members affiliated with national federations. The percentages run as follows: Cotton 100; Wool, 95; Coal Mining, 93; Iron and Steel, 78, Engineering, Railway, and other transport and general labor, 15 each. On the employers' side also these industries were covered by organizations formed mostly on a national basis. See *The 21st Abstract of Labor Statistics*, pp. 3, 136, 150, 134.

[6] The Commission on Foreign Inquiry of the National Civic Federation, *The Labor Situation in Great Britain and France*, p. 114.

[7] For a detailed study see Appendix, Table No. III.

workers in a total working population of 21 millions and a loss of less than 15 million working days, or less than one day per worker. A further detailed study shows that aggregate loss of working days for the pre-war period, if spread over all workpeople in the country (on the basis of 21 millions), would amount to less than three days in 7 years; for the war period, less than one and a half days in 5 years; for the period of industrial turmoil following the Armistice and leading to the General Strike in 1926, a little over two days each year, and for the period of industrial truce after 1926, a little over one day in 7 years. Furthermore it is important to bear in mind that British strikes are noted for the preservation of peace and order with good humor, a situation that compares favorably with that prevailing in many other industrial countries. This shows the disciplinary effect of strong trade unionism, on the one hand, and of the British sense of fair play and of their law-abiding spirit, on the other.

The principal cause of industrial disputes is of course wages.[8] Out of the total number of stoppages of work occurring in the period 1920-1923 wage items accounted for 60 per cent., while hours of labor, trade unionism, and other conditions of work accounted for only 3, 6, and 26 per cent respectively.

This brings us to the basic problem of industrial peace, namely, the division of interests which the mere creation of machinery, however well devised and complete, would by itself never be able to settle. After long experience in industrial conciliation and arbitration Lord Amulree points out that the settlement of industrial differences is primarily "not a matter of administrative machinery or legislative provision, but of good will and common sense."[9] From the

[8] For a detailed study see Appendix, Table No. IV.

[9] Lord Amulree, *Industrial Arbitration*, Preface, p. v.

practical point of view this is true, because there is no panacea to apply in the solution of industrial disputes that arise from the very nature of modern economic organization. The essential feature of the modern industrial system is specialization based on division of labor. Therefrom inevitably arise questions of the coordination through discipline and order of various productive agencies for a certain common purpose, and of the distribution among these cooperative agencies of the proceeds received from the purchasers.

Certain socialist members of the Whitley Committee, it will be recalled, expressed their opinion that "a complete identity of interests between capital and labor" could not possibly be obtained so long as the modern economic system was governed by a private profit motive. We have also seen that this view is shared by advanced workers in the well-organized industries. A complete identity of interests as between the various productive agencies is, of course, hardly to be expected under any form of industrial organization. The substitution of a cooperative society for the private employer, for instance, would not answer the question of what would be a proper wage for a shop assistant or for the driver of a delivery van, as we have seen in the numerous decisions of the Industrial Court; nor would a Government shipyard in the place of a joint stock company settle the question of demarcation. The nationalization of coal mines would not solve the difficult questions of trade slump or foreign competition, or dispense with labor discipline or the wages system itself. These difficulties of industrial relations are inherent in the nature of modern industrial life and no final solution can be expected. They are difficulties that can be adjusted only by endless and continuous effort on the part of those immediately concerned or by their representatives, who may take various relevant and constantly changing facts into account in order to reach an equitable settlement.

Such is the general view held by British industrialists and trade unionists whose practical idealism and love of freedom favor voluntary rather than compulsory cooperation between employers and workmen. Voluntary cooperation, incidentally, produces diverse methods for the settlement of disputes and therefore provides more freedom for experimentation in new ways.

On the other hand, it is also generally recognized that good will is not likely to prevail where industry is governed by the practical dictatorship of the capitalist, where industry is thought of as a mere process of material production without regard to the human rights involved. This brings us back to the basic proposition of democracy. The workers claim, and rightly, that they are "living souls" with personalities that lie at the base of all social cooperation and human civilization and that they therefore must be cared for as such. They are not to be regarded merely as a part of factory equipment or as mere profit-making machinery. Their skill, strength, capacity, training, and daily work are things into which their personality enters and through which their personality is expressed. In other words their very lives are invested in the process of industrial production, and this fact alone, if nothing else, they maintain, entitles them to a share in the management of industry. Furthermore they are members of the community and their position as such should be given the full recognition and security due a free citizen who owes the country not only good workmanship but also the true realization of his best self by living a "free and full life." It is in the soil of such social conditions, it is claimed, that good will may originate and grow to the fullest measure of peace and attainment.[10]

[10] Parl. Deb. Commons (121), 667-80, Nov. 17, 1919, per Mr. Arthur Henderson.

This claim of labor is really a claim for the civilization of the industrial process of production, a process that vitally effects, not only the wages, hours, and working conditions of the worker but his growth in personality as well. The claim, which is irrefutable, has, to some extent, already been recognized by modern British democracy which realizes more and more the public responsibility of industry and therefore the importance of its regulation in the interest of the community as a whole. As we have already seen leisure, health, safety, and livelihood itself, which are indissolubly bound up with employment under the existing industrial organization, have been brought under the protection of Parliament. The inevitable sequence of events may therefore sooner or later force the State to take a definite stand on the moot question of reconstruction of the capitalistic order of society today.

Many reconstruction proposals have been made, some based on the Russian model of socialism and others on the Italian idea of the Corporate State. In view of the traditional British love of individual freedom and initiative it is improbable that these proposals will meet with general approval.[11] According to the usual British fashion of practical experiment by piecemeal legislation different industries may receive different treatment according to their own special

[11] "I do not believe," says Sir Arthur Salter, "that the only alternative before us is a Communism which destroys both political and economic freedom, or a Fascism which, at the expense of political liberty, leaves a limited freedom for capitalists; or the inefficiency which follows the assumption of new and more complex tasks by a representative Government as it now functions. I believe that we can both plan and preserve freedom on three conditions: that Parliament will delegate some of their functions to the Executive; that the Executive will fit itself for its task by welcoming the assistance of those who direct the actual economic activities of the country; and that these in turn will assume the task of collectively controlling and planning their own activities, in association with Government and through an appropriate organization." *The Framework of an Ordered Society*, p. 21.

requirements. A start has indeed been made in this direction in certain recent legislation passed for the revival of agriculture, coal mining, and the cotton trades.[12] The important point to note in these measures is that the organizations of employers and workmen are made the basis of operation for policies adopted, either jointly or separately, with some official representation to safeguard the public interest. The basic idea of the measures is to enable the industries concerned to carry through necessary reformation and reconstruction by the decision of a real majority of the members of the trade or industry. Such decision, if proved, to the satisfaction of the official elements, to be necessary, may be legally binding by Ministerial Orders.

Self government of industry on these lines may be taken as an indication of the future, if not the ultimate, British

[12] The Agricultural Marketing Act, 1931 (21 & 22 Geo. 5, c. 42) provides for the group action of agricultural producers by authorizing them to elect boards with power to devise and administer schemes necessary for the regulation of the marketing of their products. See *The Ministry of Agriculture and Fisheries*, Economic Series No. 33, the Agricultural Marketing Act, 1931.

Part 1 of the Coal Mines Act, 1930 (20 & 21 Geo. 5, c. 34) provides for the regulation of the production, supply, and sale of coal by means of schemes to be devised and administered by boards representative of the coal mine owners' associations. *Cf.* "The Coal Mines Act, 1932 (22 & 23 Geo. 5, c. 29)"; *The Ministry of Labor Gazette*, April, 1930, p. 281, June–July, 1932, pp. 208, 244.

The Cotton Manufacturing (Temporary Provisions) Act, 1934 (24 & 25 Geo. 5, c. 30) authorizes the Minister of Labor to issue Orders directing wage rates agreed upon by organized employers and workmen engaged in the cotton weaving section to be legally binding upon the entire trade with due safeguards of public interest. See *The Labor Gazette*, June–July, 1934, pp. 157, 231. Another interesting piece of legislation is the Special Areas (Development and Improvement) Act, 1934 (25 Geo. 5, c. 1) which provides for the appointment of special commissioners with wide powers to initiate, organize, prosecute, and assist measures designed for the economic development and social improvement of certain of the depressed areas. See *The Labor Gazette*, Dec., 1934, p. 438.

democratic policy for an "Ordered Society."[18] Free adjustment of supply and demand may remain, as heretofore, a general policy. "Rugged individualism" will be kept, however, within due bounds and be made the operative force of business upon conditions that may be prescribed by those who, representing the majority opinion of the organized employers and workmen, jointly interpret the social and economic needs of their industry as a whole. This plan will have the advantage of preventing, on the one hand, bureaucracy and political wire pulling, and of enlisting, on the other, the best representative abilities of the industries for their internal government. The plan, therefore, while conserving unity, common purpose, and constructive planning for an orderly progress, will still leave a large measure of freedom for individual efforts. In other words the existing trade unions and employers' associations, which have been developed as a combatant power, will be given a new status of professional organizations, responsible, separately, for the standards and conditions of work of their membership, and, jointly, for the general welfare of their industry as a whole. Such a policy, which is only a step forward under the Whitley scheme, may be taken as another instance of the typical British "muddling through" by half measures of compromise. In all history, however, the finest and the most difficult task in political art is to combine the great principles of liberty and regularity in due proportion, as the changing conditions of society may require. Therein lies the secret of a moving equilibrium of social justice.

In pursuance of such a policy the Government may grant to existing national organizations of employers and workmen in individual industries powers enabling them to decree wages and hours of labor, to determine conditions of apprenticeship and retirement with honor after long service to

[18] *Cf.* L. S. Amery, *The Forward View*, pt. ii, ch. ix.

relieve unemployment, to resettle displaced workers, to conduct technical education and research, to plan the future course of production in anticipation of trade cycles and general economic conditions, and generally to carry through measures of rationalization and reconstruction. For the purpose of adjusting labor disputes the position of existing negotiation machinery may be greatly strengthened by the creation of more works councils at individual workshops and the establishment of a closer relationship between regional or sectional councils and the national council. These self-governing industries may then be linked up with a national joint council which, representing the industries on a national basis, may coordinate the separate policies of the individual industries and advise the Government on questions affecting the industrial life of the country as a whole. This may mean, on the one hand, the much desired relief of Parliament and the Executive Departments from congestion of work, and, on the other, a larger measure of self-government of industry on a basis of joint representation of employers and workers, on a more or less equal footing.

Such improvement of industrial relations may not, of course, lead to the complete elimination of disputes or a complete identity of interests but it will tend to create a better temper among the workers and a greater understanding between employers and workmen, without which the most elaborate peace machinery may fail of its entire purpose. Such improvements in temper and mutual understanding may cause the industries to commit themselves more deeply to the cause of peace, composing differences peaceably, in the majority of cases, by conciliation, and, failing such settlement, submitting them to impartial public inquiry and arbitration whether by authorities of their own appointment or by the Industrial Court, whose facilities hitherto have not been taken advantage of by many of the well organized industries.

Born of the Industrial Revolution, and led by the crude social theory of free competition for "the survival of the fittest," without much prevision of its future course, British industry has, after a long experience of toil and turmoil extending over a period of more than a hundred years, worked out a broad scheme of cooperation between employers and workers on the basis of consent and representation of those engaged in industry and on the recognition of the greater responsibility of industry for the community at large. It is still incomplete in the sense that it holds great possibilities of further development; it is unbalanced in the sense that it is extremely flexible and diverse in form. These are signs not of weakness, but of strength. With that strength it is anticipated that the British people, devoted as they are to moderation, fair play, and practical idealism, will gradually erect a more enduring democratic structure of industrial government. Free Britons in free cooperation, recognizing their full responsibility in the exercise of industry, may then enjoy the fruits of their labor in the peace and good will that will follow their deeper understanding of the true meaning of life.

APPENDIX

TABLE I

NUMBER OF CASES SETTLED BY GOVERNMENT AGENCIES

Year	Arbitration Settlements No. 1	No. 2	No. 3	Total	Conciliation Settlements No. 4	No. 5[1]	Total	Courts of Inquiry	Total
1920 ...	540*	73	15	628	11	275	286	6‡	920
1921 ...	122	19	7	148	5	118	123	1	272
1922 ...	37	9	8	54	—	48	48	1	103
1923 ...	113	14	6	133	—	33	33	1	167
1924 ...	143	7	12	162	5	78	83	7	252
1925 ...	165	8	8	181	9	64	73	3	257
1926 ...	104	5	4	113	5	19	24	—	137
1927 ...	82	6	1	89	5	9	14	—	103
1928 ...	52	10	5	67	4	32	36	—	103
1929 ...	39	14	5	58	3	35	38	—	96
1930 ...	43	6	3	52	2	28	30	1	83
1931 ...	35	7	6	48	1	47†	48	—	96
1932 ...	28	5	1	34	—	2	2	—	36
Total ..	1,503	183	81	1,767	50	788	838	20	2,625

[1] Nos. 1-5 stand respectively for the Industrial Court, Single Arbitrators, Ad-Hoc Courts, Conferences presided over by an independent chairman appointed under the Conciliation Act, 1896, and Settlements reached by Efforts of Officers of the Ministry of Labor.

* Includes Decision No. 180A.

† Includes 4 settlements providing for reference to arbitration which are also included under arbitration settlements.

‡ One of the Courts was appointed in 1919 and reported in 1920; the number includes three cases of "investigation" conducted by the Ministry of Labor.

TABLE II

TOTAL NUMBER OF CASES SETTLED BY VARIOUS AGENCIES IN 1920-1932 AS CLASSIFIED BY TRADE GROUPS

Industry	Arbitration Cases [1] No. 1	No. 2	No. 3	Total	Conciliation	Courts of Inquiry	Total
Building	50	8	—	58	89	2	149
Mining	10	12	4	26	37	4	67
Iron & Steel	28	23	40	91	16	—	107
Engineering & Shipbuilding	418	13	16	447	63	3	513
Other Metals	86	9	—	95	48	—	143
Textile	43	12	2	57	50	1	108
Clothing	9	3	—	12	28	—	40
Boots & Shoes	3	19	3	25	26	—	51
Railway Serv.	195	—	—	195	1	1	197
Transport	72	13	5	90	111	8	209
Paper Making & Printing	11	5	—	16	11	—	27
Woodworking	28	10	4	42	54	—	96
Bricks & etc.	10	5	—	15	20	—	35
Glass	5	—	—	5	17	—	22
Oil, Chemical, & etc.	30	5	—	35	21	—	56
Food, Drink, & etc.	36	14	—	50	103	—	153
Leather	2	—	—	2	10	—	12
Public Utility	182	25	2	209	38	—	247
Civil Service	186	1	—	187	—	—	187
Miscellaneous	99	6	5	110	106	1	217
Total	1,503	183	81	1,767	849*	20	2,636*

[1] Nos. 1-3 stand respectively for the Industrial Court, Single Arbitrators, and Ad-Hoc Courts of Arbitation.

* Fifteen cases are included under this heading, which are also included in the arbitration settlements as they were referred to arbitration under conciliation arrangements.

TABLE III

THE NUMBER OF STRIKES AND LOCKOUTS IN GREAT BRITAIN AND NORTHERN IRELAND FOR THE 41 YEAR PERIOD, 1893-1933[1]

Year	No. of Disputes	No. of Workers Affected (in thousand)	Working Days Lost (in thousand)
1893-1913 (21 years) ..	13,721	7,527	183,561
	%	%	%
Percentage	51.02	31.63	30.77
1914-1918 (5 years) ...	4,071	3,159	26,799
	%	%	%
Percentage	15.14	13.21	4.49
1919-1926 (8 years) ...	6,471	11,069	356,540
	%	%	%
Percentage	24.06	46.45	59.76
1927-1933 (7 years) ...	2,629	2,077	29,691
	%	%	%
Percentage	9.78	8.71	4.98
Total	26,892	23,832	596,591
	%	%	%
Percentage	100.00	100.00	100.00

[1] *The 21st Abstract of Labor Statistics*, p. 125.

TABLE IV

STRIKES AND LOCKOUTS CLASSIFIED BY CAUSES [1]

Year	Wages	Hours of Labor	Employment of Particular Persons	Other Working Conditions	Trade Unionism	Other Causes	Total
			No. of Disputes				
1920	1,079	41	259	93	89	46	1,607
1921	560	31	91	40	24	17	763
1922	385	18	77	52	31	13	576
1923	353	16	87	52	91	29	628
1924	436	13	121	58	57	25	710
1925	305	15	141	54	72	16	603
1926	148	16	80	29	28	22	323
1927	165	22	68	22	26	5	308
1928	169	15	69	29	13	7	302
1929	224	12	107	40	40	8	431
1930	249	19	79	45	28	2	422
1931	232	33	84	52	18	1	420
1932	230	10	89	43	14	3	389
1933	188	4	90	44	24	7	357
			No. of Workers Directly Involved (in thousands)				
1920	1,450	13	176	45	27	68	1,779
1921	1,705	10	23	14	7	11	1,770
1922	206	6	23	263	10	4	512
1923	147	6	24	43	105	18	343
1924	422	2	35	26	18	55	558
1925	275	9	57	22	31	7	401
1926	1,087	1	16	8	13	1,599	2,724
1927	31	13	29	5	6	6	90
1928	38	1	13	7	1	20	80
1929	440	4	25	7	15	2	493
1930	156	96	17	11	5	—	286
1931	239	24	16	140	5	—	424
1932	292	4	16	17	6	2	337
1933	46	—	34	26	5	3	114

[1] *The 21st Abstract of Labor Statistics*, p. 130.

BIBLIOGRAPHY

I. Primary Sources

A. Acts of Parliament

1. *Conciliation and Arbitration*

Date	Short Title	Reference	
1800	Cotton Arbitration Act (English)	39 & 40 Geo. 3,	c. 90
1803	Cotton Arbitration Act (Scottish)	43 Geo. 3,	c. 151
1804	Arbitration (Amendment) Act	44 Geo. 3,	c. 87
1813	Cotton Arbitration Act (Irish)	53 Geo. 3,	c. 75
1824	Arbitration (Masters and Workmen) Act ..	5 Geo. 4,	c. 96
1837	Arbitration (Amendment) Act	7 Will. 4 & 1 Vict.,	c. 67
1845	Hosiery Act	8 & 9 Vict.,	c. 77
1845	Silkweavers Act	8 & 9 Vict.,	c. 128
1867	Councils of Conciliaion Act	30 & 31 Vict.,	c. 105
1872	Arbitration (Masters and Workmen) Act ..	35 & 36 Vict.,	c. 46
1896	Conciliation Act	59 & 60 Vict.,	c. 30
1915	Munitions of War Act	5 & 6 Geo. 5,	c. 54
1916	Munitions of War (Amendment) Act	5 & 6 Geo. 5,	c. 99
1917	Munitions of War Act	7 & 8 Geo. 5,	c. 45
1918	Wages (Temporary Regulation) Act	8 & 9 Geo. 5,	c. 61
1919	Wages (Temporary Regulation Extension) Act	9 & 10 Geo. 5,	c. 18
1919	Industrial Courts Act	9 & 10 Geo. 5,	c. 69

2. *Trade Unions*

Date	Short Title	Reference	
1800	Combination Act	39 & 40 Geo. 3,	c. 106
1817	Seditious Meetings Act	57 Geo. 3,	c. 19
1824	Combination Act	5 Geo. 4,	c. 95
1825	Combination Act	6 Geo. 4,	c. 129
1859	Molestation of Workmen Act	22 Vict.,	c. 34
1871	Trade Union Act	34 & 35 Vict.,	c. 31
1871	Criminal Law Amendment Act	34 & 35 Vict.,	c. 32
1875	Conspiracy and Protection of Property Act .	38 & 39 Vict.,	c. 86
1875	Employers and Workmen Act	38 & 39 Vict.,	c. 90
1876	Trade Union Amendment Act	39 & 40 Vict.,	c. 22
1906	Trade Disputes Act	6 Edw. 7,	c. 47
1913	Trade Union Act	2 & 3 Geo. 5,	c. 30

Date	Short Title	Reference	
1917	Trade Union Amendment Act	7 & 8 Geo. 5,	c. 24
1919	Restoration of Pre-War Practices Act	9 & 10 Geo. 5,	c. 42
1920	Emergency Powers Act	10 & 11 Geo. 5,	c. 55
1927	Trade Disputes and Trade Unions Act	17 & 18 Geo. 5,	c. 22

3. *Principal Social and Industrial Legislation*

1802	Health and Morals of Apprentices Act	42 Geo. 3,	c. 73
1833	Factory Act	3 & 4 Will. 4	c. 103
1842	Lord Ashley's Act (Mines)	5 & 6 Vict.,	c. 99
1847	Factory (Ten Hours) Act	10 Vict.,	c. 29
1860	Regulation and Inspection of Mines Act	23 & 24 Vict.,	c. 151
1864	Factory (Dangerous Trades) Act	27 & 28 Vict.,	c. 48
1870	Elementary Education Act	33 & 34 Vict.,	c. 75
1872	Coal Mines Regulation Act	35 & 36 Vict.,	c. 76
1875	Public Health Act	38 & 39 Vict.,	c. 55
1878	Factory and Workshops (Consolidation) Act	41 Vict.,	c. 16
1880	Employers' Liability Act	43 & 44 Vict.,	c. 42
1885	Housing of the Working Classes Act	48 & 49 Vict.,	c. 72
1892	Shops Regulation Act	55 & 56 Vict.,	c. 62
1894	Coal Mines (Checkweigher) Act	57 & 58 Vict.,	c. 52
1896	Friendly Societies Act	59 & 60 Vict.,	c. 25
1897	Workmen's Compensation Act	60 & 61 Vict.,	c. 37
1900	Mines (Prohibition of Child Labor Underground) Act	63 & 64 Vict.,	c. 21
1900	Workmen's Compensation (Agriculture) Act	63 & 64 Vict.,	c. 22
1901	Factory and Workshops (Consolidation) Act	1 Edw. 7,	c. 22
1902	Metropolitan Water Board Act	2 Edw. 7,	c. 41
1904	Shop Hours Act	4 Edw. 7,	c. 31
1906	Workmen's Compensation Act	6 Edw. 7,	c. 58
1908	Old Age Pensions Act	8 Edw. 7,	c. 40
1908	Coal Mines Regulation (Eight Hours) Act	8 Edw. 7,	c. 57
1909	Labor Exchanges Act	9 Edw. 7,	c. 7
1909	Trade Boards Act	9 Edw. 7,	c. 22
1911	Coal Mines (Consolidation Act)	1 & 2 Geo. 5,	c. 50
1911	National Insurance Act	1 & 2 Geo. 5,	c. 55
1912	Coal Mines (Minimum Wage) Act	2 Geo. 5,	c. 2
1916	Police, Factories, etc., (Miscellaneous Provisions) Act	6 & 7 Geo. 5,	c. 31
1916	New Ministries and Secretaries Act	6 & 7 Geo. 5,	c. 68
1918	Trade Boards Act	8 & 9 Geo. 5,	c. 32

Date	Short Title	Reference	
1918	Maternity and Child Welfare Act	8 & 9 Geo. 5,	c. 29
1919	Electricity (Supply) Act	9 & 10 Geo. 5,	c. 100
1920	National Health Insurance Act	10 & 11 Geo. 5,	c. 10
1920	Unemployment Insurance Act	10 & 11 Geo. 5,	c. 30
1920	Mining Industry Act	10 & 11 Geo. 5,	c. 50
1920	Employment of Women, Young Persons, and Children Act	10 & 11 Geo. 5,	c. 65
1921	Education Act	11 & 12 Geo. 5,	c. 51
1921	Railways Act	11 & 12 Geo. 5,	c. 55
1924	Agricultural Wages (Regulation) Act	14 & 15 Geo. 5,	c. 37
1925	Workmen's Compensation (Consolidation) Act	15 & 16 Geo. 5,	c. 84
1925	Widows', Orphans', and Old Age Contributory Pensions Act	15 & 16 Geo. 5,	c. 70
1926	Mining Industry Act	16 & 17 Geo. 5,	c. 28
1926	Electricity (Supply) Act	16 & 17 Geo. 5,	c. 51
1930	Coal Mines Act	20 & 21 Geo. 5,	c. 34
1931	Agricultural Marketing Act	21 & 22 Geo. 5,	c. 42
1932	Wheat Act	22 Geo. 5,	c. 24
1933	Children and Young Persons (Consolidation) Act	23 & 24 Geo. 5,	c. 12
1933	London Passenger Transport Act	23 & 24 Geo. 5,	c. 14
1934	Unemployment Act	24 & 25 Geo. 5,	c. 29
1934	Cotton Manufacturing (Temporary Provisions) Act	24 & 25 Geo. 5,	c. 30
1935	Special Areas (Development and Improvement) Act	25 Geo. 5,	c. 1
1936	Railways Agreement Act	26 Geo. 5,	c. 6

B. PARLIAMENTARY PAPERS AND GOVERNMENT REPORTS

1. *The Parliamentary Debates*

1st Series, vols. 1- 41 (1803-1820)
2nd Series, vols. 1- 25 (1820-1830)
3rd Series, vols. 1-356 (1830-1891)
4th Series, vols. 1-199 (1892-1908)
5th Series:
Commons, vols. 1- (1909-1935)
Lords, vols. 1- (1909-1935)

The Journal of the House of Commons.

The Journal of the House of Lords.

2. *Reports from the Select Committees of the House of Commons*

Report from the Select Committee appointed to inquire into the state of the existing laws between masters and servants, 1801 (62) III, 135.

Minutes of Evidence taken before the Select Committee on the operation of the Cotton Arbitration Act, 1800, 1802-3 (114) VIII, 889.

Report from the Select Committee appointed to consider of the most speedy and effectual mode of adjusting such difference as may arise between masters and workmen engaged in the cotton manufacture, 1803-4 (41) IV, 211.

Reports from the Select Committees appointed to consider the cotton weavers' and spinners' petitions, 1808 (177) II, 95, 1809 (111) III, 331; 1801-11 (232) II, 389.

Reports from the Select Committee appointed to inquire into the state of the laws respecting artizans leaving the Kingdom, the exportation of tools and machinery, and the combination of workmen: First Report to Sixth, 1824 (51) V, 1.

Report from the Select Committee appointed to inquire into the effects of the Combination Act, 1924, in respect to the conduct of workmen, 1825 (437) IV, 499.

Minutes of Evidence, 1825 (417) IV, 565.

Report from the Select Committee appointed to consider the means of lessening the evil arising from the fluctuation of employment in the manufacturing districts, 1830 (590) X, 221.

Report from the Select Committee appointed to inquire into the operation of the Combination Act, 1925, and into constitution, proceedings, and extent of any trade unions or combination of workmen, or employers of workmen, 1837-38 (488) VIII, 1.

Second Report from the same Committee, 1837-38 (646) VIII, 315.

Report from the Select Committee on Masters and Operatives (Equitable Councils of Conciliation), 1856 (343) XIII, 1.

Report from the Select Committee appointed to consider the best means of settling disputes between masters and operatives, 1860 (307) XXII, 443.

Report from the Select Committee on laws as regards contracts of service, 1865 (370) VIII, 1.

Second Report from the same Committee, 1866 (449) XIII, 1.

3. *Reports by Royal Commissions*

Reports from the Royal Commission appointed to inquire into the organization and rules of trade unions: First Report to Fourth, with Minutes of Evidence, 1867, XXXII, 1; Fifth Report to Tenth, with Minutes of Evidence, 1867-68, XXXIX, 1; Eleventh and Final Report, vol. i, Report, 1868-69, XXXI, 235, vol. ii, Appendix, Digest of Evidence, *ibid.*, 363.

First Report of the Royal Commission appointed to inquire into the working of the Masters and Servants Act, 1867, and the Criminal Law Amendment Act, 1867, with Evidence, 1874 (c. 1094) XXIV, 391; Second and Final Report, 1875 (c. 1157) XXX, 1, Appendix, *ibid.*, 35.

General Reports of the Royal Commission on Labor: First Report, 1892, XXXIV, 1; Second, 1892, XXXVI, pt. 1; Third, 1893-94, XXXII, 1; Fourth, 1893-94, XXXIX, pt. 1, 1; Fifth (final), 1894, XXXV, 9; Summaries of Evidence and Appendices, *ibid.*, 263.

Evidence before Group A (Mining, Iron, Engineering, Shipbuilding, and cognate trades): Minutes and Appendices, vols. 1-3, 1892, XXXIV, 313, XXXVI, pt. 1, 5, 1893-94, XXXII, 5; Digest, vols. 1-3, 1892, XXXIV, 5, XXXVI, pt. III, 1, 1893-94, XXXII, 531.

Evidence before Group B (Agriculture, Railway, Shipping, etc.): Minutes with Appendices, vols. 1-3, 1892, XXXV, 1, XXXVI, pt. II, 1, 1893-94, XXXIII, 1; Digest, vols. 1-3, 1892, XXXIV, III, XXXVI, pt. III, 197, 1893-94, XXXIII, 681.

Evidence before Group C (Textile, Clothing, etc.): Minutes, with Appendices, vols. 1-3, 1892, XXXV, 711, XXXVI, pt. II, 441, 1893-94, XXXIV, 1; Digest, vols. 1-3, 1892; XXXIV, 209, XXXVI, pt. III, 369, 1893-94, XXXIV, 781.

Evidence before Commission sitting as a whole: Minutes, 1893-94, XXXIX, pt. 1, 5; Digest, *ibid.*, 629; Appendices, *ibid.*, 805.

Answers to Schules of Questions: Group A, 1892, XXXVI, pt. III, 533; Group B, *ibid.*, 1007; Group C, *ibid.*, pt. iv, 1.

Rules of Associations of Employers and Employed, with Introductory Memoranda, prepared for the Royal Commission, 1892, XXXVI, pt. v, 317.

Report of the Royal Commission on Trade Disputes and Trade Combinations, 1906 (cd. 2825) LVI, 1; Evidence and Appendices, 1906 (cd. 2826), LVI, 137.

Report of the Royal Commission on the working of the Railway Conciliation and Arbitration Scheme, 1911 (cd. 5922), XXIX, pt. 1, 663.

The Coal Industry Commission: Reports and Minutes of Evidence on the first stage of the inquiry, vol. i, 1919 (cmd. 359) XI; Reports and Minutes of Evidence on the second stage of the inquiry, vol. II, 1919 (cmd. 360) XII, Appendix, 1919 (cmd. 361) XIII.

Report of the Royal Commission on the Coal Industry: vol. 1, Report, 1926 (cmd. 2600) XIV, 1; vol. II, 1927 (cmd. 2899) XI, 303.

4. *Reports by Committees and Councils Appointed by the Government*

Report by Sir George Askwith on the Industrial Dispute Investigation Act of Canada, 1907, 1912-13 (cd. 6603) XLVII, 303.

Report from the Industrial Council on the methods of securing the due fulfilment of industrial agreements, and of enforcing agreements throughout particular trades or districts, 1913 (cd. 6952) XXVIII, 1; Evidence, 1913 (cd. 6953) XXVIII, 23.

Report by Lord Balfour of Burleigh and Mr. L. Macassey on the causes and circumstances of the apprehended differences affecting munition workers in the Clyde district, 1914-16 (cd. 8136) XXIX, 297.

Reports of the Commission of Inquiry into industrial unrest: 1917-18 (cd. 8662-69) XV, 1.

Summary of the Reports of the Commission by Rt. H. G. N. Barnes, 1917-18 (cd. 8696) XV, 149.

Report of the Provisional Joint Committee presented to the meeting of the Industrial Conference, 1919 (cmd. 139), XXIV, 1.

Similar Report, with an Appendix on the causes of and remedies for labor unrest, and a provisional scheme for trade union representation on the National Industrial Council, 1919 (cmd. 501) XXIV, 21.

Reports of the Whitley Committee on Relations between Employers and Employees: Interim Report on Joint Standing Industrial Councils, 1917-18 (cd. 8606) XVIII, 415; Second Report on Joint Industrial Councils, 1918 (cd. 9002) X, 659; Supplementary Report on Works Committees, 1918 (cd. 9001) XIV, 951; Report on Conciliation and Arbitration, 1918 (cd. 9099) VII, 763; Final Report of the Committee (signed July 1, 1918), 1918 (cd. 9153) VIII, 629.

Interim Report of the Committee on Commercial and Industrial Policy on Certain Essential Industries, 1918 (9032).

Final Report on commercial and industrial policy after the war, 1918 (cd. 9035).

Board of Trade Committees: Report on the position of the coal trade after the war, 1918 (cd. 9093); Report on the position of the engineering trades after the war, 1918 (cd. 9073); Report on the position of the iron and steel trades after the war, 1918 (cd. 9072); Report on the position of the shipping and shipbuilding industries after the war, 1918 (cd. 9092).

Committee on Industry and Trade: Survey of Industrial Relations, 1926; Survey of Metal Industries, iron and steel, engineering, electrical manufacturing, shipbuilding, with a chapter on the coal industry, 1928; Survey of Textile Industries, cotton, wool, artificial silk, 1928; Final Report, 1929 (cmd. 3282) (published by H. M. Stationery Office, London).

5. *Reports by Government Departments*

Ministry of Munitions:

Rules and Regulations relating to the Munitions Tribunals, 1914-16 (348) LV, 895; No. 2, 1917-18 (cd. 8716) XX, 85.

Rules for constituting and regulating Munitions Tribunals, 1916 (32) XXIII, 391.

Returns of Cases heard before the Munitions Tribunals, 1914-16 (cd. 8143) LV, 979, 1916 (cd. 8360) XXIII, 407.

Health Committee Reports: Industrial Canteens, 1914-16 (cd. 8133) XXIX, 289; Sunday Labor, 1914-16 (cd. 8132) XXIX, 283; Welfare Supervision, 1914-16 (cd. 8151) LV, 985.

Health Committee's Memoranda: Nos. 4-15, 1916, XXIII; Nos. 16-20, 1917-18, XX, No. 21, 1918, XV.

History of the Ministry of Munitions, 5 vols., published by the Ministry in 1922.

Board of Trade:

Memorandum on Conseils de Prud'hommes in France and Belgium, 1854-55, L, 371.

Memorandum explaining the arrangements made for collecting and publishing statistics relating to labor, 1886 (48).

Memorandum on the progress of the Work of the Labor Department, Board of Trade, 1893 (194).

Annual Reports on strikes and lock-outs (with notes on conciliation and arbitration) for 1888-1913.

Annual Reports on trade unions for 1887-1913.

Annual Reports of proceedings under the Conciliation Act, 1896, for 1896-1918.

A Special Report on the establishment of railway conciliation boards, 1909 (cd. 4534).

Report on Rules of Voluntary Conciliation and Arbitration Boards and Joint Committees, 1907 (cd. 3788).

Second Report on Rules of Voluntary Conciliation and Arbitration Boards and Joint Committees, 1910 (cd. 5346).

Report on Collective Agreements between employers and workpeople, 1910 (cd. 5366) XX, 1.

Ministry of Labor:

Industrial Reports (1917-1920):

No. 1. The Whitley Report, together with the letter of the Minister of Labor explaining the Government's view of its proposals.

No. 2. The report of the enquiry conducted by the Ministry into existing Works Committees.

No. 3. The Joint Memorandum of the Minister of Reconstruction and the Minister of Labor explaining the Government's view of the proposals of the Second Whitley Report.

No. 4. Industrial Councils: suggestions as to the constitution and functions of a National Joint Industrial Council, of district Councils, and of Works Committees in industries in which National Joint Industrial Councils are established.

Reports on Conciliation and Arbitration for 1919, 1921 (221), for 1920, 1921 (185).

Report on the establishment and progress of Joint Industrial Councils, 1917–1922, H. M. Stationery Office, London, 1923.

Report on Collective Agreements between Employers and Workpeople, vol. 1, 1934.

Annual Reports commencing from 1923-24.

6. *Reports by Industrial Courts*

Committee on Production:

Memorandum on the proceedings of the Committee on Production, May, 1917–April, 1918, 1918 (cd. 9126) XII, 703; 1919 (cmd. 70) XXVII, 959.

Industrial Court:

Decisions yearly published by H. M. Stationery Office.

Courts of Inquiry:

Reports, see chapter 4, p. 138.

C. PERIODICALS

Weekly

Cotton Factory Times, published by the Amalgamated Association of Operative Cotton Spinners and Twiners.

Miner, published by the Miners' Federation of Great Britain.

Railway Review, published by the National Union of Railwaymen.

Monthly

Amalgamated Engineering Union Monthly Journal, published by the A. E. U.

Industrial Review (1928-1933), now incorporated with the *Labor Magazine*.

Labor Magazine (incorporating the *British Trade Union Review* and the *Labor Party Bulletin*), published by the Trade Union Congress and the Labor Party.

Man and Steel, published by the Iron and Steel Trades Confederation.

The Ministry of Labor Gazette.

II. REFERENCE BOOKS AND ARTICLES

Aberconway (Lord), *The Basic Industries of Great Britain*; coal, iron, steel, engineering, shipbuilding, an historic and economic survey, Benn, London, 1927.

Addison, C., *The Manufacture of Munitions*, Truscott, London, 1916; *British Workshops and the War*, Unwin, London, 1917; *Politics from Within*, 2 vols., Herbert Jenkins, London, 1924.

Alcock, G. W., *Fifty Years of Railway Trade Unionism*, Co-Operative Printing Society, London, 1922.

Allen, G. C., *British Industries and their Organization*, Longmans, London, 1933.

Amery, L. S., *The Forward View*, Geoffrey Bles, London, 1935.

Amulree (Lord), *Industrial Arbitration in Great Britain*, Oxford University Press, London, 1929.

Ashley, Sir W. J., *The Adjustment of Wages*, Longmans, 1903; *British Industries*, Longmans, 1903; *The Economic Organization of England*, Longmans, London, 1928.

Askwith (Lord), *Industrial Problems and Disputes*, J. Murray, London, 1920.

Baillie, J. B., "Industrial Unrest—some causes and remedies," in *Labor and Industry*, Manchester University Press, 1920.

Baldwin, S., *This Torch of Freedom*, Hodder and Stoughton, London, 1936.

Bell, R., *Trade Unionism*, T. C. & E. C. Jack, London, 1907.

Beer, M., *History of British Socialism*, 2 vols., Bell, London, 1929.

Booth, C., *Industrial Unrest and Trade Union Policy*, Macmillan, London, 1913.

Burns, C. D., *The Philosophy of Labor*, Allen, London, 1925; *Industry and Civilization*, Allen and Unwin, London, 1925; *Democracy*, Butterworth, London, 1935.

Burns, E., *Russia's Productive System*, Dutton, New York, 1930.

Burns, E. M., *Wages and the State*; a comparative study of the problems of State wage regulation, P. S. King, London, 1926.

Carter, G. R., "The Triple Industrial Alliance," *The Advertiser Press*, Huddersfield, 1917.

Catlin, W. B., *The Labor Problem in the United States and Great Britain*, Harper Brothers, New York, 1926.

Chapman, S. J., *Labor and Capital after the War*, J. Murray, London, 1918.

Cheyney, E. P., *An Introduction to the Industrial and Social History of England*, Macmillan, 1901.

Citrine, W. M., *Trade Union Movement in Great Britain, International Federation of Trade Unions*, Amsterdam, 1926; "The Next Step in Industrial Relations," in the *Manchester Guardian Weekly*, Industrial Relations Supplement, Nov. 30, 1927; "Where are the Trade Unions Going?," *The Labor Magazine*, Oct., 1927; "Democracy or Disruption," *ibid.*, Dec., 1927, Jan.–Mar., June, 1928; "Truth about the Turner-Mond Talks," *ibid.*, Oct., 1928; "In Defence of Freedom," *ibid.*, June–August, 1933.

Clark, J. B., "Is Compulsory Arbitration Inevitable?," in *Employers and Employees*, Public Policy, Chicago, 1902.

Clay, H., *The Problem of Industrial Relations*, Macmillan, London, 1929.
Clynes, J. R., "Organized Labor in Relation to Industrial Development," in *Labor and Industry*, Manchester University Press, 1920.
Clow, W. M., *The Quest of Industrial Peace*, Hodder, London, 1921.
Cole, G. D. H., *Self-Government in Industry*, Bell, London, 1919; *Labor in the Coal Mining Industry*, The Clarendon Press, Oxford, 1923; *Workshop Organization*, The Clarendon Press, Oxford, 1923; *Organized Labor*, Allen and Unwin, London, 1924; *A Short History of the British Working Class Movement, 1789-1925*, The Labor Publishing Co., London, 1927; *The Payments of Wages*, Allen and Unwin, London, 1928; *The Next Ten Years in British Social and Economic Policy*, Macmillan, London, 1929; *British Trade and Industry, Past and Future*, Macmillan, London, 1932; *Studies in World Economics*, Macmillan London, 1934.
Cole, G. D. H. and Arnot, R. P., *Trade Unionism on the Railways*, Allen and Unwin, London, 1917.
Commission on Foreign Inquiry of the National Civic Federation, *The Labor Situation in Great Britain and France*, Dutton, New York, 1919.
Crompton, H., *Industrial Conciliation*, H. S. King, London, 1876.
Crook, W. H., *The General Strike*, The University of North Carolina University Press, 1931.
Dimock, M. E., *British Public Utilities and National Development*, Allen and Unwin, London, 1933.
Engineering and Allied Employers' National Federation, 30 Years of Industrial Conciliation, Broadway House, London, 1927.
Feis, H., *The Settlement of Wage Disputes*, Macmillan, New York, 1921; *Principles of Wage Settlement*, H. W. Wilson, New York, 1924.
Finer, H., *Representative Government and a Parliament of Industry*, Allen and Unwin, 1923.
Fisher, A. B. G., *Some Problems of Wages and their Regulation in Great Britain since 1918*, P. S. King, 1926.
Freeman, J., *The Soviet Worker*, Liveright, New York, 1932.
Furnis, E. S., *Labor Problems*, Houghton Mifflin, Boston, 1925.
Gemmill, P. F., *Present Day Labor Relations*, Chapman and Hall, London, 1929.
Gilman, N. P., *Methods of Industrial Peace*, Houghton, Mifflin and Co., Boston, 1904.
Gilson, M. B., *Unemployment Insurance in Great Britain*, Industrial Relations Counselors, Inc., New York, 1931.
Goodrich, C. L., *The Frontier of Control*, Harcourt, New York, 1920.
Haider, C., *Capital and Labor under Fascism*, Thesis for Ph. D., Columbia University, New York, 1930.
Hammond, J. L., *The Rise of Modern Industry*, Methuen, London, 1925; *The Skilled Laborer*, Longmans, London, 1920.

Hammond, M. B., *British Labor Condition and Legislation During the War*, Oxford University Press, 1919.

Hand, F. H., *The Work of Joint Industrial Councils*, The Manchester Guardian Commercial, July 28, 1927.

Hartley, L. A., *Human Engineering and Industrial Economy*, Chicago, 1928.

Hatch, L. W., *Government Industrial Arbitration*, Thesis for Ph. D., Columbia University, 1905.

Hedges, R. Y. and Winterbottom, A., *Legal History of Trade Unionism*, Longmans, London, 1930.

Henderson, A. and Slesser, Sir H. H,, *Industrial Law*, Benn, 1924.

Hicks, J. R., *The Early History of Industrial Conciliation in England*, Economica, March, 1930, pp. 25-39.

Higgins, H. B., *A New Province for Law and Order*, Constable, London, 1922.

Hilton, J. and Others, *Are Trade Unions Obstructive?*, Gollancz, London, 1935.

Hobson, J. A., *The Evolution of Modern Capitalism*, Scott, London, 1926; *The Conditions of Industrial Peace*, Allen and Unwin, London, 1927; *Work and Wealth, a human valuation*, Allen, London, 1933.

Hobhouse, L. T., *The Labor Movement*, Macmillan, London, 1912; *The Elements of Social Justice*, Holt and Co., New York, 1922.

Hohman, H. F., *The Development of Social Insurance and Minimum Wage Legislation in Great Britain*, Houghton, Mifflin and Co., New York, 1933.

Howell, G., *Labor Legislation, Labor Movement and Labor Leaders*, Unwin, London, 1902; *The Conflicts of Capital and Labor*, Macmillan, London, 1890.

Hutchins, B. L. and Harrison, A., *A History of Factory Legislation*, P. S. King, 1926.

Hutt, W. H., *The Theory of Collective Bargaining*, P. S. King, London, 1930.

International Labor Office, *Conciliation and Arbitration in Industrial Disputes*, an international survey, Geneva, 1927; *Studies and Reports*, Series A (industrial relations), No. 5, No. 10, The British Government and the Miners' Federation of Great Britain; No. 13, *The Miners' Strike in Great Britain*, 1920; Nos. 28-32, *Freedom of Association*, 5 vols.; *International Labor Review*.

Jeans, J. S., *Conciliation and Arbitration in Labor Disputes*, Crosby Lockwood, London, 1894.

Jevons, W. S., *The State in Relation to Labor*, Macmillan, 1910.

Johnston, T. B., *Industrial Peace*, Arrowsmith, Bristol, 1919; "Industrial Councils and their Possibilities," in *Industrial Administration*, Manchester University Press, 1920.

Kettle, Sir R., *Strikes and Arbitration*, Simpkin, Marshall and Co., London, 1866; *Masters and Men*, P. S. King, London, 1871.

Kiddier, W., *The Old Trade Unions*, Allen and Unwin, London, 1930.

Knoop, D., *Industrial Conciliation and Arbitration*, P. S. King, London, 1905.

Ko, T. T., *Government Methods of Adjusting Labor Disputes in North America and Australasia*, Thesis for Ph. D., Columbia University, 1926.

Labor Research Department, *Labor and Capital in the Engineering Trades*, The Labor Publishing Co., London, 1922; *The Federation of British Industries*, 1923.

Laski, H., *A Grammar of Politics*, Yale University Press, 1925; *Communism*, Williams and Norgate, London, 1927.

Lauck, W. J., *Political and Industrial Democracy*, Funk and Wagnalls, New York, 1926.

League of Nation Union, Toward Industrial Peace, London, 1927.

Liberal Industry Inquiry, Britain's Industrial Future, Benn, London, 1928.

Lindsay, A. D., *Karl Marx' Capital*, Oxford University Press, 1925.

Lloyd George, David, *War Memoirs*, 4 vols., Ivor Nicholson and Watson, London, 1934.

Lucas, A. F., "British Movement for Industrial Reconstruction and the Control of Competitive Activity," *Quarterly Journal of Economy*, 49: 206-35, F. 1935.

MacIver, R. M., *Labor in the Changing World*, Dutton, New York, 1920; *The Modern State*, The Clarendon Press, Oxford, 1926.

Mackenzie, Sir W. W. (Lord Amulree), "British Industrial Court," *3 International Labor Review*, 41-50 (1921); *The Industrial Court: Practice and Procedure*, Butterworth, London, 1923.

Macmillan, H., *Reconstruction, A Plea for National Policy*, Macmillan, London, 1934.

Macassey, Sir L., "The Industrial Court Act, 1919," *2 Journal Comparative Legislation and International Law*, 72-76 (1920).

Milne-Bailey, W., *Trade Union Documents*, Bell, London, 1929; "The Economic Advisory Council," *Labor Magazine*, May, 1930, p. 19; *Trade Unions and the State*, Allen and Unwin, London, 1934.

Morris, Sir H., *The Industrial Court*, Economica, March, 1928; *cf. The Monthly Labor Review*, 27: 102-105 (1928).

Morrison, H., *Socialization and Transport*, Constable, London, 1933.

Moses, M., "Compulsory Arbitration in Great Britain during the War," *26 Journal Political Economy*, 882-900 (1918).

Mote, C. H., *Industrial Arbitration*, Bobbs-Merrile Co., Indianapolis, 1916.

Perlman, S., *A Theory of the Labor Movement*, Macmillan, 1928.

Pigou, A. C., *Principles and Methods of Industrial Peace*, Macmillan, London, 1905; *Economics of Welfare*, 3rd ed., Macmillan, London, 1929.

Price, L. L. F. R., *Industrial Peace*, Macmillan, London, 1887.

Pugh, Sir A., "Trade Unionism in Transition," *Labor Magazine*, Jan., 1928; "What is Wrong with the British Iron and Steel Industry?," *ibid.*, July, 1931.

Rankin, M. T., *Arbitration Principles and the Industrial Court*, P. S. King, London, 1931.

Rayner, R. M., *The Story of Trade Unionism from the Combination Acts to the General Strike*, Longmans, London, 1929.

Renold, C. G., *Works Committees*, Pitman, London, 1921.

Richardson, J. H., *Industrial Relations in Great Britain*, International Labor Office, Geneva, Studies and Reports, Series A, No. 36, 1933.

Rowe, J. W. F., *Wages in the Coal Industry*, P. S. King, 1923; *Wages in Practice and Theory*, G. Routledge & Sons, London, 1928.

Rowntree, B. S., "Social Obligation of Industry to Labor," in *Industrial Administration*, Manchester University Press, 1920.

Salter, Sir J. A., *Toward a Planned Economy*, John Day, New York, 1933; *The Framework of an Ordered Society*, Macmillan, London, 1933.

Schulze-Gaevernitz G. von, *Social Peace*, S. Sonnenschein & Co., London, 1893.

Selekman, Ben and Sylvia, *British Industry Today*, Harper Brothers, New York, 1929.

Sells, D., *The British Trade Boards System*, P. S. King, London, 1923.

Seymour, J. B., *The Whitley Councils Scheme*, P. S. King, London, 1932.

Shotwell, J. T., *The Origin of the International Labor Organization*, 2 vols., Columbia University Press, 1934.

Slesser, Sir H. H., *Trade Union Law*, Nisbet, London, 1927.

Steed, H. W., *A Way to Social Peace*, Columbia University Press, 1935.

Thomas, J. H., "Railwaymen's Wages," *Labor Magazine*, July, 1922.

Tracey, H., "Makers of the Labor Movement: the Miners and their Union," *Labor Magazine*, July, 1923; "The Railwaymen in Action," *ibid.*, June, 1924; "Arthur Pugh, a Statesman of Industry," *ibid.*, Nov., 1925; "Trade Unionism Produces a Statesman," *ibid.*, June, 1927.

Trade Union Congress, *Industrial Negotiation and Agreements*, 1922; Industrial Conference: *Annual Reports* for 1928, pp. 209-230, for 1929, pp. 186-209, for 1930, pp. 160-162; The public control and regulation of industry and trade: *Annual Reports* for 1932, pp. 206-19, for 1933, p. 210; Report on Socialization of the Iron and Steel Industry: *Annual Report* for 1934, pp. 189-205; Scheme for Cotton Corporation: *Annual Report* for 1934, pp. 376-380, for 1935, pp.

202-208; Socialization of Coal and Allied Industry, *Annual Report* for 1935, pp. 208-9.

U. S. Bureau of Labor Statistics, *Monthly Labor Review.*

U. S. Department of Commerce, *British-Wages*, Trade Promotion Series No. 42, Washington, D. C., 1926.

Warbarton, W. H., *The History of Trade Union Organization in the North Staffordshire Potteries*, Allen and Unwin, 1931.

Webb, Sidney and Beatrice, *Industrial Democracy*, Longmans, London, 1920; *History of Trade Unionism*, Longmans, London, 1920; Lady Passfield (Mrs. Webb), "The Trade Unions in Russia," *Labor Magazine*, Sept., 1932; Lord Passfield (Sidney Webb), "The Wage Earner in Soviet Russia," *ibid.*, Jan., 1933.

Weeks, J. D., *Labor Differences and their Settlement*, New York, 1886.

Welbourne, E., *The Miners' Unions of Northumberland and Durham*, The Cambridge University Press, 1923.

White, L. D., *Whitley Councils in the British Civil Service*, The University of Chicago Press, 1933.

Whitley, J. H., "Works Committees and Industrial Councils, their Origins and Possibilities," in *Labor and Industry*, Manchester University Press, 1920.

Wolfe, A. B., *Works Committees and Joint Industrial Councils*, U. S. Shipping Board Emergency Fleet Corporation, Industrial Relations Division, Philadelphia, 1919.

Wolfe, H., *Labor Supply and Regulation*, The Clarendon Press, Oxford, 1923.

Wright, C. D., *Some Ethical Phases of the Labor Question*, American Unitarian Association, Boston, 1902.

Wright, C. W., "Labor and Capital under Fascism in Italy," *Annals of Acad. of Political and Social Science*, 174: 166-72, July, 1934.

Zueblin, C., "Relation of the public to Capital and Labor," in *Employers and Employees*," Public Policy, Chicago, 1902.

INDEX

Bei Fragen zur Produktsicherheit wenden Sie sich bitte an:
If you have any questions regarding product safety,
please contact:

Walter de Gruyter GmbH
Genthiner Straße 13
10785 Berlin
productsafety@degruyterbrill.com